"I can't imagine a better guide to lifestory writing. Sharon Lippincott pushes, cajoles, encourages, shares, and stays with you every step of the way. Don't worry if writing and computers are new to you. Do your children and grandchildren a favor. Get this book, take a deep breath, and give them your story."

– John Kotre, Ph.D.; author of *White Gloves, Make It Count, Seasons of Life*; Emeritus Professor of Psychology, University of Michigan, Dearborn

"*The Heart and Craft of Lifestory Writing* is an indispensable roadmap to guide a writer successfully and quickly to a completed manuscript. The book inspired me to write. It is the driving force that keeps me on track. I carry it with me all the time in my briefcase with my writing material."

– Paul Ohrman, lifestory writer

"This book is the boarding point for the trip that records the journeys of life in lifestory writing. Her work makes it easy for others to follow."

– Herchel "Herm" Newman, contributor,
Chicken Soup for the African American Soul

"A multi-faceted reflection into the mind of Sharon Lippincott as she educates the aspiring author through her own personal lifestories, *The Heart and Craft of Lifestory Writing* encourages writers to abandon their apprehensions and embrace their own literary truths. This step-by-step volume, with editing, grammar, and computer software techniques, also offers a wide variety of exercises to jumpstart a writer's mind; a perfect companion for both the novice and more advanced writer."

– Tara S. Zawacki, lifestory writer

D1444545

The Heart and Craft of Lifestory Writing

How to Transform Memories into Meaningful Stories

By Sharon M. Lippincott

Lighthouse Point Press
Pittsburgh, PA

The Heart and Craft of Lifestory Writing

How to Transform Memories into Meaningful Stories

Published by:

 Lighthouse Point Press
100 First Avenue, Suite 525
Pittsburgh, PA 15222
www.lighthousepointpress.com

This publication is designed to provide accurate and authoritative information in regard to the subject matter covered. It is sold with the understanding that the publisher and author are not engaged in rendering legal, accounting, or other professional service.

The purpose of this book is to educate and entertain. The author and Lighthouse Point Press shall have neither liability nor responsibility to any person or entity with respect to any loss or damage caused, or alleged to be caused, directly or indirectly by the information contained in this book.

Copyright © 2007 Sharon M. Lippincott
Printed in the United States of America
Library of Congress Control Number: 2007926892

Publisher's Cataloging in Publication Data
Lippincott, Sharon M.
The Heart and Craft of Lifestory Writing: How to Transform Memories into Meaningful Stories / by Sharon M. Lippincott
    p.   cm.
Includes bibliographical references and index.
    1. Writing
    2. Reference
ISBN-13: 978-0-9792998-0-3
ISBN-10: 0-9792998-0-2
Paperback, $16.95

This book is printed on acid-free stock.
First printing, July 2007

Contents

Acknowledgements

Nobody writes a book alone. Without the encouragement and inspiration of my wonderful students, members of my face-to-face and online writing groups, and friends, this book would have remained a pile of random handouts. I especially thank these people for keeping my feet to the fire, because in the process of creating this book, my own understanding of the craft of writing, and especially the craft of lifestory writing, has deepened immeasurably.

Special thanks are due to my friend and publisher, Ralph Yearick, at Lighthouse Point Press, the most supportive and flexible publisher I've heard of. Working with Ralph and his staff is a delightful part of my own lifestory.

Without my growing list of grandchildren, I never would have been inspired to start writing lifestories. Thank you, Keith, Stephanie, Tosh, Sarah, and Marley.

Last, but not least, I couldn't have done it without my chief supporter, resident proofreader, and husband, Parvin.

Chapter 1:
Setting the Stage

"Good stories have the power to save us … . We can all make a difference by simply sharing our own stories with real people in real times and places."

—*Mary Pipher*

Lifestory writing is the process of transforming your own essence into words on paper for other people to know—daring to expose not only your actions and experiences, but your thoughts, your choices, your perceptions, and your feelings. It takes courage to bare your soul for the examination of future generations, and making the effort to share yourself with them is an act of great love. This act of love and confidence is the heart of lifestory writing, whether that be a single story about a specific event, a complex compilation of stories, or something in between. You may fear contempt or ridicule, but rest assured, if you feel the urge to share, someone out there needs to hear what you have to say. Some may be indifferent to your words, but many more in times and places you may not be able to foresee will be grateful for the knowledge and wisdom you've shared. You may spare someone grief, comfort those who have shared your experience, or inspire a person to heights they'd never dare attempt without your example.

The craft involves sorting, polishing, and refining the raw ore of words that flow from your heart until they gain their maximum power to touch the hearts of your readers, informing, amazing, or inspiring them. Simply getting the words on paper is enough for many aspiring lifestory writers. Others want to invest the time and effort to further shape and mold their stories, bringing out highlights, emphasizing details, and framing their thoughts to best advantage and purpose. You must follow your own heart and its desires in this matter. What's right for one writer may derail the efforts of another.

The purpose of this book is to provide tools you can use to work on whatever level you choose. Nobody will use every planning and organizing tip, and few will be concerned with all aspects of editing and polishing. Consider your purpose, your available time, and your interest in the craft of writing, and use only the parts that fit. Listen to your heart and let it be your guide. This is *your story*, and of all the things you ever do, this should be done *your* way!

Why We Write

Interest in writing lifestories is mushrooming. This may partly reflect the growing ease of writing, as home computers become ubiquitous and people of all ages gain confidence in using them. Some people feel the urge to write as a means of exploring and making sense of their own lives. Others write for their own personal enjoyment. The interest may also reflect a growing desire to reach forward and establish connections with generations we may never know.

Perhaps there is still another reason that's more obscure. When Alvin Toffler wrote *Future Shock*, back in 1970, he foresaw an ever-increasing rate of cultural change that would continually intensify stress. As one of the antidotes to this stress, he imagined resorts that functioned as a sort of time machine.

They would be completely isolated from the outside world, and people would go there to immerse themselves in the leisurely, low-pressure lifestyle of earlier eras. Toffler's vision of change and stress has proven to be alarmingly accurate, but his time-out facilities largely remain an unfulfilled dream.

Or, perhaps they are manifesting in a form he failed to see. Perhaps some older writers are using lifestory writing as a way to reconnect with a past that seems less stressful in retrospect than it did at the time. Each time we sit down to write, today's worries dissolve into the nurturing warmth of the past we've safely survived—a past filled with fewer options and seemingly simpler choices. Younger readers may find escape from their own frenzy by reading of these calmer lifestyles, or put their own dilemmas in perspective by reading about conditions that seem harrowingly primitive or brutal to them.

Probably the largest number write at the behest of friends and family, or because they feel the urge to leave their footprint on the sands of time, and perhaps leave a sort of survival manual for those with the need or desire to step outside the increasingly wired order.

Even more people are thinking about writing, but haven't yet gotten around to actually beginning. A nurse I met in the allergist's office vividly illustrated this interest, as well as a common barrier. Several times I'd noticed her looking my way as I underwent allergy testing.

"What are you working on so diligently?" she finally asked.

"I'm revising the handouts for the lifestory writing class I teach," I explained.

She lit up like a Christmas tree when I mentioned lifestory writing and told me how much she cherishes a copy of the autobiography her grandmother wrote decades ago. Grandmother was born in France, raised in Paris, and came to Amer-

3

ica as a young woman. She had an exciting and colorful life, and wanted her descendants to know about it.

When the story wound down, I said, "One of these days you'll have grandchildren of your own, and they'll be just as thrilled as you were if you write the story of your life for them."

"I know," she said. Her voice became subdued and she dropped her eyes. "I've thought about doing that, but I don't have any idea how to go about it, and I really don't have time."

She's not the first person I've heard tell a story like this. Many people bubble with enthusiasm over lifestories written by relatives, and mean to follow suit, "one of these days." You may be one of them, reading this book in an effort to get your arms around the project. If so, you've taken the first step, and will hopefully soon be writing away. My own collection of lifestories written by relatives is a primary source of my inspiration and passion for lifestory writing.

Although few lifestories make it to finished form, one of my grandmothers did finish hers. As today's writers may splurge on a computer before they begin writing, she splurged on an electric typewriter for the specific purpose of writing her autobiography. When she was finished, she put copies of all twenty-five pages in bright orange report covers with the title, *Clara The Great*, pasted on the front, and gave them to everyone in the family. The finished product includes examples of nearly every pitfall a lifestory writer should avoid. She jumped around and used sentence fragments. She mentioned siblings without naming them, and she recorded incomplete thoughts with unclear references that are meaningless to readers today. In spite of its plethora of shortcomings, I treasure every word. Short though it may be on substance, the fact that she went to the effort of writing it says a lot, and it does give a sense of who she was and how she thought.

My husband's grandmother penned the story of her life, by hand, on lined notebook paper over a period of several months. She completed this labor of love in the form of a uniquely personalized letter to each of her three grandchildren. The handwriting is easily read. The grammar and spelling reflect the fact that by her own choice, Grandma's formal education ended with the eighth grade, but her indomitably cheerful spirit and warm-hearted generosity shine through as brightly as her joy in life and love for her family.

Shortly after my mother died, I found a folder of material with a couple of chapters about her childhood and an overview of her father's life. Most of the details in these accounts were new to me. I was sad that her time had been cut short before she was able to finish what she set out to do, but grateful to have even this little bit. To my astonished delight, a couple of years later a stack of computer printouts as thick as my thumb, with several more chapters of Mother's story, turned up in genealogy files. Other folders held dozens of sheets of handwritten notes, along with a treasure trove of family history documents. Although I don't have Mother's finished story, I do have her own account of the years before she was married, and the notes and other resources she left behind are valuable in their own right. My father had no idea she'd been working on this project, which all goes to show that you never know what you may find squirreled away in odd places, and if you don't tell people what you are up to, they may never know.

Even my father is getting on the bandwagon. He loves to tell stories about the olden days, and every now and then he sends out an e-mail with a story about something like cowboys, hunting jack rabbits, or raising chickens. Daddy is a masterful storyteller, and his work is polished, entertaining, and worthy of publication. We look forward to each story.

My own interest in lifestory writing surfaced shortly after I became a grandmother. I started writing when our oldest grandchild was a toddler, intending that by the time he was three or four, I could read him stories about what things were like when I was his age. Because my purpose was to write this story for Keith and future preschool grandchildren, I decided to write it as I might have told it when I was very young, one child to another.

Once I decided to work on this project, without further ado, I sat down at the computer and started writing. I kept at it fairly continuously until I ran out of things to say. I wrote descriptions of our house and the chickens we raised, the soap opera my mother listened to on the radio every day (often while wearing pin curls covered by a bandana) and how I learned to count by gathering eggs. I told how my father slaughtered chickens, and about learning to sew. I wrote about my dolls, the night my baby sister was born, learning to roller skate, hanging clothes on the clothesline and all sorts of things. When I finished writing, I added a few pictures of my family, house, the yard, and myself and named the resulting project *The Albuquerque Years*, because that's where I lived from the time I was a year old until I was six—when that story ended.

A few years later, while visiting Keith and his younger sister Stephanie, I asked if they'd like to hear my story. "Yes!" they chorused. My heart raced. This was the moment I'd waited for. To my dismay, they soon began fidgeting, but their father listened intently. The kids seemed relieved when I handed the manuscript to him to take in the other room and finish reading. Although I thought I'd written from a child's point of view, to appeal to children, it didn't pass the road test with my target age group, but older readers liked it.

Fortunately, I saw that a story appealing to older readers would have far more staying power than one written for tots.

My efforts were not wasted—I'd simply overshot my target, and I wasn't surprised at the confirmation that I don't have a gift for writing for children as some other people do. It helps to recognize both your innate strengths and your limitations as a writer. You'll discover your own best style as you experiment and practice.

It's worth mentioning that you shouldn't assume that every family member is going to be overjoyed to receive your finished work. One of my students gave copies of her finished lifestory to her three children on her own seventy-fifth birthday. Later she wryly explained, "One son wanted to know why I'd wasted my time, one set it aside 'to read later,' and the other one *The author may never know the ultimate success of a lifestory project.* opened it with a huge smile and began reading right then and there. His wife had to make him put it aside for later. He was really excited." Her experience was a microcosm of the varying reactions people generally have. She was a perceptive woman and realized that the first son may not have been interested right then, but quite likely he will discover its value later, maybe after she is gone. She also speculated that her grandchildren and future great-grandchildren would appreciate it most in the future.

Over the ensuing years, I've continued to experiment with various forms of lifestory writing in hundreds of stories. I've continued to read books and articles on lifestory and memoir writing. I've been active in writer's groups, both online and real-time, and I've begun teaching lifestory writing. My handouts have become almost as voluminous as my stack of stories, and the time has come to organize both the stories and the handouts. This book is my way of incorporating the best of the two, stories and handouts, into a single volume covering both the heart and the craft of lifestory writing.

What Are You Waiting For?

Please keep in mind that writing even a little bit, even a single letter or story, is better than writing nothing. As I described earlier, none of my forebears wrote lengthy stories, but however short, I treasure them, and they are *better than nothing.*

> # Any lifestory you write is better than writing nothing!

Don't worry about what to say, or whether it's worth the effort, or whether you have time to write a document the size of a James Michener novel. Anything you write will be *better than nothing!* Pick up a pencil and paper, or sit down at your keyboard, and start writing. You can start with the day you were born (as you've been told about it), or you can write about anything that comes to mind and use the guidelines in later units to piece random stories together.

Many people are like the nurse I mentioned earlier, thinking about writing their lifestories "someday." Off the top of their heads, they may not be able to give specific reasons why they don't get started. When pressed, the reasons amount to fears that fall into five main categories:

- *Ignorance*—they don't know how to go about it
- *Writing skill*—they don't think they write well enough
- *Content*—they don't think they've done anything worth writing about

- *Criticism and ridicule*—they're afraid of what people will say
- *Time pressure*—they don't think they have time

Each is a valid concern, but not a reason to continue putting the project off. The main point of this book is to show you how to go about it. Let's look more closely at each concern.

Ignorance

When you think of all the things that you've experienced over the course of a lifetime, the thought of organizing it all in a coherent fashion that will have meaning for others can be daunting. The fact that you are reading this book is a huge step toward overcoming this obstacle. Between these covers you'll find every- *Books and classes can give you direction, but only you can write your story.* thing you need to know to get your story written, whatever form you decide it should take. You'll even find help on making that decision about form. The only limitation you face is to think about writing without taking action.

Writing skill

You may break out into a cold sweat at the thought of writing anything more complicated than a two-line e-mail. Maybe it's been fifty years since you got that C in grammar, and your correspondence is limited to signing greeting cards and writing "Wish you were here" on picture postcards.

The Inner Critic that lives on the left side of our brains causes most of the butterflies and self-doubt people feel when they think of writing. *How stupid of you to think you could write something anyone wanted to read ... You were always the first one to drop out in spelling bees! ... You'll never write as well as Uncle Jack did when he wrote his lifestory. You'll just look stupid in comparison.* This Inner Critic works hard to strangle the Inner Creator that lives on the right side of our

9

brains. Fortunately, you can choose whether to listen to your Inner Critic or not. Just listen to those quiet inner whispers, and then say firmly, out loud, "Enough already! I can do this!"

Don't worry—if you can talk, you can write. Some of the most touching and memorable stories are the ones that pour straight from the heart, without edits or polish, but if you want to tidy them up, lots of help is available. Word processing programs have spellcheckers and grammar checkers. Some basic grammar tips are included in later chapters here, and references to helpful books are included in the bibliography.

Content

In a scene in the movie *Breathing Space*, Joanne Woodward confides to a friend that earlier she had said something to her daughter, who then "looked me straight in the eye and asked, 'Mother, was there some point in your life when you made the decision to settle for being ordinary?' " The friend clucked appropriately and Joanne tearfully continued, "I don't know why she said that. I don't think I'm ordinary!" We can brush off unwelcome or unaware remarks made by friends, but we hope for more from family, especially our children. Offspring often go through a phase of thinking (on a good day!) that their parents' lives are unacceptably dull. By the time they are old enough to think beyond this assumption, it's often too late to ask. Do them the favor of preparing the answer, so they can find it when they're ready and understand it when they're able.

Elaine is the flip side of Joanne Woodward's character. Several years ago she was reminiscing about a mutual friend who hitchhiked alone around Europe after college graduation and generally lived life in the adventure lane. Elaine sighed and remarked about the contrast between Wendy's exotic wanderings and her own "plain vanilla life." To my thinking, Elaine has led quite an interesting life. She taught high school chemistry for twenty-two years and inspired several students to pursue careers in the field. She raised successful children and show dogs, sang in her church choir, and won prizes in quilt shows. In her retirement she began teaching quilting, and she'll probably live another thirty years. Her life may be less flamboyant than Wendy's, and ordinary in her own eyes, but dull would never be a word I'd use to describe it.

Many people will read about Elaine and think, *Well, she's a superstar, for pity's sake. She's nothing like me. My biggest excitement was winning a spelling bee in sixth grade, and I've worked in a grocery store (or been a homemaker, car mechanic, secretary, farmer or whatever) all my life.* Here's a secret, just for you—if you start thinking about the different houses you've lived in, the friends you've had, maybe some mischief you and those friends got into, and things like that, you're going to discover your life wasn't as dull as it seems. If you grew up in a family with limited income, you've learned valuable lessons in making do. Perhaps you've learned to see as much beauty in a fistful of dandelions as others see in a dozen premium roses, ensconced in a crystal vase. Every life has lessons and value, and when you begin writing about your own life, you may find it has more value than you imagined. If nobody else admires it, you will!

In the unlikely event you happen to be right, and your life *is* plain as mud, in fifty years somebody will be fascinated to read what "plain old life" was like back in "The Olden Days." A simple account of daily life as you live it now could seem amazing to future generations. In the quarter-century between my childhood and my children's, many things were lost. They never

In a hundred years, today's ordinary life will sound amazingly exotic.

gathered freshly laid eggs from a warm nest under the hen. I didn't think to have them blow soap bubbles with an empty spool and bar of Ivory, and they never knew what it was like to hang clothes out to dry or grab them in before the rain began. Future generations may well wonder what a person did to pass the time during summer vacation without computers, television, Game Boys, iPods, cell phones, and other electronic pacifiers. There is some possibility that learning how we coped in simpler times could be useful to later generations during future disasters or economic downturns. Use the memory magnet tools and lists beginning on page 39 and you'll soon have a notebook brimming with stories of the olden days that will charm your readers.

Fear of criticism

Nearly everyone has stories they hesitate to write because they don't want to hurt or embarrass various family members, or make someone angry, or because people tell them their memory is poor. These are all legitimate concerns, but they aren't an excuse not to write. You can write anything you want, and only show it to people

Fear of being wrong is the prime inhibitor of the creative process.

who will appreciate it. In fact, you don't have to show it to anyone. It's perfectly okay to write purely for the joy of writing, and never show it to another soul. Chapter Seven explores ways to work around touchy topics.

Remembering things differently from other family members is another matter. Memory is a complex topic, filling whole books. There are two fundamentally different types of memory: factual memories like dates and places that you can empirically validate, and narrative memories. Narrative memories are the way we make sense of the world and explain it to ourselves. If you don't agree about factual memories, you can usually work things out. You are never likely to fully agree about narrative memories, because of their personal nature. Exploring differences in narrative memories can be a powerful way of resolving differences between people. You'll read more in later chapters about these differences and ways of working with them.

Time

Finding time for something new is always a challenge. Some find it easy enough to get started, but the project quickly gets shoved to the side in the press of everyday life. Suggestions for managing your time are included in the next chapter, along with other tips for managing your lifestory project.

How This Book Works

The one thing you absolutely must do to create a finished story, whether that's a short account of a single event, or an overview of your whole life, is to have an idea, then write it down. If you do no more than that, you'll leave a treasured legacy behind. You don't need a how-to book if that's all you intend to do. This book is intended for those who plan to invest more time, thought, and effort in a larger project* consisting of a single ongoing story or a composite of shorter ones. It includes sections on how to plan and manage a lifestory project from the original concept, write the component stories, and pull it all together into a completed volume. You'll read tips on how to edit and rewrite your stories until they meet whatever standards of perfection and polish you set for yourself, along with additional resources on grammar, punctuation, layout, publishing options, and working with word processing programs.

Figure 1 gives an overview of how the whole project process fits together, from planning and collecting story ideas, through

---

* I have tried throughout to use the term "lifestory" to refer to an entire project of one long continuous story or several stories combined into a book, and the term "story" to mean a stand-alone episode that might some day be part of an entire lifestory book project.

the various levels of writing and editing individual stories, and finally compiling them into a published volume. You may choose to write as many or as few stories as serve your purpose, and you will discover how to develop a clear understanding of what that purpose is.

Throughout the book you'll be reminded that there is no "right" way to do things, but there are ways of making your work easier to understand and more interesting to read. All planning and editing guidelines are optional. Use the ones that make sense and appeal to you and ignore the rest. To a point, even the writing sequence is flexible. You can start in the middle and work your way back through an individual story or the project process.

You'll also find tips on overcoming writer's block and writing about topics that may be intensely personal or embarrassing or invade someone's privacy. You'll find an extensive bibliography, grammar and punctuation guidelines, and even tips for laying out stories with your word processing program. Finally, I've included a few of my own favorite life stories, with notes to show how they illustrate points discussed in the book.

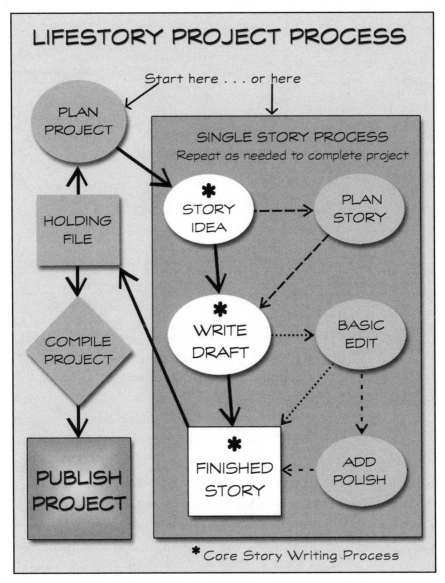

Figure 1: Lifestory Project Process

Chapter 2:

Get Organized

Better to write for yourself and have no public, than to write for the public and have no self.

— *Cyril Connolly*

Which came first, the chicken or the egg? This ancient question is directly relevant to lifestory projects—they may begin with a plan or with spontaneous writing. Somewhere along the line the two threads twist together.

Once you decide to write your lifestory—whether that's an overview of your whole life or one or more stories about specific elements—you have the rudiments of a plan. You have an idea, and a commitment to write something. That alone is enough to get started, and plenty of people have produced finished volumes with no more planning than that. If you are reading this book, you probably have an idea of a story or two you'd like to write, and getting the words flowing right away builds powerful momentum for the project.

This chapter is about planning and organizing, but if you begin to write before you begin to plan or study writing and editing tips, you may subdue attacks by your Inner Critic that often develop after reading how things "ought" to be written. If you feel like writing now, pick up your pen and write, then use

the planning and editing tips to carry on when your initial gush of words subsides. By doing this, you'll also have examples of your natural style of self-expression that will show how your *Write quick, before your Inner Critic discovers you don't know how.*
writing style changes over time as your skill grows.

If you don't feel quite ready to write, use the material in this chapter to plan and organize. Jokes about women reading instruction manuals while men toss them aside also apply to lifestory writers—but only if you leave gender out of the equation. The fact is, whether male or female, some people are more comfortable starting with a well-thought-out plan in hand, while others typically dash right in. Some enjoy detailed planning and would rather or- *Planning smoothes the path, but some people enjoy bumps.*
ganize information and make a plan than follow one. Others find the structure of plans constraining. There is no moral imperative here. Neither approach is better than the other, so follow your own inclinations. This topic of individual preferences is discussed in more detail later in this chapter.

Whether you begin with planning or writing, eventually the points in the list below will come into play. Most people find it works well in the early stages to balance their time around the three functions of writing, planning, and organizing. Whether you make formal lists and write everything down, or sort things out in your head, this chapter is full of helpful ideas to speed you on your way. The items on the list are arranged in order of immediate importance, with writing tools and a place to write being the minimum starting point for everyone.

- Writing gear—your tools of the trade
- A place to write
- A clear sense of purpose

- Project plan
- Framework for organizing stories
- Memory magnets

We'll examine each of these in turn.

Tools of the Trade

As I write these words, I'm gazing out at flaming autumn leaves. Even at an age where I enjoy senior citizen discounts, flaming autumn leaves remind me of the beginning of school and new school supplies, something you can read about in *Fall, Then and Now* (page 222). I loved buying pencils, pens, paper, a notebook, and all the other paraphernalia associated with study, writing, and learning in general. I still do. Office Depot is more tempting to me than a candy store, and hazardous to my wealth. My inner aesthete hopes you'll go out and fill a shopping cart with paper, pens, and other writing supplies.

My practical, frugal side knows that all you really need is a pencil and paper. Plain paper or a yellow pad are standard, but the back of an envelope or an empty lunch bag will do in a pinch. This part of me wants to have you writing immediately. Fortunately, there is an in-between position. Grab any piece of paper and pen or pencil and write the letter described in the exercise below. You can type it if you prefer. Whatever tools you use, just *write the letter.*

> ### Exercise
> Write a letter to a friend or relative telling how excited you are to be starting your lifestory project. Describe your plan. Copy and mail it, or simply file it away with your planning material.

When you finish, gather items for planning and writing your lifestory project. Any sort of work goes more smoothly and is more enjoyable when you have the proper tools at hand. Arrange your writing gear conveniently, so you won't be distracted by the need to dig around for a pencil or paper. If you don't have a desk, find a box or drawer to store your materials when you aren't writing.

The supplies listed below will help keep your ideas and stories organized, and they are listed more or less in order of importance. They don't need to be new—just gathered together.

Pen or pencil

Even if you use a computer, you'll need a pen or pencil for editing, and sometimes ideas flow more freely through handwriting. Use a pen that feels "write" in your hand. You could invest in a wonderful pen just for this project and make it part of your writing ritual. Some favor a pencil for the ease of erasing, but erasing on first drafts is discouraged. The true advantage of a pencil is its ability to write at any angle—handy if you feel the urge to write in a recliner or bed. A red pen is good for editing, but any color different from the text will do. I like to edit with pencil because I change my mind, and erasing edits is okay. Mechanical ones are my favorites.

Paper

You'll need paper for writing drafts and typing or printing. Punched notebook paper or yellow pads are good for handwritten drafts. Some people like to write on lines, some prefer unbounded space. Use whatever unleashes your creativity. I write on the backs of printer discards, and some of my most creative work happens on the backs of large mailing envelopes. I always have at least a few index cards with me, in case I feel a story coming on while I'm waiting somewhere. It really doesn't matter what you use to write. What matters is that you do write, and unless you always have a computer at hand, you need paper to write.

Typewriter/computer

If you write drafts by hand, you'll want to type them into a computer for finished copy. If you don't have a typewriter or computer, or can't type, you can do the whole project by hand. Your final copy will be easier to read if you find someone to type it for you. Since the prices keep falling and home computers have become so common, I'm writing with the assumption that you will be using one. If you need help learning to use one, check for classes at your local community college, senior citizen center, or library. You may be fortunate enough to have grandchildren who would be happy to help. If computers are not and will not be part of your life, ignore the computer references, and carry on by hand or typewriter.

Memory grabbers

The muse of lifestory writers is notoriously fickle and a terrible tease. If you don't do homage by jotting down ideas she dangles before you, she'll jerk them back, coyly hide them, and perhaps not visit you again for a long time. She prefers to deliver her tantalizing tidbits at awkward moments, and you must honor her by recording and making good use of her gifts to encourage frequent visits. Always keep a note pad, cards, or a small notebook nearby to catch stray ideas, wherever you are.

Index cards or small notepads are perfect for this purpose, because you can jot key words in the corner and sort them by category if you're a tidy type. They are easy to incorporate with the stack of memory cards you'll read about on page 39.

Filing system

Stories and planning sheets pile up fast, so you'll need a way to keep them organized. One popular choice is a three-ring binder. Binders with plastic pockets on the cover are especially nice because you can give your project a title and make a colorful cover insert. Splurge on tabbed dividers to sort your stories by topic or time as your collection grows. Other options include file folders in a box or file drawer, a portfolio pouch, or organizers with pocket pages for conveniently filing loose sheets of paper. Choose a system you love and imagine how stunning it will look, and how pleased you'll feel when it's chock full of stories. When you see it in your mind, you'll feel compelled to make it real. Think of this often.

Exercise
Gather the items in this list, and take a stab at the planning activities. But don't spend all your energy shopping and sharpening pencils. Do that while *you write, not instead of writing stories.*

The Write Spot

You don't need a room of your own, or even a special desk, to write the stories for your project. If you happen to have your own office, that's great, but you can do just fine writing on the kitchen table, or even a tablet in your lap. If you don't have an office or desk where you can leave your project sitting out, use a box or container for keeping everything together between writing sessions, and find a spot where you feel comfortable writing. Think about where you used to do your homework. That may conjure up old writing memories and identify a productive writing spot.

Some people find it helpful to have a specific place they use for writing, and only for writing. When they sit there, they're programmed to write. They may have trouble writing in any other location. Others respond well to variation. I generally write on my desktop computer, but now and then using paper and pen in a different location frees up fresh ideas. On especially nice days, I sometimes take my laptop outside under the trees. Once in awhile I venture forth to write in a bookstore coffee shop. There are usually a couple of other people tapping away on laptops, and I imagine one of them could be the next Hemingway, writing a bestseller right beside me. Some of my best work has flowed forth in tiny letters on scraps of paper while I waited for appointments.

Whether you respond best to stability or variety, the important thing is to arrange your physical surroundings to support your decision to do the writing required by this project. Don't let the lack of a dedicated writing station deter you!

A Clear Sense of Purpose

A clear sense of purpose is a major driving force behind any project, and writing your lifestory is no exception. Without a sense of purpose, you may sit down and write a story or two, but you are doing little more than scratching an itch in your brain. Once you finish scratching, you're likely to move on to something else. When you have a purpose, when you see the result in your mind, you'll discover awesome staying power. Beyond the motivational, your purpose will guide you in deciding which stories to include, what form to use in telling them, and how to organize them for your final package.

There are many reasons to write a lifestory. Peter is writing his in response to pleas from his children to record the details of his globetrotting career and generally adventurous life. Marcie is writing a series of essays about her beliefs. She regards her project as an ethical will—a way of passing on the importance of these beliefs to her grandchildren and later generations. Alan is writing stories of "life in the olden days" so his descendants will have a better idea of what life was like in the era before the World Wide Web, cell phones, and two-income families. Jodie is writing primarily for herself, to examine her memories and experiences in the hope that she will gain deeper understanding of what at times has seemed a chaotic existence. Evelyn is writing about the challenges of growing up with substance-abusing elders. So far she has kept these stories carefully hidden from outsiders, not wanting to disclose short-comings of others. Now she feels a growing desire to enlighten her family about the extended costs of substance abuse and their hereditary vulnerability.

From these examples, it's clear that purpose is as personal as life. Each purpose statement is unique. Your purpose statement will answer questions about *why* you want to write your lifestory, *who* you are writing for (this could be an audience of one—yourself), *what* you want them to learn by reading it, and *when* they are likely to be reading it.

Exercise

Write a letter to yourself explaining why you want to write your lifestory. Include a description of the type of stories you want to include, who you are writing it for, why this matters to you, and when you hope to be finished with the project. Keep your finished letter in a safe place so you can refer back to it.

Exercise

Using the letter from the previous exercise, write a concise Purpose Statement on an index card or small piece of paper. Post this card where you'll see it often and be reminded to write.

The mental effort you invest in your written statement is important, but the most powerful part of your purpose is your vision of the results of your work. As you read your completed purpose statement, think how your finished volume will look between covers, whether those covers are on a three-ring binder, a hand-bound leather volume, or something in between. (It's okay to change your mind on the style later—this is a starting point.) Think about other results, like seeing delight on your grandchildren's faces as they read it, and feeling the warm glow in your heart from realizing your dream. Or it may involve a sense of inner peace and satisfaction springing from a new level of self-understanding and acceptance. Take a moment to savor this vision when you sit down to write. It will draw you toward completion like a magnet attracts iron filings. Savor the vision in living color, complete with good feelings of satisfaction and joy. Savor it with a huge smile on your face!

Fundraising campaigns often use huge posters with something like a thermometer that rises as contributions pour in. A similar gimmick may help keep your writing on track. Keep a tally or chart to show where you are in the process, in story count and on the calendar. A scorecard, as small as an index card attached to your refrigerator door or strategically placed on your desktop, will do the trick.

A clear sense of purpose helps you set goals that keep you on track and a vision to pull you forward.

As I explained earlier, my initial purpose in writing *The Albuquerque Years* was to tell my grandchildren about life when I was their age. Although unwritten, this purpose was clear and specific. I was writing to and for my grandchildren, when they were preschool age, and the material I planned to cover was my life as a preschooler. I felt a bubbly sense of warm delight as I imagined sitting on a sofa with a tot on each side. They giggled with delight as I read stories from my binder. What could be more motivating than the desire to bring this Rockwellesque vision to life? It propelled me to completion.

Once I finished this project, I found my purpose expanding. Today my core purpose for everything I write is to share my personal insights for the enlightenment and benefit of others. I write because I love the gratification of helping people solve problems, or learn something new. I especially enjoy writing entertaining stories, and I love the way words flow out of my fingers, sometimes taking on a life of their own, surprising me with unanticipated insights. I have a passion for writing, especially writing stories from and about my own life and experience. I love each story I write, and each one is shaped by its own purpose. In its own way, following a passion is a purpose. Like making love, you do it because it feels good.

So, you see, purpose may evolve as you proceed, but it helps to define one in order to get started. The Purpose exercise is truly powerful and takes only a few minutes to do.

Planning Your Project

Planning your project creates a roadmap for implementing your purpose. Typically, at this point, you'd expect instructions on how to prepare a to-do list for the project and how to schedule your writing and various checkpoints along the way. Making those lists is an excellent investment of your time, and likely to speed you along the path and make it smoother. However, I also know that they work better for some people than others. Many others could draw up a letter-perfect plan, worthy of an "A" in Project Management 407, and then become distracted by the urgencies of daily life or enthusiasm for another project within a short period of time. Not following the plan creates guilt, which creates a tendency to avoid the project, and ... you get the picture.

The brain dominance factor

Are people in the latter group lazy? Lacking in character or self-discipline? Not at all! It's simply that their brains work differently. You've probably heard or read about the differences between right- and left-brain functions, and how some people's thought processes are guided predominately by their right brain, while others are left-brained. This is the core source of the different approaches to planning. Regimented planners are primarily left-brained people. Spontaneous, "Let's see where this road leads" people are usually right-brained.

This brain dominance factor will influence every aspect of your project, and it's worth exploring your own thought style. Many evaluation tools are available, some extensive and expensive, but most people can look at the list in Figure 2 and know where they stand. To use the list, make a check by the word in each pair that most closely resembles your way of looking at things and operating. The more items you have checked in one column, the more strongly dominant you are on that side. By the way, nobody is all one or all the other. We each have some of both, enabling us to work in either style. Even if you are strongly dominant on one side, you can call upon the

LEFT BRAIN	RIGHT BRAIN
logical	emotional
detail oriented	"big picture" oriented
linear	mosaic
facts rule	imagination rules
words and language	symbols and images
present and past	present and future
math and science	philosophy and religion
comprehends things	intuitively "gets" things
knows	believes
acknowledges	appreciates
order/pattern perception	spatial perception
knows object name	knows object function
reality based	fantasy based
forms strategies	presents possibilities
practical	impetuous
safe	risk taking

Figure 2: Left- and right-brain functions

26

other functions when you need them. It just won't feel as natural or easy as using your innate strengths, like using your nondominant hand involves tension and awkwardness.

From Figure 2 you can see that a writer with left-brain dominance (hereafter referred to as a left-brainer) will benefit from a logical, orderly, detailed, clearly-written schedule. A right-brainer may jot down a few notes, but the important part of the plan will be that "big picture" or vision of the project, the sense of what it's all about. Left-brainers plan their project with zeal, but may lack a sense of vision. Right-brainers may rely on an intuitive mental map for planning, but have a well-developed vision of the completed project. Here's where you'll benefit from stretching to involve your whole brain: left-brainers will get a motivational boost from developing their vision, and right-brainers will find it easier to stay on track by incorporating a structured plan into their vision.

A left-brainer's vision may seem a bit flat and uninspiring to a right-brained observer, and a right-brain project plan may look slap-dash to the fastidious left-brainer, who revels in checking the details. Right-brained checklists are more likely to be stored in a pile of scrap paper than neatly filed in a project folder. Regardless of your brain dominance, checking a list now and then does keep important project elements from falling through cracks.

A full-blown left-brained project plan will include:
- Written purpose statement
- Personal timeline
- List of stories (with the option of adding others as they come to mind)
- List other material to be included (pictures, documents, etc.)
- Organization plan
- Estimated length
- Plan for compiling and publishing

- Target completion date
- Milestones

A right-brained project plan may be as insubstantial as recognizing an impulse and deciding to act on it. That was the extent of the plan that led me to write *The Albuquerque Years*, and for that project it was enough. One step naturally led to the next. For larger projects, I do use planning tools.

Right-brainers are notorious for impetuous writing binges, and respond eagerly to the call of the muse. They are likely to have piles of unfinished stories sitting around. They'll often experiment with various styles of writing, and may not have a clear idea of how, when, or why they'd want to print and distribute collections of their stories. That represents an extreme. Most right-brain lifestory writers do have a purpose in mind, and a general idea of where the project is going to go. However, instead of committing a plan to the rigidity of paper, they tend to work from a mental image or gut feeling of what they should be doing to get where they want to go. They aren't above borrowing left-brained planning tools, or even scheduling steps when it matters and will serve a purpose.

Left-brainers are likely to work in short spurts, at regularly scheduled intervals (be that a day or weeks apart). Unlike their right-brained cousins who have piles of unfinished work, left-brainers are likely to have one piece of work and may get stuck perfecting it rather than moving on. I work best when I immerse myself in a project for hours or days at a time. Sometimes, especially with longer stories, large chunks take shape in my mind, and I have trouble focusing on other things until I get the words on paper. You may work best when you spend smaller periods at regular intervals. The only right answer is what works best for you. Let past experience guide you.

A well-documented plan based on a timeline will serve you well if you have a commitment to producing a finished product and a deadline in mind. If you are writing for recreation or self-exploration, you certainly don't need that sort of plan. Neither approach is inherently better than the other. Left-brainers and right-brainers are likely to work from different purposes in the first place, and your plan should serve your purpose as well as your personal work style.

It's a matter of time

The most common writing obstacle anyone faces is time, and if you are serious about writing your lifestory, time management is a factor. Writing does take time, but it only takes as much as you give it. It's a simple truth that we make time for the things that are important to us, whether that involves exercise, family activities, playing golf, or writing. Be honest about the importance of this project, consider how much time you can devote to it, and plan accordingly.

Clear priorities are the primary key to managing time. Working through the planning steps in the exercise at the end of this chapter will help you prioritize events in your life so you can begin writing about the most important, and work your way down the list. If you run out of time, at least you'll have the major bases covered.

Don't be deterred if you determine you'll need one hundred stories and you only have time to write one a month. Even if you skip a couple of months, then spend six months editing and organizing, you can finish in nine years. If you don't start writing, in nine years, your lifestory will still be an empty book. If you begin, but never finish the project, as my mother didn't, at least you will leave something behind, and your family will be as tickled (and maybe surprised) as I was.

You don't have to write your whole lifestory as a single project, or even to finish a specific theme or time period without straying. Thelly Reahm, a lifestory writing friend in California, known locally in Cardiff-by-the-Sea as Story Lady, has written over five hundred of her own lifestories, assembled with the collective title *Tidbits of Time.* Her stated purpose is to build character in her readers and pass down family traditions, morals, political holdings, and spiritual beliefs to her descendants. Despite this noble-sounding purpose, Thelly's stories tend to be humorous and/or touching, admired by a large following on the Internet. Every Christmas she gives her children, grandchildren, and great-grandchildren a volume of the current year's stories, along with instructions on where to file them in the binders she previously gave them.

Thelly began this project in 1996 and her stories fill several binders. She has posted a large collection of her stories on her website and blog. You can easily locate and read them by doing an Internet search for her name.

Selecting a Framework

Your framework is the organizing principle for your project and closely related to your purpose. While you don't need a specific framework in mind to get started, having a preliminary idea of the form for your finished project will help you determine which stories to write, and how to piece them together. To choose a framework, consider *whom* you are writing for, *what* effect you want the material to have, and *how* you can best achieve that effect for those people. A brief description of the most common frameworks follows.

Chronological

This style is biographical, and shows the full scope of your life as it flowed from one year to the next. In general, chronological lifestories tend to be more documentary and less descriptive, though that doesn't have to be the case. Peter is using a chronological framework for the story his children mandated. He started writing with a short description of his ancestors, followed by such details of his birth as he had. He went on from there to write straight through grade school, high school, college, and his career. Peter has strong left-brain dominance, and works well with structure and planning.

Vignette

Vignette stories are a descriptive slice of life, written as stand-alone stories about topics like a person you knew, a job you held, or a special experience. They work well in theme or assorted topic collections. A vignette may be as long or short as you wish. Let the story itself dictate the length. Nearly everything I write is a vignette, and I love that I can usually write one in a single sitting.

Thematic

A thematic framework consists of a collection of stories written around a central theme, such as recipes. Ruth Reichl, the editor-in-chief of *Gourmet* magazine, has written three best-selling memoirs on the theme of food. Each chapter is part of an overall story, and she includes a related recipe at the end of each chapter. Other people have written cookbooks that feature a story per recipe. Your theme could center on cars in your life, coin-collecting adventures, influential teachers, or anything you can imagine. Amanda has written a collection of fourteen stories about her adventures on cruise ships. A common thread runs through all these cruises, and she is organizing the solitary stories into a unified whole by reminiscing on her reflections and insights between cruises as a way of weaving the parts into a coherent overall story.

Like Amanda, I find that themes develop within groups of stories I spontaneously write. For example, I have a seasonal theme comprising stories about seasons of the year, and a humorous series of adventures with friends. Two stories from my chilihead theme begin on page 218. I also have a growing pile of stories about my mother, my children, and so on. *Crunchy Frosting* (page 199) is on a cooking/recipes theme. You'll read more about themes in Chapter Eleven.

Scrapbook

Some people accrue a collection of assorted stories with no particular theme or writing approach. The stories may use different styles of expression as well as addressing different topics. My bulging portfolio includes humorous stories, essays, family stories, descriptive stories, and others that defy classification. Scrapbook memoirs are the easiest to fill up, and a challenge to organize effectively. They may be organized chronologically, by topic, by relationships, or by any other method that makes sense. Alternatively, you could leave them as they are, for future readers to read at random.

Some people know immediately and instinctively what form they want to use in their projects. If you aren't sure which approach will work best for you, select scrapbook as your default, and start writing. Sooner or later a plan will fall into place for you. If it doesn't, your descendants will be happy to have a collection of loose stories.

You aren't limited to working with just one form. Your scrapbook is similar to the sketchpads of Michelangelo or DaVinci. Some of their most fascinating work is *Writers are word artists.* in their sketchpads, which show their thought process and the evolution of style. What a loss it would have been if these sketchpads had been tossed out! Your pile of unfinished or unsorted stories may be viewed the same way, as inspiration for future compilations or a later glimpse into your mind at work. Your holding file may contain a chronological account of a specific period, several vignettes, and a pile of assorted stories and essays. Someday you may organize the vignettes and stories into a collection with a pet theme, a grade school theme, stories about your children, and so on. Perhaps the themes will become chapters or sections in a finished volume.

Lifestory writing may become addictive, but hey—you are producing something tangible, which is more than you can say for watching television, playing computer games, or many other leisure activities. Furthermore, research is showing that writing is the type of activity that encourages formation of new brain cells, even in people past the age of seventy, and it may delay the onset of Alzheimer's symptoms. It could prove to be a genuine fountain of youth, for your mind if not your body.

Memoir, Autobiography, or Lifestory?

When I wrote *The Albuquerque Years*, I agonized over what to call it. Was it a memoir or an autobiography? I hadn't heard the term lifestory, though when I did, it intuitively sounded right to me. But my left brain screamed for accuracy in conforming to truth-in-labeling practices, so I kept looking for precise definitions to guide me. As I read and dug, I determined that distinctions among memoir, autobiography, and lifestory are fine ones, and a matter of degree. I once had a neat list defining the differences among these categories, but when I began to write an article for a webzine about this topic, the differences began to blur. The article, reprinted on the following pages, took the form of a personal essay, which is another form of lifestory writing, loosely defined.

Autobiography, Memoir, or Lifestory—
Beyond the Confusion

When I first became interested in writing my own life history, I wanted to write the perfect story. After all, I was writing about the most intense and important topic I knew – myself! I was writing from and about my heart. A big part of writing the perfect story involved knowing what to call it. I wasn't sure whether I wanted to write my autobiography or memoirs, or just what the difference might be.

I headed for the library and book store in search of help on defining my writing form and learning how to go about it. Over the next few weeks I found and read several excellent volumes, but I became more confused about terminology. Some books referred to the type of writing I was attempting as autobiography, others as memoir, and still others as life story or lifestory writing. They all seemed to be talking about more or less the same thing, and none defined the term they chose. My next stop was **Webster's Unabridged**, which offered the following definition:

> **Autobiography** A biography written by the subject of it; memoirs of one's life written by oneself.

So, I thought, autobiography and memoir are two words for the same thing. Reading the full definitions for biography and memoir supported this conclusion. Perhaps lifestory writing was yet another word for the same thing. If so, why so many terms?

My search for clarity continued. Eventually I derived some intuitive definitions, based on my perception of common usage. It appeared to me that *autobiography* was primarily linear in nature, covering the full space of a life up to the time of writing, and was largely documentary. *Memoir* was a more artistically developed literary form that could address limited periods of time and specific experiences. It left more room for creativity, interpretation and emotion. *Lifestory writing* seemed to me to be the most spontaneous, natural, cozy form, informally written from the heart, like a letter to a friend. This was the style I felt at home with. I settled into it and began writing stories.

I accepted the challenge of writing an article to explain the differences in form I had derived. Soon after I began writing, I became aware of a funny feeling in my tummy – a feeling I've learned to identify as a sign that the limb I'm creeping out on is beginning to dip precariously toward the ground. Rather than stay on that shaky limb, I returned to the research I thought I'd finished a couple of years ago. I pulled my collection of books off the shelf, and began flipping through them, one by one, wondering where my subconscious was leading me.

At first I found nothing new. Then, at the bottom of the stack, I found **Your Life as Story** by Tristine Rainer (Tarcher/Putnam, 1997). Glancing at the Table of Contents, I noticed Chapter Two, *The Evolution of a New Autobiography*. My pulse quickened. Would I finally find the answer to my question? Maybe what I was trying to write about was actually this – new autobiography! She apologized for including a historical treatise at the beginning of a highly personal instructional book. I didn't recall reading this material before. I plunged in and read the history of autobiography, starting with the ancient Egyptians, who considered a copy of their memoirs essential to bargaining with the gods in the next life. I read about the early confessional writings of sinners-turned-saints and later ones of financially desperate fallen women. I learned about the exhortational works of religious early Americans and financially successful later ones.

Rainer explained that from colonial times, fiction reading was considered wanton, and little fiction was available. Aside from scripture and news, exhortational autobiography was the reading of choice. In the mid-1800s, adventures of escaped slaves and captivity narratives by women held hostage by Indians became enormously popular. In frenzied attempts to make material ever more compelling to readers, the boundary between fact and fiction blurred. Sensationalism blazed as brightly then as now.

Around the turn of the century, the novel emerged from this literary quagmire as a respectable and almost revered form of writing. Half the population dreamed of writing the Great American Novel. By the middle of the 1900s, the situation once again reversed, and writing from a personal perspective became the rage, even among successful novelists. Today the list of forms this personalized writing takes seems endless: "faction" (fact-based fiction), docudrama, nonfiction novels, personal journalism, dramatic nonfiction, literature of fact, creative nonfiction, autobiographical novels, nonfiction narrative, personal essay, literary memoir and probably others. The plethora of terminology dazzled and befuddled me, yet I found it reassuring. Shackles of confusion shattered from terminology overload. Could insight be far away?

Heartened by the hope I gained from Trainer, I turned to the Internet for more information. As usual, I had no trouble finding over 12,000 listings for websites offering tips on writing autobiography, memoirs, life stories, or personal history, but I found no site that defined differences among these forms. Major sites are cross-listed on all terms, apparently considering them interchangeable. Finally I discovered the site for the journal *Creative Nonfiction* (http://creativenonfiction.org/the-journal/whatiscnf.htm) and listened to a series of RealAudio interviews with Lee Gutkind, the editor and founder of the journal. Like Rainer, Gutkind emphasizes the value of using literary techniques like story telling, scene setting, dialogue, and description to elevate the quality of non-fiction stories, generally told from a personal perspective. Suddenly I found what I'd been seeking. I caught the emphasis on the word *story* – as in *lifestory.* Everything fell into place.

All the dozen or more "new" forms I found listed, along with traditional autobiography and memoir, are ways of telling *stories* that come from the fiber of our lives. They have roots in tribal customs as old as mankind. They remind me of the ancient Hawaiian tradition of "talking story" as Aunty Jo, a Hawaiian elder, did with an Elderhostel group I attended on the Big Island. We sat spellbound one night as she spontaneously described life in early Kailua, her faith, being sold by her mother for a few dollars into a forced marriage of virtual slavery, her escape from that marriage, her return to Kailua from California and more. None of the passions of life were overlooked. This was not a rehearsed story. She told it in answer to a simple question. Did she recount her autobiography? I wouldn't call it that. Did she recite a memoir? Hardly! She simply *talked story.*

Aunty Jo and the Islanders talk story. I write story. Now that I've become acquainted with all these new words describing so many more ways of writing stories, I realize that the attempt to define terms is meaningless. I've come to understand that writing stories from our experience, from our lives, is far too personal a matter and too complex a challenge to be bound by form. Our form will be as personal as the stories we write, and our reasons for writing them. The forms we evolve will be perfect for our unique stories.

The challenge as I see it today is not to master a specific form of writing, it is to master writing itself, and to master the discipline of persistence in writing. Our challenge is to become crystal clear about our personal message and to continually refine our skills so we can present that message in the most compelling way, whether in an essay, an adventure story, a personal letter or some entirely new form. We may even choose to tell several stories, several different ways. The more we develop our ability to separate the wheat from the chaff, refine the essence of the message, and master skills like dialogue, character development, or sensory description, the more compelling our stories will become.

At the bottom line, if we write nothing, we leave no message. Anything at all that we write about our lives will be appreciated by at least some of our descendants later, no matter how humble the effort. No beginner should let ignorance of form or style delay the writing of a single word. Go beyond the confusion and simply write the story that is in your heart. Call it what you like and let it grow as it will. Learn as you go, and it will become your own perfect story.

Since writing that essay, I have found further clarification and support for my intuitive assessment. Lifestory is a collective term, spanning a continuum from autobiography to memoir. The autobiography designation applies specifically to lifestories that follow a linear flow through the course of a life and emphasize objective, verifiable material. They tend to be historical and documentary in nature.

Memoir takes quite a different slant by including extensive reflection on the events of life, emphasizing personal truth. In his book, *White Gloves*, about the development of memory, psychology professor John Kotre explains that memory serves as a structure for making sense of life and understanding who we are. Memoir incorporates memories from this point of view rather than a precise, empirical one. Although a memoir writer should always respect the reader's expectation of honest reporting, in the service of conveying your own point of view there is room for a certain amount of flexibility in interpretation and description.

Most lifestories written primarily for family distribution fall somewhere between these two designations. Write your own story, your own way, in your own words, conveying truth as you understand it, and you will never go wrong. Keep in mind that *words printed on a page are nothing more than words.* The most they can do is create an illusion of a life once lived. There is always a story behind the story. No matter how much and how long you write, you can never include more than a few facets of your life.

One other writing form, the personal essay, also has relevance for lifestory writers. The primary difference between essay and memoir is purpose or focus. In memoir, the focus is on specific experiences. Interpretation is a means of making sense of experience. In personal essay, the focus is on the interpretation, and experience gives substance to the interpretation. In a nutshell, if you are simply describing things that happened to you, that's lifestory. If you add material about what the experiences meant to you, you are moving into memoir. If you write about how you think or feel about a topic, and add descriptions of your experience to explain your views, that's essay.

Don't worry about labels. Just write what's in your heart and let people with degrees in literature and writing worry about labels.

Caveat: Planning is good. I strongly advise it. But planning is not better than writing. Don't fall into the trap of planning *instead* of writing. You can keep coming up with story ideas for the rest of your life, but the ones you think of in the first few days or weeks are likely to remain the most interesting and urgent for you, and the ones that give the most vivid sense of who you are. As soon as you have a reasonable sense of direction and list of ideas, turn your thoughts to writing, and work further planning around it.

Making Sense of Memory

One of the most powerful planning tools is to make a list of memories to generate story ideas. But memories come in several packages, and not all serve the same purpose in story writing. Before moving on to the various ways of capturing and organizing memories, let's take a closer look at their nature.

At first glance, lists of memories seem rather simple. From preschool years, I remember my parents, some toys, the birth of my sister, going to Sunday School, swinging, learning to roller skate, and so forth. As an adult, I remember belonging to League of Women Voters, taking care of sick babies, beginning grad school, joining Toastmasters, a string of jobs, and so forth.

On closer examination, you can notice differences within this list. Some are factual memories of events that can be verified with documentation or other evidence, such as birthdays, wedding dates, or school attendance. Others are composite narrative memories, formed from a consolidation of clustered events such as learning to roller skate, performing routine tasks, or driving a car. These are generally ongoing activities that define and shape our lives. A third category is examined memories, those narrative memories that we keep going back to and exploring in our mind to make sense of things.

Your initial memories and the order in which you remember them are significant in conveying this meaning to yourself and to others. In light of that, if you are writing primarily for self-exploration, you are well advised to simply pick up a pen and begin writing about the first thing that comes to mind and go from there, without trying to capture memories. Order is significant in disclosing meaning.

If your story is primarily for others, you may want to include aspects of daily life and other trivia that don't always come to mind easily. Lists of trigger questions and similar material will give you more ideas than you'll ever have time to write about. As your list of memories grows, you'll find that many cluster together and fit well into a single story. You may want to start a second list for specific story topics or titles. Whether you use one list or several, lists help you organize your approach, keep track, and give you something to write about on days when your creativity is at a low ebb and you're tempted to let your writing slide.

Capturing and Organizing Memories

Once your memories start flowing, they may begin gushing like a fire hose. Without a way to capture them on the fly, many will vanish as quickly as they appeared. The three tools below are especially useful for capturing core memories in a flexible form. As you develop momentum, your organization strategy may become fluid and take on a life of its own. This is good. This means the system is gaining power and impact.

Card stack

Take a stack of 3x5 cards and write one story idea on each. Keep writing as long as you can think of ideas. Include a few key story points on the card if they easily come to mind, as in Figure 3, but don't succumb to the temptation to begin writing the story on the card. Stick to a rudimentary outline. When a card like the one on the left has a large number of sub-points, you may want to zoom in more deeply and break it down into several stories, depending on your purpose.

When you're finished, assuming you are planning an organized project and not simply looking for random story ideas, lay the cards out and sort them into related piles. These piles form

MOVED TO TULSA 1951
NEW SCHOOL, TOUGH TEACHER
TREE HOUSE IN YARD
TOMMY JONES NEXT DOOR.
SHORTY GOT LOST

GRADUATION! 1958

Figure 3: Typical stack of note cards

logical section or chapter headings. Label each pile and use it as a starting place for that section or chapter. As you sort, you'll probably think of new ideas.

As mentioned earlier, keep blank index cards or note paper in your pocket or purse, and jot ideas on them any time. Then add these cards to your collection. Use these cards for story ideas when you are ready to write. In a pinch you can certainly scribble ideas on paper napkins, envelopes, etc. The safest, most orderly way to ensure these don't get lost later is to transfer the information to cards and add them to your stack. Orderly left-brainers will do this. Others who are less compulsive will do well to have a box, envelope, or some other place to put them for safekeeping.

> ### Exercise
> Take a stack of blank index cards or memo tablet sheets and jot down ideas for at least five minutes. Sort the stack, and prioritize for writing.
> For an extra challenge, try doing this with a stack of one hundred cards, making sure you fill each of the cards with one fact about your life. You don't have to stop at one hundred.

Trigger questions

Doing a memory scan for spontaneous memories is helpful, but deeper ones surface only in relation to other memories. Many of these may eventually arise as you begin writing, but trigger questions provide a fast, reliable way of digging out that sort of information. You'll find a list of typical trigger questions beginning on page 243. If you like this approach and want more questions, do a web search for trigger questions, and check the library for additional books on writing lifestories and memoirs that feature trigger questions.

Reminder resources

Like trigger questions, items on the following list of resources will help you remember additional stories and refresh your memory on details. Several of the items listed, like photos, letters, or journal excerpts, can be included as illustrations to add extra interest to your stories.

- *Old photographs.* If you have boxes full, select the most significant. Use these as memory joggers while writing, and include a few in your finished copy.

    If you want to use photos or documents in your story, and you aren't able to scan them yourself, try a copy shop. Most copy shops and photo centers can scan them and save the files on a disk for you, or you could leave space on the finished page and paste them in before copying. General instructions for inserting photographs and other types of graphics are found on page 264.

- *Scrapbooks* may include programs from plays, dance cards, invitations, announcements, newspaper clippings, and other trivia that ties in with stories. Even if you didn't keep a scrapbook, you or your mother may have kept a box or trunk full of similar mementos.

- *Diaries or journals* can be a treasure trove of memories and insights. One key difference between lifestories and journals is that journals generally take one of two forms—some record spontaneous reactions and feelings while others are little

41

more than a log of events. Stories take those events and reactions and emphasize their significance by giving form and shape to add meaning for readers.

- *Calendars* remind you of forgotten events, and they are the gold standard for documenting dates.

- *Music* and songs can trigger gushing floods of long-forgotten memories. Chances are that if you still have old recordings, they'll be on records, and relatively few people still have working turntables. You can probably find copies in updated formats. Check the library, or search the Internet. Numerous websites allow you to listen to music over the Internet and download selections at little or no charge.

- *Letters*, written to or by you. Perhaps relatives have saved letters you wrote to them or have other relevant material they would return or loan you. Ask them, and get them involved with your project.

- *Documents* like birth and marriage certificates, graduation diplomas, property deeds and transfers, paycheck stubs and records, military service records, and similar material can bring back memories, and provide interesting illustrations in your finished story.

    If you're a packrat, you may still have receipts, warranties, travel brochures, maps and all sorts of things your family swore you'd never look at again. Here's your chance to prove they were wrong and put the items to good use.

- *Family members and friends* can remind you of stories or recall details you don't remember. Tell them about your project, and ask about their memories. It's enlightening and fascinating to explore how differently people remember things. You may want to incorporate some of these differences into your story. Just remember that *you* own the story!

    After reading one of my stories, my sister once began correcting my faulty memory. "You may be right, but that's not the way I remember it, and this is *my* story about what *I* remember," I told her. "I guess you need to write your own story." She laughed and agreed that she just may do that.

- *Websites.* Search for sites on memoirs, genealogy, historical events, locations, etc. If you don't have Internet access at home, go to the library. The librarians are happy to show you the basics of how to use it, and many libraries offer free classes on doing Internet research.

Caveat: A search for "Lifestory writing tips" will yield thousands of hits. Unfortunately, as time goes by, an increasing number of these sites are simply selling classes, services, or products, and few have useful information posted on the site. Read the information below about autobiography kits before investing in any products.

Autobiography kits

One popular approach to writing lifestories is to use a comprehensive list of questions, such as "What was your favorite toy as a child?" to produce something amounting to a fill-in-the-blanks story. There are kits on the market with printed questions and a few inches of space to write answers under each one. A lifestory written with one of these kits will give a lot of information about you, but it doesn't record spontaneous memories or priorities about what you consider important. These kits have only a small amount of space allocated to each question. Some questions may get you so excited you could easily fill six pages, and others may be irrelevant. One solution to that dilemma is to jot notes in these books for some questions, and write full stories for others.

Those are the negative aspects of using kits. One of the benefits is that this may be the only way some people will ever write down anything at all, and *any lifestory you write is better than writing nothing,* even if it's just fill-in-the-blank answers to someone else's questions. If these kits appeal to you for yourself, or you want to give one to a relative who's not likely to write more than that, by all means, use them.

Mind map

Mind maps are helpful for organizing memories on any scale from your whole life to specific stories, and a powerful way of capturing watershed memories. They form a non-linear outline of clustered memories relating to specific topics, people, or events. Begin by writing a name, event, or similar core concept in the center of your paper. Draw a circle around this. As related ideas come to mind, draw a line out from the circle and write the new idea at the end of it, using just one or two words. You can keep drawing additional clusters off the new ideas.

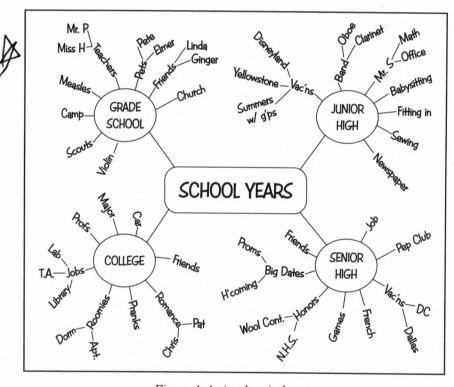

Figure 4: A simple mind map

Some people use colored pens to draw mind maps, using different colors for different types of ideas. Maps can be as simple or complex as you care to make them. You could make a map of your whole life that covered an entire wall. You could make a pile of smaller maps with more focused content, or you may just do a quick one when you feel stuck. You can include copies of mind maps with your collection of stories to make your thought process visible. Another way to do mind maps is to use Post-It® notes for each idea, and cluster the notes around core concepts. Figure 4 captures highlights of typical school years. Each word represents a potential story.

Because they are intuitive and non-linear and allow for indicating many links for each object as your brain does, mind maps will especially appeal to right-brain thinkers. The example in Figure 4 is tidy. Spontaneous maps tend to be messy, with lines all over the place, because you don't know where the ideas will fit, or how many there will be when you first start.

Exercise
Use the largest piece of paper you can find to make a mind map of your life. Cut open an old grocery bag for lots of room.

Watershed memories

Watershed memories, often referred to as turning points or insights, are the ones that shape and give meaning to our lives. They may be events such as the birth of a sibling, move to a new town, death of a parent or spouse, graduation from school, marriage, birth of children, and so forth. They also include moments of striking insight such as a religious conversion, feeling especially loved, discovering that you enjoy being onstage, or realizing that it is okay to hate swimming.

Watershed memories may also be small, quiet events that pass almost unnoticed at the time. These are memories of events where you realized something new about the world, and your understanding changed forever. They aren't necessarily connected with major events, but they are generally sudden.

One of my own watershed memories from the year I was six was tiny, quiet, and instantaneous. I glanced across the living room and noticed my father lift my younger sister into his lap to tie her shoe. *He'll never hold me in his lap that way again,* I thought. *I'm too big for that now.* There was neither pain nor joy attached to this realization. I just knew that's how things were, and the insight redefined my relationship with my father from that moment on. Another occurred when I suddenly realized I was pregnant with my first child. I came of age at that moment, the last vestiges of girlhood falling aside in my mind like a snake's discarded skin.

If you begin listing watershed memories, you may see your life pass before you as a sort of parade, similar to the life review process described by near-death survivors. The watershed memories are the ones that stand out. Not everyone experiences this linear flow. Some people find their thoughts jumping all over, often with no obvious relationship between adjacent memories. In either case, the process of listing them should proceed quickly, because these memories lie on the top of the heap. If you have to dig, it probably isn't a watershed memory, although some less happy ones may lie below the surface.

Exploring watershed memories is especially helpful to those who write for self-discovery, healing, or to convey a philosophy of life, because these memories generally identify the root of attitudes and self-concept. Other writers may find this list helpful for shaping a timeline or identifying topical areas to organize random memories.

> **_Exercise_**
> *Make a list of your own watershed memories. File the list away and transfer those you want to use in stories to your card stack and/or story list.*

Story list

I refer to your story list several places in this book. This list includes all the story ideas you want to include in your project. It serves as a checklist, allowing you to write in any order and still cover all the material. Place a checkmark next to the item or cross it off the list as you complete that story. If you are an orderly thinker, you may prefer to prioritize your stories, placing the most urgent at the top of the list and working your way down as you write. Or, you could arrange them in chronological order, using the personal timeline described in the following section. If you are of a more spontaneous nature, just make the list and use it as a touchstone now and then to renew inspiration and ensure you don't miss anything important.

Personal timeline

A timeline is a powerful aid for arranging your memories in chronological order. You may not choose to order them this way in final form, but a timeline is still helpful for keeping things straight in your own mind. Readers appreciate having a timeline to help them place events within the timeframe of your life, especially when your story flow is non-linear. If your project covers a limited period, a timeline for that specific period of time will suffice.

The basic mechanics of making a timeline are simple. Make a table, two columns wide, with a row for each year of your life. Starting with the year you were born, number the left column, one year per row. Now, adjust the width of that column to be just wide enough for the numbers.

In the right column, list the events of the year. In my own timeline, I begin the entry with the season, month, or specific date of the event, if I remember and it's relevant. I've used the hanging indent format for paragraphs so entries that wrap to a second line stand out. I add just enough detail in the entry to give a general sense of the event without going into the story, and I keep adding new items as I think of them. Examples, taken from two different years are shown in Figure 5.

1953	Spring: Miss Hones marries Mr. Young. Takes Cheryl Jackson and me to help her clean her new home before the wedding.
	Fall: Begin Fourth Grade with Mrs. Wheelock.
1957	Sept: JUNIOR HIGH – eight classes per day!
	Geography class – Mr. Otis. We do class maps. Father teaches me to use grid for enlarging images.
	Second chair, first violin.

Figure 5: Sample Timeline

Note how subtopics for Junior High are indented one level to make organization more visually obvious. I'm a formatting junkie. I personalized my table with a few embellishments. I've omitted vertical lines, and left horizontal lines between each year. The year entries in the left column are in bold. I've used a special font (CAC Futura Casual) for a hand-written look. You can jazz yours up, or leave it plain and simple. Format is less important than function. It works fine to simply put the year on a separate line and list events underneath without using a table at all. See Appendix Three for further instructions on formatting stories with your computer.

If you aren't comfortable with the computer, work with pencil and paper. Index cards work well for this purpose. Start with one card per year, and add more as needed. When you finish, transfer this collection of information to a computer file, type a copy, or write one by hand. Later you may want a typed copy to include with your project.

Timelines are valuable as a reference tool even if you never write a single story. My own took considerable time and research to complete, but now I don't have to agonize over which year I worked for Tri-Com, broke my ankle, friends moved to town, or we went to Yellowstone. At least once a year I update it. When I print story collections for family members, my timeline will immediately follow the Table of Contents, serving as a map to place events in the stories within my life's timeframe.

As you work on your timeline, you'll probably find that over a life spanning many decades it isn't easy remembering what happened in a given year, or which year specific things happened. You may have to settle for approximate dates and general periods. Dig through your files, talk to relatives and do other research. You'll produce a valuable family resource that your siblings and offspring will also find useful.

Some people include major historical events. The website hosted by www.OurTimeLines.com is especially helpful for getting started on this. If this website disappears, search for a world events almanac or "events of 1969," or some such thing. Ask your reference librarian if you get stumped. They are eager to help, in person, by telephone, and probably by e-mail (check the library website). Your tax dollars pay their salaries, so don't hesitate to make use of this valuable resource.

Exercise
Take a pile of paper and begin laying out your own timeline, from the day you were born through the present. Alternatively, set up a two-column table with one row per year of your life, and begin filling it in on your computer, listing as many or as few major events as you remember. If you are uncertain about any dates, do research on them. Add to this timeline until you are satisfied with it, then keep it current from one year to the next.

Compiling Your Plan

If you've used some or all of the tools described above, you'll have a huge amount of material. The following exercise will help you organize it into a working document to guide you through your project with the smoothest possible path.

Exercise
Answer as many of the questions below as you can, then add a list of stories compiled from your card stack to formulate a complete plan of action for your project. If you have trouble with any, it's okay to leave them blank for now. Start on it, go as far as you can see, and you'll be able to see further when you get there.

- *What purpose do you have for this project?*
- *Who will your readers be?*
- *What are their specific interests?*
- *What point of view will you take?*
- *List at least a dozen stories you want to write, ranking them in terms of importance.*
- *What framework will you use to organize your collection of stories, e.g., chronological or scrapbook?*
- *How much time per day or week do you plan to devote to this project?*
- *When do you plan to finish this project?*
- *What steps do you plan to take to clear the time to work on this project?*
- *How can you make your writing environment pleasant so you'll enjoy sitting down to work?*

Working the Plan

No matter how immaculately you plan, as your project progresses, you'll find new story ideas you want to incorporate, and you may think of alternate ways to organize your material. This is natural, so expect it. This is one reason I encourage you to begin writing fairly soon, doing additional planning in small chunks along with your writing. All lifestory writers, whether they make an entire plan first, write and plan simultaneously, or confine most plans to their heads, share one aspect of the process: all will cycle through the basic story writing process dozens of times before the end of the project. In Figure 1 back on page 15, you'll notice a loop going from the project plan through the core story-writing process to the holding file, then back up to the project plan. However you go about it, the story list in the project plan will eventually be empty, the holding file will be full, and you'll progress to compiling and printing your final volume.

Keep in mind that writing always takes precedence over planning. Don't obsess over your plan. Do as much as you are able or inclined, and that will be enough. Somehow, in the end, it all works out.

Chapter 3:

Where Heart Meets Paper

A scrupulous writer, in every sentence that he writes, will ask himself at least four questions, thus: 1. What am I trying to say? 2. What words will express it? 3. What image or idiom will make it clearer? 4. Is this image fresh enough to have an effect?

— *George Orwell*

Pouring your words onto paper is the point at which you begin exposing the contents of your heart for others to see. This is an act of faith. When you speak with people directly, you monitor their reactions and adjust your words accordingly. You write bravely and blindly, without feedback, hoping to make these words true and understandable to all readers for generations to come. Some find this challenge daunting. Others know intuitively what they want to say, and the story takes on a life of its own with words gushing from fingers as soon as they begin moving. Those who experience this latter phenomenon will quickly tell you that they don't actually write the stories—the stories are simply "there," waiting to be recorded.

I experience this gushing story syndrome now and then. I sense a story building in my mind, and the urge to sit down and write becomes intense. I generally know the subject, but the shape of the story may be fuzzy. I'm often surprised at the form it takes and sometimes I gain new insights into past events as a result. These stories seldom need much editing.

Nobody can explain precisely what causes this phenomenon, but it appears to come from material the brain has processed on a level below awareness, perhaps during sleep, and the recording phase is handled by the intuitive right side of the brain. Writers who experience this state of flow often refer to it as "being in the zone."

Unfortunately, not all writing is like this. The initial draft is frequently the most challenging and intimidating part of writing. Some people never get "in the zone," and others do only rarely. I've heard of no one who claims to be there all the time. Sometimes there are no words. You can sit and stare at your computer screen or paper for a solid day without producing a single coherent sentence. More often, you have an idea of what you want to say, but words tangle and jam in your fingers. That may be the situation you face as you begin your lifestory writing project. Many people feel swamped by the idea, and use procrastination to soothe their anxiety.

If you want to begin writing but feel uncertain what to write about, the answer is simple: It doesn't matter. You can begin anywhere. A completed lifestory is similar to a necklace made up of a strand of dozens of unique, individually hand-crafted beads. You can begin with any piece, jumping around as you write, and arranging the order only when you are ready to string the necklace. You can begin with your birth and hammer your way through the calendar. Or you can begin at the top of a list arranged in some other order. If no idea comes readily to mind, look at your list of story ideas or your stack of cards and pick out an easy one. If you decide to write a chronological lifestory, start at the beginning, with a story about your family.

Include details like who your grandparents were, and where the family originated.

Here is where the path forks. You stand at a decision point regarding this specific story. Will you take time to plan the story, or begin writing spontaneously? Two criteria will provide guidance. If you feel that gushing story syndrome bursting your brain, let it rip. Don't read any further—begin writing without delay. You should also begin to spontaneously write if your primary purpose is self-discovery. Let your purpose be your guide and follow the story-planning loop with your chosen topic in mind.

Story Planning

Just as planning a lifestory project helps make the process run more smoothly and directly, planning a story can help you get it on paper more easily, with less rewriting, and ensure it conveys the intended message. Written notes or an outline are helpful, especially for less experienced writers, but for very short stories, they may not be needed. The relationship of this plan to the overall story-writing process is illustrated in Figure 6, a flow diagram of the story-writing process excerpted from the larger project plan flow diagram in Figure 1. The rest of this chapter discusses the key elements of well-structured stories. With the exception of dialogue, which is always optional, these elements apply to stories of any length, from short vignettes to full-length autobiographies. If you write a spontaneous story, use this material as an editing checklist.

Define the purpose

Just as a clear purpose gives focus to your project, a clear purpose gives shape and focus to a story. For example, it helps you decide what details are important, what tone it should have. You may assume that the purpose of any story in your project

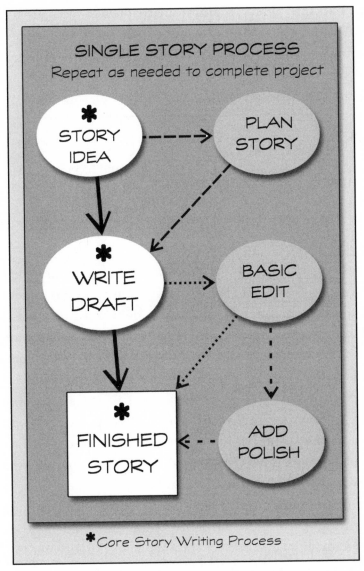

Figure 6: Writing the single story

is simply to tell what happened, what things were like, and so forth. A purpose may shade the way you present that information. If your only readers are close to your age, you can skip much of the detail about how things were done in your childhood that your grandchildren would need to make sense of the story. You may want to entertain readers as you present the facts. You may want to alert them to dangers, or inspire them to certain beliefs or courses of action. Knowing this purpose while you plan and write the story increases the likelihood of attaining the desired result.

Exercise

Ask yourself "Why am I writing this story? What does it mean to me, and what do I want people to understand after they read it?" State the answer in a single sentence, and keep it in mind as you write. Analyze the final story against the yardstick of your purpose.

Choose a title

The title constitutes the first words of the story and serves as an advertisement, so it should draw readers in, and make them want to keep reading. Your title can be a word or phrase that sums up the content of the story, or it might be the name of a character in the story. There are no standard rules, and until you make final copies, you can always change the title.

The story topic will probably suggest the title. For example, a story of how you met your spouse when you were thirty-six, got acquainted, and fell in love may be titled "Love at Last." A story of a camping trip with a buddy the summer you were sixteen, when you spent the night in the car because there was a bear in camp, might be titled "Bearly Alive." Telling how you nearly froze getting out of bed in your unheated bedroom on winter mornings and racing your sister to the kitchen to dress near the stove could be called "Icicle Mornings."

If the title serves only to keep track of a piece of a larger story while it's stored in your scrapbook pile, any utility title will work. If the title will be included with the story, use your imagination. Chronological writers may use story titles as headers within chapters when the final version is assembled. You'll find more discussion of that in Appendix Three.

Key points

One of the most common lifestory shortcomings is a lack of facts. Many writers neglect to tell where or when the story took place. They identify story characters by name only, forgetting that readers may not know their relationship to the author. Be sure you've covered the basics of who, what, where, when, and why. Not every story requires each element, but if you skip one, make sure the story doesn't suffer. If you write a series of stories to be read together, identity and similar information can carry over. Cover relevant bases clearly within isolated stories.

Who

If your only brother is named Edwin, you don't need to name him in every half-page story within a collection. However, if you have three sisters, Alice, Alexa, and Alvina, make sure we know which sister you are talking about at any given time. This was one of my grandmother's pitfalls. She wrote:

> The next thing I remember was seeing a big, tall, handsome cowboy come riding up on horseback. I was playing on a long porch, a gallery they called it then. I was delighted to learn that he was my brother who had been gone to far-off places for a long time and I didn't recognize him. He became my hero at once. He always brought home gifts which little girls loved.

Nobody will ever know which of her seven brothers he was. Does this matter? Not really—but since she brought it up, I'd like to know, and had she been able to read this book, she would have known to fix it.

I also wonder what gifts little girls loved and I'd like to know what far-away places the brother had visited. A short sentence giving his location would be quite satisfactory. She did do well to tell us that the porch was called a gallery in earlier times.

When

Include at least a general timeframe. This opening paragraph is non-specific, but tells the ages of all the characters:

> Kay and I are already outside playing when Martha comes out.
> She lives next door and she's eleven, two years older than I am.
> Sometimes she won't play with us, especially when Kay is out,
> because she thinks Kay is just a little kid. She's not even seven!

You can easily see the author is nine, two years younger than Martha. The timeframe is the summer the writer was nine, and for general purposes, the specific year is of little concern. If this story is part of a larger collection, the age will disclose the year.

Where

This question must fit the story context. It may be as broad as the country where you were traveling, or as narrow as "the bottom bunk bed." In the opening lines above, the location is obviously near the house, probably in the front yard. In this case, the name of the town doesn't matter. The nature of the story is such that it could have taken place in nearly any town, and people who know the author will know where the story took place. Besides naming the location, include a few relevant details to give a sense of the place.

In my grandmother's story about the cowboy brother, the "where" is explained in earlier sections. It's an example of a mini-story included in a longer collection.

What

This is a multi-faceted point. Primarily it addresses what the story is about, but it also covers other "whats," like what people said, what they did at specific points, or what something looked like. The title often tells what the story is about, as in *Crunchy Frosting* (page 199).

To make sure you are clear on what your story is about, ask yourself the questions in the purpose exercise on page 56: "Why am I writing this story? What does it mean to me, and what do I want people to understand after they read it?" Besides helping focus your story, these questions often spark other memories. A list or outline may help you remember and keep track of all the "whats" and put them in the best order.

Why

This question isn't relevant to every story. Sometimes telling what happened is enough. You may not even know why something happened, but your speculation about reasons can add value and impact. Your understanding of situations defines how you make sense of life, so if you have them, do include strong feelings about reasons. If you felt baffled by the situation, at the time or later, include that reaction to personalize the story and shed light on your thinking.

How

Explanations of how something happened can be entertaining. They are also enlightening when your purpose is to give a picture of how things used to be done. But unless you are writing an instruction manual, too much technical detail may put readers to sleep.

Ask someone who knows nothing about the situation to read the story. You are recording cultural history. People not yet born may read this story in sixty years or eighty years with no idea who your subjects are, where anyone lived, or how things were done. Someone unfamiliar with your family or living conditions can point out ambiguities and missing information.

Look for opportunities to explain terminology and technology. Grandma Moses did a commendable job of this in her autobiography. For example, she had never heard the term "pig in a poke" until they moved down south. Because she explains to her readers that "poke" is another word for bag or sack, I learned the meaning of a phrase I'd often heard and never understood. My own grandchildren are unlikely to sit around a blazing wood stove playing dominoes by kerosene lantern, or find tomato worms crawling on their ears in the middle of the night after picking quarts of the critters from a field of green tomatoes all afternoon, so I explain kerosene lanterns and tomato worms in that story.

If you use terms that may not stand the test of time, include a glossary at the end of the book. Tell people in the beginning that it's there.

Maintaining Story Integrity

Talking with friends and family often helps fill in forgotten details, but as you listen to their versions, don't lose sight of the fact that this is *your* story, based on truth *as you perceive it.* They can provide dates and other factual information. They can share their thoughts, feelings, and related experiences. However, they cannot tell you what *your* experience was, what *you* thought, felt, and saw. If you write your story based on their experiences, it will turn into family history rather than your lifestory.

If you draw heavily on someone else's thoughts in something you claim as your own lifestory, readers will sense a jangling note and begin to doubt your honesty. Collaborative family stories are valuable if they are identified as such, and not presented as your own lifestory. The most significant difference is point of view—lifestories are written in first person while family history is necessarily written in third. Family histories benefit from including many people's input and points of view, along with excerpts and references to official documents. Their purpose is to document the family, and opinions of family members (clearly labeled, by source, as opinions) are an important component. In contrast, lifestories will sound cluttered and confusing if you contradict yourself by including differing versions from several people.

Caveat: As you confer with friends and family, beware the trap of rehashing things so much your story loses freshness! Over time, the root memory is continually updated. Every time you tell or write a story, the story changes just a little. The way you tell it affects how you feel about it, even just a little, and those feelings are incorporated into your evolving memory. Other people's thoughts and reactions are incorporated as you hear them. Eventually the reconstructed memory may bear little resemblance to the event as you initially remembered it, without you ever being aware of the changes. These reconstructed memories may sound flat and unconvincing.

Choose your tense

It's your choice whether to write in the present or past tense. Past tense is most common, but either is correct. The present tense may give a sense of immediacy and poignancy. It feels spontaneous, intimate, and conversational. To decide on the best tense for a particular story, imagine telling it to someone. If you're excited about it, you'll probably tell it in present tense, as a sort of delayed play-by-play account. You may find yourself slipping into the present tense quite naturally as you write about gripping incidents. Most of the time, it feels natural to narrate and write in past tense. It generally seems more appropriate for a project spanning a longer period, and gives you wider leeway to jump around in time as needed.

Compare the following two paragraphs, which are identical in content:

> An hour or so later I woke up. Both boys were reading on their beds. Thank heavens, I thought, marveling at their cooperation. I glanced into the hall bathroom just then, and saw a startling sight. The kitchen stool stood directly in front of the water heater closet. The door to the cabinet above it hung open. I held my breath as I edged cautiously into the room and looked around. The container of baby aspirin sat on the counter next to the sink, with the childproof cap alongside. My heart skipped a beat as I picked up the bottle. I let out a sigh of relief

when it appeared there were about as many as I remembered seeing when I last put it away, several weeks ago.

An hour or so later I wake up. Both boys are reading on their beds. Thank heavens, I think, marveling at their cooperation. I glance into the hall bathroom just then, and see a startling sight. The kitchen stool stands directly in front of the water heater closet. The door to the cabinet above it hangs open. I hold my breath as I edge cautiously into the room and look around. The container of baby aspirin is on the counter next to the sink, with the childproof cap alongside. My heart skips a beat as I pick up the bottle. I let out a sigh of relief when it appears there are about as many as I remember seeing when I last put it away, several weeks ago.

The difference is subtle, and more apparent when the stories are read aloud. Choice of tense is another way to personalize your writing, and it's worth experimenting to find the result you like the best. You may prefer to vary the tense from one story to the next, or keep it uniform for anthologies. Just don't jump around within a single story without a clear strategy.

Optional Elements

The optional elements in this section relate to story structure, and it's easier to incorporate them from the beginning, though you can add them later. These elements will feel more natural to some writers than others, and they aren't appropriate for every story. Take your pick and use them like herbs, to liven up stories that call for them.

Dialogue

A few lines of dialogue pull readers right into the heart of a story. Even a couple of lines can make it sizzle. Which would you rather read:

Cub hung up the phone and told us the first baby was a boy who weighed three pounds, thirteen ounces.

Or

Cub was grinning when he hung up. "The first one's a boy. Three pounds, thirteen ounces."

Writing dialogue comes more naturally to some people than others, but with a little practice, it will soon sound convincing. I'm quite biased on this matter. Of the twelve stories included in Appendix One, only one is written entirely without dialogue. Most stories use it extensively. I've included notes with several explaining fine points about the dialogue.

People always ask, "How can I possibly remember an actual conversation that took place when I was only nine years old?" Of course you won't remember the exact words. That doesn't matter at all. If a conversation stuck in your mind, it was a significant event, and what matters is that you remember the occasion and the impact it had, not the specific words. Write it the way you recall it, and you'll be right on target.

When you write dialogue, draft it as it plays in your head. Include idioms and the person's unique way of saying things. Clean it up enough to focus the message—take out the static words like "uhm" and "err," and use typical dialogue openers like "Well ..." or "You know ..." as sparingly as salt. People use these verbal cues to alert others to start listening. They serve that purpose well, but they don't read well in print. You want it to sound like a real person talking without making the reader work to wade through it.

If you feel squeamish about using dialogue, read a few good novels and pay attention to how the authors use it. The same techniques work in either fiction or memoir. The main difference between the two genres is the reliance on truth and actual events in memoir. A well-crafted novel makes the characters seem so real you feel you'd recognize them on the street, and a well-crafted lifestory keeps people turning the pages. Try it a few times and see how it goes—you can always delete it.

Dialogue is presented as part of your initial planning checklist to remind you of this powerful option. If you chose not to use it to start with, or it doesn't seem to flow, don't worry about it. You can always add some (or remove it) during the rewrite.

Caveat: A little dialogue kicks life into a story, but too much will make it read like a play script. Use narrative text to give background and detail provided by the set and other audio-visual cues in a play or movie. Don't have characters chatting about their surroundings.

Humor

You don't have to write like Erma Bombeck or Dave Barry to liven up your stories with humor. Many events that are vivid enough to stick in your mind seem inherently humorous after the dust has settled. Once you see this, the humor will flow naturally, lending extra zip to the stories. Using humor expresses your outlook as a person who is able to laugh and enjoy life. However, humor is one of the most personal elements of writing and not all writers come by it naturally. Some people have a gift for making an intrinsically humorous situation more so, or interjecting humor into an otherwise neutral story. Others have to work at it. It's perfectly possible to have a sunny outlook on life and uplift everyone who lays eyes on your work without a single amusing word. Conversely, curmudgeons, as exemplified by Andy Rooney, can be screamingly funny. Be true to yourself and your story.

You can find books and websites with tips on humorous writing, but the safest advice is to try it if you are so inclined. Let a trusted friend or relative read it, and if it doesn't work, don't use it. Forced humor is worse than none.

Time travel

Many stories jump around in time, just like memories do. Feel free to do this on paper, the same way you would if you were telling someone the story. Just make sure your readers know where you are going, and clue them in when you circle back. Don't make too many loops, or you may lose them.

Memoirist Lori Jakiela makes extensive use of time travel in *Miss New York Has Everything,* an account of growing up in the tiny Pittsburgh suburb of Trafford. In one chapter, she uses the story of a visit from her aunt, an alcoholic, drug-abusing nun, as a thread to string half a dozen flashback memories in the form of vignettes about Shaun Cassidy, her parents' fascination with legal drugs, and so forth. Each is a story in its own right. During a book signing program, she explained that when she's planning a story, she begins with a vivid memory and then asks herself, "Why is this memory important to me? What else does it remind me of?" Then she weaves those other memories into the fabric of the main one. This threaded story technique is illustrated in Figure 7.

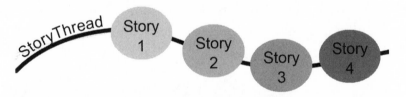

Figure 7: Threaded Stories

Another way to give depth to a topic is to use nested stories, as shown in Figure 8. *The Rocking Chair* on page 213 is an example of this technique. This story is like a Russian nesting doll with a third layer nested in the second. In a sense, this story also has a fourth layer, because I used an epilogue, or afterward. The main story took place when I was about sixteen, with flashbacks to earlier years. Since the story recounts some typically teenage resentments of my mother, I wanted to tem-

Story 1	Story 2	Story 3	Story 4	3	2	1

Figure 8: Nested Stories

per the harshness of that judgment by pulling the story into the context of adult understanding. I did this in the epilogue rather than spoiling the authenticity of the memory by interjecting current thoughts into the story body. If I had begun the story with an opening paragraph set in the present, the epilogue would reflect back to the beginning and tie the story together by completing a full fourth layer.

Some stories, or series of stories, follow a theme that weaves through your life, such as your experiences playing the piano, as shown in Figure 9. The stories are linked with a few lines of transition, but lack the ongoing story line of the threaded stories. You may tell about your lessons when you were young, then there may be little involvement with the piano for a dozen years until you begin playing for the church choir. Later you may be asked to accompany a choral group, and eventually play for group sings on Thursday evenings in your retirement complex. As you begin each new episode, include some time stamp, like the year it began, or some other marker to help readers keep track.

Figure 9: Sequential Stories

Adding photos and other illustrations

You know the old saying, "A picture is worth a thousand words." Sometimes pictures convey things that you can't say any other way. You can describe the house you lived in until you are blue in the face, but seeing a picture will snap it into focus faster than anything. You don't need to turn your lifestory project into a photo album, but one or two well-chosen photos will add immense value.

The photo in Figure 10 gives a sense of room size and décor: wood floors, a mix of early Danish Modern and western furniture. The pile of ashtrays may seem odd today. The Christmas candle flags the season, and the mother's maternity dress typifies the era.

Figure 10: Inserted Photo

You can tell quite a bit about this family without knowing who they are. In your own story, you'd explain the picture, tell when it was taken, who the people are, and point out anything relevant, like maybe Aunt Martha made those candles by the dozens every December. The pile of ashtrays is misleading. Nobody in this nuclear family smoked, but the grandfathers did. Such anomalies should be mentioned.

You can also use sketched floor plans of houses you lived in, maps of areas where you vacationed or lived, hand-drawn sketches or illustrations by you or someone else, and various items mentioned in the Reminder Resources section starting on page 41 are also appropriate. You'll find general directions for inserting graphics into your document on page 264.

Chapter 4:
The Write Path

"I have written my life in small sketches, a little today, a little yesterday, as I have thought of it, as I remember all the things from childhood on through the years, good ones and unpleasant ones, that is how they come out and that is how we have to take them."

—Anna Mary (Grandma) Moses

Whether you've spent hours or days planning your project or story, or no time at all, eventually you have to get those fingers moving and do some writing. This chapter will help you get the words flowing to produce the initial draft. For some readers this may be the only draft, but for most, it's likely to be the first of two or more.

Warming Up

When you have a story idea clearly in mind, the words generally flow right out, but there will be days when this doesn't happen. Sometimes looking a blank piece of paper or monitor in the face can intimidate even a veteran writer! When your story feels stuck, freewriting, the following warm-up exercise, will get the words flowing. This warm-up exercise is liberating. Since nobody will ever read it, you can write without self-consciousness. Don't worry about grammar, or spelling, or what other people might think. You write about your own experience and feelings. Plan to wad that paper up and toss it when you're done. Use freewriting anytime you need to loosen up, choosing a topic at random.

Exercise

Take a sheet of paper (ideally scrap paper) and set a timer for five minutes. Then write about the thoughts you have as you look at that blank sheet of paper. Don't stop. Keep your fingers flying and write whatever comes to mind. If the flow of words stops, shift to a new topic or repeat a single word until more thoughts come.

Write That Draft

It doesn't matter how or where you write. You can sit at a fancy desk with elegant paper and pen; you can write drafts on the backs of envelopes with a pencil stub; you can use a typewriter or a computer. The important thing is that you write.

As you write, keep your purpose in the back of your mind to maintain energy and enthusiasm. Think of your words as pebbles thrown into the river of life. When pebbles hit the water, ripples spread out from the impact and keep spreading, even after they are too weak to be seen. These ripples bump into others, and each affects the course of the others. Your words could ripple out into other lives now, or generations down the road, to enlighten, inspire, provide guidance, or entertain multitudes, but only if you write them.

Use the following tips to get that story on paper. Don't worry about editing or specific content. That will come later.

Write without stopping

It is tempting to write a sentence, erase several words and then start over. After an hour, you may find that you've written only three sentences—umpteen times each. Don't fall into this trap.

Write the story from beginning to end, as it flows. Don't stop to reread, and don't edit as you go, not even on a computer. If you can't resist rewriting on the fly, or you become distracted by the red and green lines that flag suspected errors, turn off automatic spell and grammar checking.

Put this book down and take a writing break!

(Look on the Tools menu under Spelling and Grammar to change these options in Microsoft Word. In OpenOffice the setting is under Tools>Options>Language Settings, and in WordPerfect you'll find it under Tools>Language>Settings.)

Write Now. Revise Later.

Some people write by hand with ink to avoid the revision temptation. Whether you use a keyboard or paper, once you begin, keep writing. If the words stop before the story does, keep your fingers moving. Doodle or drum lightly on the key tops for a moment and remain relaxed until the words resume. The important thing is to keep your fingers and pen *moving*.

Write in first person

There is only one absolute to writing memoir and lifestories: Always write in first person. Always refer to yourself as I. Some people are under the impression that it is egotistical to use the first person singular pronoun. Nonsense! You're not being self-centered, you are being clear. Paul Auster's memoir, *The Invention of Solitude*, tells of his own memories after the sudden and unexpected death of his father. In the second part, he writes about his own experience in the third person, presumably for artistic effect. I found it confusing, and was never quite sure whether he was referring to himself or his father as "he."

Write like you talk

One way to keep a natural tone is to write your story in the form of a letter to a good friend who hasn't heard it before. While writing letters, you feel more relaxed about grammar, form, style, punctuation, and spelling. It helps to have a specific reader in mind as you write. It's like telling a story aloud—you

Your goal is lively writing that reveals YOU—not technical perfection.

choose words and points to interest that specific person. When you tell a story aloud, you often remember things out of order and add them by saying, "Oh! I forgot to mention ..." and then continue with your story. It's fine to add things this way when you write your draft. You may decide to leave it that way, or rearrange things when you rewrite.

You may find it helpful to record yourself telling the story and transcribe the recording for your first draft. With practice, writing the way you talk will become second nature. People who know you will be able to pick up something you wrote and identify it as your work, without seeing your name on it.

Write like a child

This means writing with a child's wonder and enthusiasm, not childish language. Have you ever watched a child of eight or ten sit down to write a story? He may not write very long, but while he's writing, he isn't worried about spelling or grammar, or punctuation. He simply puts that story down on paper the way it comes out of his head, and hands the finished story to you with a grin. He knows you'll love his story. There may be

71

many missing details, and misspellings and grammar errors may abound, but the story rings true. That's the warm spontaneity you strive for.

Focus on your story, get your fingers on your pen or keyboard and *write*. Write like you did in the warm-up exercise, without stopping to think about grammar, spelling, or what it sounds like. You can fix all that later.

Give it a rest

After you finish the first draft, set it aside for a while. If this is as far as you plan to take it, or you have a hunch you may not get back to it, go ahead and do a spell check and a quick scan for obvious mistakes, but don't obsess about edits right away. Remember that your descendants would rather have a pile of unfinished stories than two or three perfect ones.

Back It Up

Even if you plan to work on it more later, if you wrote your draft on the computer, make a backup copy of the file and print it out. You can use the printed version to make corrections later. I can't overstress the importance of backing up. Over half a dozen of my friends have lost huge chunks of work when their hard drives died and they didn't have backup copies. "I felt like my whole life had been trashed," lamented one. "I had over two years of stories and hundreds of scanned photos. I'd borrowed some of those photos and may not be able to get them back." My heart bleeds when I hear about these preventable tragedies.

A couple of these people had printed copies of most stories, and were able to either retype the things that mattered, or scan them in with optical character recognition, but that was a huge amount of work, especially compared to the ease of backing up the files in the first place. Most computers today have CD or

DVD writer drives, and blank disks cost only pennies. These are especially good for archiving finished copies, but they'll also do for drafts. The price of hard drives has fallen to the point that an extra drive for backup is increasingly affordable. Do not use a separate partition on a single hard drive for backup, and never trust an old-style floppy disk.

Saving your work as you go along is a critical habit. I generally save the file as soon as I start a story, then use Ctrl-S every few minutes to save what I've written. Your word processing program probably makes backup copies automatically every ten minutes or so, but "hard" saves are more reliable and convenient. When I'm doing edits, I save at least once a page so I don't have to go back and wonder what I already did.

Save and back up rigorously. You'll never regret it.

Chapter 5:
Firming the Basics

Telling a true story about personal experience is not just a matter of being oneself, or even of finding oneself. It is also a matter of choosing oneself.

—*Harriet Goldhor Lerner*

Some time ago, Roxie showed me a story she had written. The touching story came straight from her heart, and I suggested it would be a welcome contribution to one of the websites that feature inspirational writings. "But before you send it, maybe you could tighten it up and focus it a bit," I suggested.

She took a deep breath and blurted out, "I'll never edit this, or anything else. It will just have to stay as it is, and I think it sounds like me; like I talk." She went on to explain that she couldn't edit it even if she wanted to, because she has no idea where to start, or how to do it.

Touché! I was pained to realize my words had provoked defensiveness. The story truly was written exactly as she speaks, and she speaks with energizing passion. If she only intended to share it with friends and family, it didn't need editing, and may be appreciated even more, precisely because it does sound exactly like her. However, those who don't know her may become distracted by pockets of conversational rambling, and streamlining the message would increase the likelihood it would appear on one of those websites to uplift countless others.

Her story is a good test of the underlying theme of this book that anything you write is okay. While utterly true, that message must be placed in context. Anything you write is indeed better than not writing anything. Your first priority should always be to get stories written, however the words flow forth. Once written, you have the choice of going back and revising them, or simply leaving them as they are. Neither choice is better than the other, and your choice must be guided by your purpose in writing as well as your interests and abilities. If you are writing for your own eyes only, if you have no interest in editing them or time to do it, so be it. That's okay! It's also okay, maybe even a good idea, to write a huge pile of story drafts, saving all the editing for later. When you are ready to polish and tighten them, the material in this chapter will guide you down that path so you can deliver crisply written stories that still sound "exactly like you talk."

Why Edit?

Roxie didn't understand the difference between listening to someone talk and reading the same words on paper. While we listen to someone tell a story, our attention may stray to the picture on the wall, what we'll say next, or what we'll have for dinner. We generally hear less than half of what's said, so a lot of the rambling is filtered out. We hear the key points, string them together and our mind fills in the blanks to make our own sense of things. Then, according to research, we forget most of it within a single day.

If we read a verbatim transcript of the same words, all the extraneous "stuff" is there, in black and white. Our eyes and minds focus in one place, and there is less external distraction. The word clutter may overwhelm the story thread. That's why we edit—to clear away the clutter and make the story easier for readers to follow. Streamlining will increase the odds they'll understand what we are trying to say rather than drawing some different conclusion of their own.

People with a conversational writing style can often reduce the word count in the first story draft by thirty percent and generate more feedback that "This really sounds like you!" than they would hear about transcripts of actual conversation. The edited version filters out all the things that people don't hear when you talk. Fortunately, when people read lifestories, they intuitively understand the difference between carefully crafted edits and raw accounts that reflect the spontaneous nature of the writer. They appreciate either one for what it is, so you can't go wrong with either choice.

When you tell stories, listeners generally interact and ask questions to keep you on track and fill in missing facts. They may ask, "Who was Sarah?" or "Did that happen in Oshkosh or Minneapolis?" They'll urge you on by asking, "And then what happened?" or "What did she say to that?" Readers can't help you out that way, so besides reducing the word count, you need to check and make sure all the main points are covered.

The challenge you face in turning your raw draft into a finished story is to remove distractions like fluff words or typos, and fill in missing elements to create a final story that anyone can read with a sense of completion and satisfaction.

When to Edit

As a rule, it's a good idea to set a story aside for at least a day or two before you edit. The longer you wait, the better. Fine stories are like fine wine. Both require a certain amount of undisturbed aging to mature to perfection. Your story may not need to sit on the shelf as long as vintage wine, but do let it rest at least a few days before printing a final copy. After a few months, it may be obvious that one of my own stories I thought worthy of a Pulitzer needs serious revision.

Most how-to books about writing recommend that you write drafts of at least two or three additional stories or chapters before going back to edit anything. This allows your mind to move ahead and feel less invested in the story of the moment, making it easier to see where changes will be beneficial. Research has shown that unless they are intensely relevant or emotional, we forget around eighty percent of things we hear within twenty-four hours. Things you say or write stick longer. It may take several days or longer for your initial mental links to weaken and make it easier to see where you thought about details without writing them down.

If you're writing a complete chronological overview of your life, your best plan is to keep writing until you have a draft of the entire work, especially if you set yourself a deadline. It's easier to keep your momentum with the writing if you forge ahead. Save any serious edits until you have the complete draft, because you may want to move sections around within the larger work, or refer back or ahead, and that won't be apparent until you see the whole thing.

What's Involved in Editing

Editing takes place on a continuum. It may be as simple as a once-over spell-check or you may go through dozens of revisions and tweaks to reach the level of sophisticated artistry you chose. The amount of time and effort you spend on it is a matter of personal preference based on taste, time, and talent.

Beyond a few basic checks for structural integrity, editing is non-linear. You may cycle through a list of several techniques before you feel satisfied with the result. You may use some techniques on this story, and others on that. It's an art, it's personal, and there are no "right answers." When you are happy with a story, or sick of working on it, the story is finished, at least for the time being. As long as you keep writing, you'll keep learning. After a few months or longer, you may read a story you were happy with earlier and find half a dozen things you want to change, because you've matured as a writer and your tastes and skills have changed. The beauty of using computers is that these changes are easy to make. Until your project is bound and delivered, improvement is always possible.

Getting Started

This chapter explains the primary editing tools included in the basic edit loop shown in Figure 6 on page 55: spelling, grammar, punctuation, focus, and flow. Use these basic tools to ensure a solid story that gets your message across. The tools found in the next chapter are used to apply polish and refinement to the strong basic story.

The order of items in the basic edit loop is arbitrary. Some people begin with an initial spelling and grammar check, others prefer to wait and do this when everything else is finished, and a third contingent picks these errors off as they find them. If this is your first step, do another scan when all your other edits are complete, in case more errors occurred along the way.

Spelling

Obviously it's a good idea to check spelling to avoid appearing ignorant or careless. But rest assured, even if you don't check it, people will be able to make sense of your story. A passage from a widely forwarded e-mail proves that truth:

> I cdnuolt blveiee taht I cluod aulaclty uesdnatnrd waht I was rdanieg.The phaonemnel pweor of the hmuan mnid Aoccdrnig to rscaherech at Cmabrigde Uinervtisy, it deosn't mttaer in waht oredr the ltteers in a wrod are, the olny iprmoatnt tihng is taht the frist and lsat ltteer be in the rghit pclae. The rset can be a taotl mses and you can sitll raed it wouthit a porbelm. Tihs is

bcuseae the huamn mnid deos not raed ervey lteter by istlef, but the wrod as a wlohe. Amzanig huh?

The first and last letter of each word hold the key to understanding. The other letters can be jumbled, but our mind understands. Errors and omissions usually jump out at you, especially if you have spell- and grammar-check turned on. If **DO NOT forget to use spell check!** you have turned it off, use it now. You probably have names of people and places—even objects—that spell check won't recognize. Add these to your spell-check dictionary, so you won't have to decide again later. If you aren't sure of the correct spelling, use a dictionary. Online dictionaries, like dictionary.com, suggest words close to the spelling you type in.

It's a good idea to have someone else proofread your story, even if you use a computer with spell-check. Spill chick want fond words ewe spelled wrong if there jest the rung ward spilled rite. Our memory of what we meant to say may prevent seeing what's really there. We miss errors that stand out like neon signs to a first-time reader with average spelling skills.

Grammar

Unless they are glaring or misleading, grammar errors are generally less serious than misspellings. Lifestories have leeway for personal expression quirks. Grammar checker may also be useful, as long as you remember it isn't perfect. Grammar is a fluid thing, reflecting your niche in society, your generation, and the basic rules of structure of the English language. Especially in lifestory writing, your challenge is to establish your own voice, with your own writing mannerisms, and these may stray from conventional grammar. The challenge is to let them stray in a controlled way. You don't want to abuse the rules to the extent that you confuse readers or sound like an ignorant hick. Readers decades from now won't be familiar with today's jargon, and may be more easily confused than current ones. Look over the edits your evaluators suggest, take them with a grain of salt, and keep experimenting until you feel comfortable with your own taste and abilities.

If you feel nervous about grammar, invest in a basic grammar guide, such as *The Little, Brown Handbook.* You'll find explanations for all grammar-related topics, and the structure of this textbook is reader-friendly. Other valuable resources are Strunk and White's classic book, *The Elements of Style*, and the Internet.

Punctuation

An English professor wrote the words: "A woman without her man is nothing" on the chalkboard and asked his students to punctuate it correctly. All of the males in the class wrote: "A woman, without her man, is nothing." All the females in the class wrote: "A woman: without her, man is nothing." Punctuation is powerful.

Grammar check will pick up most punctuation errors, but as the above parable shows, there are several options in punctuation, and many flagged errors are a matter of context, personal choice, and style. Most dictionaries include punctuation guidelines, and you can find the rules for any punctuation mark by searching on the Internet. A summary of punctuation rules you are likely to need begins on page 163.

Key Point Check

Remember that list of key points from Chapter Three? If you spent time planning this story before you wrote it, you already thought about these points. Whether you outlined a plan or not, take time now to see if you've told your readers who is involved, where and when the story took place, and what was happening. Why and how are more important to some stories than others. If you have someone else read your story, encourage them to share any questions they have.

Exercise
Go through a story you've written with a highlighter and mark each of the key points. If any are missing, add the information.

Sharpen your focus

Lack of a clear focus is one of the most common shortcomings of lifestories. The overall purpose for your lifestory project is the bedrock you build on, but each story also has its own purpose or theme. That purpose defines the boundaries of the story and how much detail to include. The effect is similar to cropping photographs to focus the interest.

Figure 11: Toys in yard

For example, consider the pictures in Figures 11 through 13. In Figure 11, a boy and girl sit together in a swing. What's the story here? The kids? The yard? The clutter? In Figure 12 you see the same kids without the clutter. The children stand out clearly, the yard and surroundings are still part of the pic-

Figure 12: No toys

Figure 13: Zoomed in

ture. Figure 13 was specifically cropped to focus on the children.

Which is the better picture? Aside from aesthetics, it's a matter of personal preference and purpose. A single photo yielded all three results. The first picture shows the kids in their yard with all the toys they generally play with. It's a vignette of daily life. The second picture is "cleaned up." It does not show the realities of daily life, but it does show the kids in familiar surroundings. The third picture focuses on the affectionate relationship. None of the pictures exactly reflects the original. In the first picture, I moved extra toys into the scene from another part of the yard. In the second shot, I removed all the toys, even the ones that were visible to begin with. The third photo is enlarged and cropped from the original.

You can do similar things with stories. By changing focus and the degree of detail, you can produce a variety of results from the same story material. If your purpose is to document daily life, you'll include different details, and probably more of them, than you would if your purpose is to share a humorous anecdote or reflect on the meaning of your life. As you sort through your draft, compare each thought to your purpose and consider whether to keep or delete it.

When you can't bear to delete part of a story, but you know it obscures the story's point, stash it in the equivalent of a scrap bag. I paste displaced story chunks into a running document titled "Scraps 2007." Every now and then I do find something useful in it. My Scraps file also provides new story ideas. After I use something, I delete it from the Scraps file. At least once a year I start a new Scraps file for size control.

Another way to handle extra details is to write the story two different ways: a descriptive account of what things looked like and how things were done, and a second story about relationships, adventures, or whatever. Dual stories work especially well in a patchwork story collection.

Perhaps you noticed that I admitted adding extra toys to the first picture. Some people would question the ethics of that. Is it okay to add details that weren't actually there? That's a personal judgment call, and partly depends on your purpose. If your purpose is to show a precisely accurate portrayal of that moment, to document it, then of course you'd leave what was there in the picture and add nothing. If your purpose is to give a sense of something, add or delete as it suits you. The extra toys illustrate the selection they generally enjoyed playing with, not how cluttered the yard was.

Another stimulating discussion could be held around the significance of removing the toys in the second photo. It's been sanitized. If that yard was always littered with toys, is it honest to clean it up? I leave that for you to decide, with respect to the picture, and with respect to your choice of details for your stories. You'll read more on the topic of honesty in Chapter Seven.

Exercise

Take a story you wrote and state the purpose in six words or less. Use the phrase "This story is about ..." to introduce the six words. When you are finished, go through the story, paragraph by paragraph and consider whether the information in that paragraph promotes the purpose of the story, detracts from it, or is neutral. Delete anything that detracts.

Paragraph structure

Paragraph structure is another editing concern. You probably studied paragraph structure in high school and have a hazy memory that they are a distinct division of a story that begins on a new line, consists of one or more sentences, and typically deals with a single thought or topic. Many people lose track of the one thought/one paragraph equation and write paragraphs with half a dozen main thoughts. Every now and then a student's first story runs on for a page or more without a paragraph break. At the other extreme are stories that start a new paragraph for each sentence.

Sometimes it's hard to know just where to break for a new paragraph, so let's look at their purpose. First, they do separate individual concepts and help in mentally organizing material. Beyond that, they break up the flow of words down the page to give your eyes a rest and make it easier to keep track of your position, should you glance up.

When you find a paragraph with more than one main thought, you have a paragraph that needs to be divided into two or more. If you find a paragraph that runs on for most of a page, you can probably break it into two or more, for reading ease as much as grammatical correctness. For example, look at the following paragraph:

> Our house on Cedar Street was great because it was so cozy and comfortable. Whenever we came home from a trip we couldn't wait to get inside our own house again. It wasn't very big and it was crowded but to us it was home. We spent lots of time in the summer playing on the screened front porch with our toy cars and teasing the girls who'd take their dolls there. Sometimes we boys dug holes in the backyard for various purposes. On hot days we liked to raise the flat door from over the cellar steps and sneak into the house through the cellar. The cellar was nice and cool, even on hot days, but it didn't smell very good when you came in from outside. You didn't notice the smell very long though. You got used to it pretty quick. Today I know that's the smell of mold. We had lots of stuff stored in

there and it was pretty dusty and dark but sometimes us kids liked to sneak in there and do things. One time we got to horsing around and bumped against the shelves that held all my mother's canned fruits and knocked off a few jars that broke on the floor. Boy did we get in trouble for that!

This paragraph has three distinct topics: the house, playing in the yard and going in the cellar. Without considering any punctuation errors or other edits, it may be broken down this way:

Our house on Cedar Street was great because it was so cozy and comfortable. Whenever we came home from a trip we couldn't wait to get inside our own house again. It wasn't very big and it was crowded but to us it was home. We spent lots of time in the summer playing on the screened front porch with our toy cars and teasing the girls who'd take their dolls there.

Sometimes we boys dug holes in the backyard for various purposes.

On hot days we liked to raise the flat door from over the cellar steps and sneak into the house through the cellar. The cellar was nice and cool, even on hot days, but it didn't smell very good when you came in from outside. You didn't notice the smell very long though. You got used to it pretty quick. Today I know that's the smell of mold. We had lots of stuff stored in there and it was pretty dusty and dark but sometimes us kids liked to sneak in there and do things. One time we got to horsing around and bumped against the shelves that held all my mother's canned fruits and knocked off a few jars that broke on the floor. Boy did we get in trouble for that!

That second paragraph is only a single sentence. It isn't technically wrong to have single sentence paragraphs, but they are generally used to highlight key thoughts and powerful ideas. The second paragraph is neither. This single sentence paragraph begs for expansion. Aren't you curious about why the boys dug those holes? Were they burying dead pets or pirate treasure? Perhaps they were building a fort or digging a hole for swimming?

Exercise

Use a highlighter to mark the main idea(s) in each paragraph in a story you wrote. Do you find more than one per paragraph? Rewrite those paragraphs. Expand any one or two sentence paragraphs to provide more detail.

For some stories, writing the initial draft requires less than ten percent of the effort required to produce a finished product. Fortunately, you'll find others that flow forth free and uncluttered, within a couple of typos of print-ready copy. With practice, the percentage in the second category will increase. Personally, I've come to enjoy the artistry of turning that raw lump of words into a polished story and I look forward to rewriting.

Some people realize their drafts need work, but like my friend Roxie at the beginning of this chapter, they feel overwhelmed by the challenge. They may lack time, they may lack interest, or they may simply not feel up to it. If you are one of these people, and you don't want to leave a pile of rambling tales as your legacy, you can have someone else do it for you. If you can afford it, you could hand the job off to a professional writer or editor. These people are easy to find on the Internet (always check references with personal phone calls), or you may know someone locally. However, help may be nearer at hand. Usually when you tell people what you're doing and mention that you need help, a friend or family member will offer to edit them for you.

If you accept their offer, make it clear that you are not turning over ownership of the story. Let them know they are welcome to suggest style, spelling, and grammar changes. Depending on your level of comfort and trust, you could let them go ahead and make spelling and punctuation changes on their own, but don't let them alter other content without your approval. Ask them to flag missing or unclear points, conflicting information, and so forth. Consider any suggestions about content changes carefully before approving them to make sure they are fully consistent with your views and memories. Only work with an editor you feel confident will respect your views. Do not let anyone, friend, family or pro, talk you into changing facts and feelings to something other than your own experience and truth.

Caveat: It's easy to get so involved in revising a handful of stories that you neglect to keep writing new ones. It can be a challenge to strike a balance between polishing your stories and accomplishing your original purpose. Especially when you are writing against a deadline, it's a good idea to postpone serious editing until you finish the full draft. That should ensure you finish the full draft, and a draft of the full story is more valuable than a polished copy of thirty percent.

Chapter 6:
Polishing the Details

The man who writes about himself and his own time is the only man who writes about all people and all time.
— *George Bernard Shaw*

A story with the key points covered, clear focus, and smoothly flowing paragraphs is a strong tale that can stand the test of time. For many people and most stories, this will be enough. Some stories merit further polishing and attention to detail. That's what the tools in this chapter are about—details. You'll find a plethora of information in this chapter, but don't think you'll have to go over each story seventeen times. You won't need every tool in every story, and you may use half a dozen tools in tandem as you go down each page. As you continue to write and become more aware of sound story structure, you'll begin to think like a writer and incorporate many editing concepts into your stories as you write.

In this chapter, we'll start with the beginning and work our way through endings, description, word choice, sentence structure, and other details.

Powerful Beginnings

"I thought I'd better call you before you heard this from someone else first."

Mother's ominous tone hit me like a bucket of ice water. I'd just walked into the office that summer morning in 1963, and my heart did flip-flops as four-alarm words like heart attack, death, and divorce flashed through my mind. She didn't keep me in suspense.

"Your sister was in a car wreck last night ... ."

Did that opening line get your attention? It got mine, back in 1963 when I picked up my ringing telephone! People form impressions of strangers and stories at a glance, and that opening passes the glance test. The list below describes six of the many ways to start a story. Use the list to bait your hook and make your stories hit the page with a bang.

Set the scene

Start the story with a date, place, your age, and what was happening (in any order).

The year was 1939. I'll never forget that Sunday, December 7, the day the Japanese bombed Pearl Harbor. I was a student at Kansas State A&M College, and I was ... .

Flashback

Open with a current event that flashes you back to a memory.

My nose runs and my glasses fog from the bitter cold. The snow crunches under my feet as I walk up the hill toward home. I look up into the starry sky and suddenly I'm transported back to 1958. The stars have never shone more brilliantly than they did that night on freshly fallen snow, lying as still and perfect as a Christmas card. I walked miles under those stars with fellow members of the French Club ... .

Begin with the end

State a conclusion or interpretation to open the story and work your way back.

Mr. Patri was such a great teacher they should have named the school for him. In one short year he managed to teach a group of rowdy fifth-graders how to do library research, make visual aids ... .

Catchy phrase

Capture the reader's attention with a catchy phrase or sentence.

I never imagined that little pretend campfire could set the whole woods on fire ... .

Start talking

Begin your story in the middle of a conversation to draw readers into the story immediately.

"Do you want to go to the movies?" asked Sandra.
"Not this week," I reply. Sandra knows I already spent my allowance. I don't know why she's even suggesting doing something that requires money when she knows I don't have any.
"So, what shall we do instead?"

Ask a question

Engage the reader's attention with a question that your story will answer.

Do you remember when girls wore starched nylon net petticoats so scratchy they felt like sandpaper on their legs?

By the way, the accident and injury in my opening example were both minor, undeserving of the sensational build-up. Take the analogy to heart, and don't disappoint readers with a stronger start than the story warrants.

And Endings

Paired with a powerful start, a satisfying close defines the scope of a story and leaves readers with a sense of completion. I feel disappointed when I read a story that trails off at the end, or leaves key details hanging, yet sometimes you'll write about events that don't come to neat conclusions. Use the following tips to give you ideas on ways to end your stories with finesse whether or not the experience did.

Close the circle

Returning to an important place or referring to a key character establishes closure by reminding the reader of the beginning.

> It's marvelous to me, the way life works itself out. It ticks on, steady and sure, and if we look for mystery and explanation, we can find it, even in the face of a Mickey Mouse watch.

Tie it back

Refer to some odd or offbeat element in the body of the story. This works especially well with humor.

> As the shop door clicked shut, Diane burst into hysterical laughter. "Next time," she gasped, "make sure the sales clerk isn't French."

Run the clock out

In stories with a relentlessly advancing time structure, the end is defined by what obviously must happen last.

> I drove off to my new life in Georgia without glancing into the rearview mirror at the childhood I left behind.

Cover the map

Stories that move from place to place, for example a vacation account, typically end by arriving at the final destination.

> I'd always thought those accounts of people kissing the soil when they stepped off the plane back in the good old USA were corny, but after all I'd gone through, I understood perfectly. The floor of JFK International was covered with enough soil to serve the purpose, and I didn't care who saw me kiss it.

Payoff

Not all stories require a happy ending, but they do require some sort of closure, such as learning a secret, solving a problem or mystery, or completing a process, that makes the reading worthwhile and satisfying. The longer the story, the larger the payoff needs to be.

> There is something compelling about secrets. They just beg to be told. Kitty was bursting to tell her secret to someone, so she told Joy, thinking her secret was safe. Joy just had to tell someone, so she told me, thinking her secret was safe. I kept the secret for twenty years, then I just had to write this story, and now the world knows.

Add an epilogue

Readers become involved with characters in stories, and this is especially true in lifestories. Many stories, especially those about events when you were young, may be more valuable or meaningful to readers if you add a few thoughts at the end about the way you see things now. The simplest way to handle this is to add an epilogue explaining the insight you've gained that has changed the way you view the situation. Another possibility is to conclude the story with an explanation like

> I would be middle-aged before I fully comprehended that if you want people to know what you are thinking, what you want or need, what you are excited about, you must *tell* them, because love doesn't turn a person into a mind reader.

or

> Over twenty years later, he was diagnosed with Tourette's syndrome, and I finally understood the outbursts that caused me such terror all those years ... .

Solve the problem

This is the classic ending for mystery and adventure stories. The problem is solved, so the story is over.

I held my breath as I ripped open the envelope, suddenly not sure whether I truly wanted to know the answers it held. Then, with a gasp of delight, I read the news, wiped my eyes, and read it again to be sure. Against all the odds, Jason was alive and well!

Quote a source

For stories that include dialogue, let yourself or another character sum things up with a pithy observation.

Sammy's face glowed with pleasure. "I can't think of anything I'd like better."

Quoting a relevant maxim or famous saying is another way to end with punch.

Point ahead

Give readers a clue about what happens in the next stage of your life and/or the next story.

"But Mom, I might as well just go throw her in the river. That's what Tim's mother is going to do. I can't take her back!"
"Her? Did you say 'her'? Are they both females?"
"Yeah. That's all he had. Aren't they cute?"
The adventure wasn't over, it had just grown larger.

Mobilize readers

When appropriate, urge your readers to heed the advice or wisdom in your story and act on what they've learned.

The next happy ending may depend on you. Have you signed your donor card?

You'll notice that some of these suggestions seem best suited for short individual stories, but they also apply to the beginning of the introduction, and the conclusion of collections of stories. Lengthy stories, like a chronological autobiography or a continuous memoir, consist of a series of smaller story units. Though you needn't strive for flamboyance, each of these units, such as chapters, will benefit from a clear beginning and an established closure at the end.

Exercise
Practice writing some catchy opening paragraphs for stories. They don't need to be things that really happened. Just have fun. If you find one you especially like, take a fiction break and write a short story about it, just for kicks.

Descriptive Magic

Use phrases like, "The heady fragrance of freshly cut grass," or, "rays of the setting sun flooded the room, washing the walls with flame," to give your readers sensory involvement in the story. Comparisons (colorful as a cardinal on sunlit snow) or metaphors (Boston streets are laid out like a bowl of spaghetti) add variety, but use your imagination instead of popping in an overused chestnut.

Good descriptions are like using crayons to color black-and-white pages.

Describing people

Make characters in your story come alive with vivid description, the more specific, the better. Tell what they looked like, what your sense of them was. For example,

> Uncle Jack's face reminded me of a round, red tomato. His cowlick rose like a stem above the damp petals of hair fringing his forehead. When he spoke, his muffled voice seemed to come from deep inside his massive, round body ... .

Stay away from clichés, and use compassion when describing people—the line between colorful descriptions and meanness of spirit is thin and fragile. You won't gain points with readers by sounding vengeful or whiney. You don't need to run that risk. A better way to portray negative traits is to include scenes like the following that demonstrate their traits in action.

"Hey Short Stuff, I'm hungry!" Jack snarled. He'd been watching when I put the Hershey bar from my lunch bag in my jacket pocket to eat at recess, and I knew he was coming after it. I pulled out the Hershey bar and ripped off the wrapper as Jack headed my way. It killed me to do it, but just before he got within arm's reach, I dropped that Hershey bar to the ground and mashed it with my heel, just the way my grandpa put out his cigarettes. If I couldn't eat it, I'd be damned if I'd watch Jack enjoy it!

The author shows that Jack is a bully, and the label would be extraneous. The action passage has the added value of showing the author's coping style.

Caveat: Space your descriptions out rather than compressing them into a clump. Work them in as they become relevant.

Exercise
Think of a person from your past and find a metaphor to describe that person. Does he remind you of an animal? A machine? Does she have a particular shape, or make an unusual sound? Is some feature irregular or unusual? Let your mind wander loosely.

Set an object in front of you, or look at something out the window. Find an unusual way to describe this object.

Now try spicing up a few descriptions in stories you've written.

Describing feelings

Tell your readers how you felt or reacted to events you write about. Were you scared? Excited? Angry? Some people find it natural to include feelings in their writing, using phrases like, "I was so excited, I thought I'd explode if I had to stay inside another moment!" Others are less aware of feelings even as events occur and find it difficult to articulate them at the time or later. It's worth the effort to avoid sounding detached. Stories that don't include at least an element of personal involvement tend to read like textbooks or museum documentation. Readers are likely to ask, "What did you think about this?" or "How did you feel about it when that happened?" For example,

consider this shocking passage from a story Paul Ohrman read
in a lifestory writing group:

> Our biggest surprise and shock of the war occurred at Erfurt.
> As we approached, we heard systematic machine gun fire and
> quickly learned the awful truth. The political prisoners from the
> Erfurt Concentration Camp were forced to line up at the edge
> of a ditch and were gunned down in advance of our arrival. The
> faster we advanced the more prisoners we were able to rescue.
> Inside the camp, the extent of the inhumanity and horror was
> evident. Starved, emaciated prisoners, just skin and bones,
> begged me to take their picture to show to the outside world.
> Some were unable to stand or even too weak to roll over. They
> slept on shelves that were three and four tiers high, with just
> enough space for bodies to be jammed together. Outside there
> were lories with dead bodies stacked like cordwood and fur-
> naces still smoking with their load of human remains and cone
> shaped piles of burned and sun bleached human bones. The re-
> port was that 7,000 died every day. I printed the photographs
> and gave them to our commanding officer to forward to 3rd
> army headquarters.
>
> It was the same ugly sight at Buchenwald; another infamous
> concentration camp that we entered on April 20, 1945. Other
> American troops arrived ahead of us and liberated the political
> prisoners there. Lampshades made from tattoos taken from the
> skin of prisoners were in the officer's quarters. One prisoner fa-
> thered a little boy and successfully fed and hid him from the
> guards for three years. Over the entrance hung a sign, "Right or
> wrong—my country." Another sign, either here or at Erfurt, read
> in German, "Abandon hope—all who enter." The news has since
> reported that 5 million Jews and 6 million others were murdered
> in these concentration camps. You cannot tell me "The holo-
> caust did not occur," because I was there and witnessed it first-
> hand with my own eyes.

A respectful silence followed this reading. After some discussion, a member gently asked, "How did you feel about that?
What was your reaction?" In the context of responding to the
group, Paul was at a loss for an answer, but the group agreed
most readers who are interested in understanding Paul's personality will wonder about his unique reaction to such an in-

tense situation. In writing the story he did use emotion-laden words like shock and horror, but he didn't personalize them. One way to clearly convey his own reaction is as simple as editing the sentence "the extent of the inhumanity and horror was evident" to read "I was horrified to view the extent of the inhumanity..." You don't need to be blatant about stating feelings if it isn't natural for you.

Like Paul, many people honestly don't remember how they felt at the time. "That was forty-seven years ago!" they lament. "How can I remember that after all this time?" It may not be just the intervening time. Perhaps the emotion was so strong it couldn't be acknowledged, even at the time. Generally, if you had strong feelings like rage or delirious joy, you'll remember that. If you don't remember precisely how you were feeling, make it up. Close your eyes and call the scene to mind. Consider how you were probably feeling, and you'll be close enough.

Personalizing feelings in a story is like adding red to a forest picture. A small spot enlivens the whole scene.

Another way to recall emotions is to use reminder resources like the ones on page 41. Paul was an official army photographer, and he wrote this part of his story after he found a stack of pictures he had taken in the camps with his personal camera. Music has a powerful ability to resurrect forgotten memories and feelings. So does smell. If you're writing about a summer of Little League games, a good whiff of a mitt can have you standing back in center field! A friend claims that the "fresh country scent" of her laundry detergent sends her straight back to carefree scenes from childhood when she ran among the damp sheets hanging on the clothesline. Photographs, scrapbooks, and visits with family members or old friends often trigger emotions as well as stories.

Sometimes you can express your state of mind as a descriptive term, such as, "The day seemed suddenly brighter," or, "I felt as buffeted as a flag in a gale." Start noticing words people use in conversation to describe feelings. Pay attention to delightfully descriptive words in books you read. When you start thinking like a writer, you begin collecting colorful and precise phrases to describe everything from the color of spaghetti sauce to the way you feel when you're stuck in a traffic jam and late for a meeting.

You can also tell about your reaction to things people say and do, for example,

> I was astonished that such wise words could come from one so young.

Don't overlook opportunities to share your reaction to change. I wrote a story explaining my first encounter with a computer. Here's a synopsis:

> I felt like a butterfly on her first soaring flight the day I sat down at our brand-new Apple II+ computer and typed a couple of paragraphs with **bold** type and *italics*! I corrected misspelled words, and revised awkward passages without ever touching paper. That day I believed my dream of seeing my name on the cover of a book could and would come true. That old Apple would hardly qualify as an interesting toy today, but that day it was magic.

Advice to include your feelings in your stories does not mean you should insert the equivalent of, "I was terrified," or "I was delighted," in every paragraph. Like other forms of description, a little goes a long way.

Caveat: Take care to report only your own feelings, not those of others. You can tell readers that "Jason's knit brow, narrowed eyes, tight lips and scrunched-up shoulders gave the impression of a thundercloud" because you can see his knit brow, narrowed eyes, tightened lips, and scrunched-up shoulders. It is not appropriate to tell readers Jason was furious. Unless Jason specifically told you he was furious, you would be stating an assumption as fact. Ditto with thoughts. Only tell us what someone thought if you heard it from the source. If Jason did tell you he was furious, dialogue is a good way to let people know you heard it from Jason. If you aren't using dialogue other places, you can use some variation of "Jason told us he was furious."

Use all your senses

Sensory-based description punches your story out of the two-dimensional limits of paper and the flatness of a black-and-white movie. For example, you may describe the texture of the plaster on the wall, the gritty sharpness of gravel in your hands, the tingle of a stubbly chin rubbing your shoulder, the vanilla fragrance of sun-warmed pines, the muscle-melting warmth of sunshine on your shoulders, the nectar-sweet juice of a ripe peach running down your chin and fingers, or the serene music of a brook babbling over stones.

The passage below is rife with sensory description. It has color, texture, scent, sound, movement, even emotion—the only thing missing is taste.

> As we padded along the springy, needle-strewn path into Oswald West State Park, a flood of mystical awe and peace washed over me. Giant old-growth Sitka spruce, Douglas firs, hemlock, and cedar formed a lushly green canopy two hundred feet above our heads, sheltering enormous ferns, vines, shrubs, and younger trees. The trail wound past fallen logs, some with roots rising over a dozen feet above the ground. These logs, covered with lush, thick, verdantly green moss, served as nurseries for tree seedlings and other plants. Invisible birds trilled merrily around us. Squirrels streaked along aerial pathways. Scattered shafts of sunlight created floodlit dots of gold on the forest floor, and infused the leaves around them with a glowing, golden light. The scent of earthy forest smelled like the fragrance of life itself.

> The forest seemed to be an organic whole, a living, breathing organism. I felt as if I were floating through it, borne along by unseen, mystical plasma of life, as a tourist in a theme park of the future might be. Yet while feeling like a visitor, I also became a part of the organism, connected to it by the tenderest web of love. That elation returns as I write of this experience and recall the privilege of entering this organism's internal space on that specific day of transcendent beauty.

As you practice thinking of details this way while you write, you'll find yourself looking at the world through a writer's eyes, vividly seeing details you missed before. Even your conversation will become more colorful!

Caveat: Avoid overly creative phrases. Descriptions such as "green-tasting air," or "sweating drops of moonshine," may confuse readers. There's a fine line between evocative imagery and camp. You want to convey a sense of your experience without sending the message, "Look how arty I can write!"

Attention to Detail

According to an old proverb, the devil is in the details. Being something of a detail freak myself, I took advantage of easy access to the wisdom of the universe via the Internet and learned that this proverb derives from an earlier version, God is in the details, attributed variously to Gustav Flaubert, Michelangelo, Ludwig Mies Van de Rohe, and others. Details pose a double challenge for writers. We want to use enough detail to get the message across, but not so much that we create clutter. We want the details we use to be precise and perfect. We may work like the devil to accomplish a result that sounds as if it flowed from the pen of God. Take your pick from the detail-polishing tools in this section to buff your stories to a high shine.

Avoid the passive voice

Sentences written in the passive voice have indirect action. "The crystal vase was given to me by my aunt" is passive. "My aunt gave me the crystal vase" is active. There are times when the passive voice is the best way to say something, but when you use it, use it on purpose. The more direct your writing, the more energetic and clear it sounds. Notice the difference in these examples:

Passive Voice	Active Voice
My attention was caught by a sandstorm as it raged to the northeast.	A sandstorm caught my attention as it raged to the northeast.
I was beaten almost daily by that brute of a stepfather.	That brute of a stepfather beat me almost daily.
When I was stood up by Tom, I was humiliated.	I was humiliated when Tom stood me up.
My admission to OSU was delayed by the lack of my SAT scores	The lack of my SAT scores delayed my admission to OSU.

Most people have grown so used to using the passive voice in both conversation and writing that it has become invisible. It may take practice to see it in your writing, but it's worth the effort. Look for the word "by" used in conjunction with a verb—that's a red flag for the presence of passive tense. Once you scrub it out, your stories will have twice the pep and zest.

Exercise
Use a highlighter to mark all the passive sentences in a story. Re-write them in active voice. Do you find any that need to be passive for clarity? Only a small percentage fall into this category.

Vary sentence length and structure

When all sentences have the same form and rhythm, stories begin to sound like a bedtime book for children. Use a combination of simple and compound sentences for variety. Basic grammar books will tell you more than you ever wanted to know about sentence structure.

Make sentences simple and direct

Clean writing avoids long strings of complicated description. Clear the clutter by breaking rambling sentences into two or three shorter ones. For example,

> I begin to type, but nothing flows forth so I finally give up and head down to the kitchen to fix dinner where I finally have a thought about the slides I've been working on for days on end and how some of the pictures lack focus because they have way too much detail in their backgrounds.

could become

> I begin to type, but nothing flows forth. When I head for the kitchen to fix dinner, a thought snaps into focus. For several days I've been scanning and enhancing old slides. Heavy background detail in some pictures prevents focus.

The first example has fifty-seven words in a single sentence. The second has forty words in four sentences. I leave it to you to decide which is more clear, easily read, and understandable. This advice may appear to conflict with the advice to be true to your own voice and write like you talk. It does and it doesn't. The revised paragraph is consistent with the general thoughts and tone expressed in the first, but it's easier to follow.

This reflects back to the earlier explanation about the way we mainly hear key concepts when we listen, and the fact that intonation separates thoughts into units that are equivalent to sentences even when a transcript may record a sentence running on for over a page. Writers need to do the work of the listener's brain and string the concepts into units that make sense to the eye the way intonation makes sense to the ear. As a bonus, people who learn to write more concisely and precisely begin to think and speak more precisely.

Exercise
Read through your story and check for run-on sentences that express multiple thoughts. Divide those sentences into two or more single-thought sentences.

Creative word choice

Use vivid word pictures to capture your readers' imaginations and paint your word pictures in exotic coloration. The following list of examples drawn from my hoard of e-mails should jumpstart your imagination:

> She caught your eye like one of those pointy hook latches that used to dangle from screen doors and would fly up whenever you banged the door open again.

> From the attic came an unearthly howl. The whole scene had an eerie, surreal quality, like when you're on vacation in another city and "Jeopardy" comes on at 7 p.m. instead of 7:30.

> The politician was gone but unnoticed, like the period after the Dr. on a Dr Pepper can.

> They lived in a typical suburban neighborhood with picket fences that resembled Nancy Kerrigan's teeth.

Yes, this is a joke, but only partly. These are excerpts from writing assignments in ordinary English classes. The authors deserve credit for stretching their minds, albeit in tasteless, corny directions. I hope along with a chuckle, the reading resulted in ideas for enlivening your own words. One of the best ways to stretch your own descriptive vocabulary is to read novels and memoirs by acclaimed authors. I'm always inspired by the fresh and imaginative descriptions in stories by Susan Albert, Sue Grafton, Maeve Binchy, and many others. Tom

Clancy, John Grisham, and Stephen King give compelling descriptions with a more masculine tone.

Pruning dead wood

Chapter Five mentions the value of cropping unnecessary words and details to focus stories more precisely. Begin by looking for places where you repeat information. Even within a well-focused story, you may find quite a bit of redundancy. Then you can begin snipping out word clutter.

This challenge won't apply equally to all writers. Some people write sparsely and need to add detail. Others are afflicted with a condition referred to variously as motor-fingers or digital diarrhea. While it is a gift to be able to get words on paper easily, it doesn't simplify writing. Verbose writers spend at least as much time removing extra words, sentences, paragraphs, and even whole sections as terse ones spend adding.

Most stories written by loose-fingered authors will benefit by removing at least ten percent of the words from the initial draft. The following paragraphs are an example of a pruning exercise I undertook:

> I look up at the gnarled oak tree, starkly outlined against the sky and see a single dry leaf clinging tenaciously to the largest limb. Every other leaf in the woods fell to the ground weeks ago when we had that last fierce wind, but this leaf may still be there when the tree buds in the spring. The leaf reminds me of my mother, clinging stubbornly to life long past the time when it seemed her body was ready to let go. (83 words)

> Some lifeless oak leaves cling tenaciously to skeletal branches. Well into winter, they stubbornly resist gales, unable to separate from the structure they've known. My mother was the ultimate oak leaf. (31 words)

The first paragraph rambles. The second version is tight and to the point. Besides reducing word count by sixty-four percent, I streamlined the concept, thereby increasing impact.

I spent several days revising that single paragraph. For all but about fifteen minutes of that time, the project was fermenting in the nether regions of my brain. Brain centers involved in creative tasks work most diligently and powerfully during sleep, and you can't rush this process.

It's difficult to generalize about what to cut. Sometimes you do something similar to cropping major parts of a picture to frame a key person. This sort of edit may involve omitting whole paragraphs or sections about circumstances or descriptions only loosely related to the core story. Other times you only need to pluck words or phrases, much as you might dash around the living room to pick up a few items of clutter before guests arrive.

Exercise

Try reducing the overall word count of a story by twenty percent.

(Check the tabs under File>Properties to find the word count for your computer document.)

Snip clutter words and phrases

Along with chunks of distracting material, you'll want to delete empty words and phrases that amount to background noise. Intensifying words like very, much, really, or absolutely top the list. *I was very tired,* doesn't tell a reader significantly more than simply stating, *I was tired.* If you were unusually tired, find a comparison or description to tell just how tired you were. "I was so tired I could have happily fallen asleep leaning against one of the boulders along the trail," lets readers know the extent of your fatigue. Another clutter word, *that,* is commonly used to excess. The phrase, *I told him that he could ...* is cleaner as simply, *I told him he could ... .*

> **_Exercise_**
> Use a marking pen to mark all the intensifying words in a story you wrote, then rewrite the story without them.

On her website, Pat Holt, a veteran editor and manuscript consultant, posted a list of ten mistakes writers make and don't see. It includes a warning about empty adverbs such as those above along with actually, completely, constantly, continually, continuously, finally, hopefully, incredibly, ironically, literally, really, totally, unfortunately. She explains that these words suck meaning out of sentences and lard your word count.

Duplicate words in close proximity are also ripe for pruning or revision. There's nearly always a way to avoid using the same word twice in a single sentence, or even a single paragraph. It isn't wrong to repeat words in a paragraph. Sometimes you need to, and sometimes you'll do it for balance or emphasis (as, for example, I do in this sentence), but be alert to frequent repetition. The English language is remarkably diverse, and with thought and a thesaurus, you'll nearly always find an alternative. Sometimes checking a thesaurus will yield a more suitable word than the one you originally used.

You don't need to clutter your desk with an extra book to use a thesaurus. Look under Tools>Language to find the thesaurus in Microsoft Word or OpenOffice. It's directly under Tools in WordPerfect. Online thesauruses offer even more options than paper copies. I have a link to Thesaurus.com on my Favorites toolbar because I refer to it several times a day.

> **_Exercise_**
> Use a marking pen to mark all duplicate words in a story you wrote. Use a thesaurus to find alternatives for any that can be replaced without changing meaning or causing confusion.

Most clichés belong on the scrap heap. Clichés are descriptive phrases and expressions in common usage that have become stale, and we use them on autopilot, without paying attention. A few examples include saved by the bell, time is money, better safe than sorry, or hotter than a pistol. A web search for "cliché list" will turn up thousands of lists of clichés. Please note that I used the word most here. An occasional cliché can give your writing a warm, cozy feeling. If you often use them in conversation, then do include a few of your favorites in stories to keep them authentic. They may give later generations a chuckle if they are easily understood from the context and used sparingly.

Editing in Action

The following example shows two versions of a story Edgar brought to a lifestory writing group. The group loved his story, but had some questions about the content. Edgar took their comments to heart as he wrote the final draft.

> The summer I was fourteen was a red letter one. Scooter, Buzz and I hung around with Edna most days. Edna just seemed like one of the guys, not a girl, and we did everything together. One day we set out for Evergreen park, with nothing particular in mind. On the way we passed the train bridge over Larimore Creek. Scooter dared us to walk across it. The narrow bridge was half a block long, and high above the creek below in the middle. But we were young and full of vinegar and Edna decided we should do it and she started out toward the bridge. I wasn't so sure, but I wasn't about to let some girl show me up, and I couldn't let her do it alone. I went after her. We put our ears to the track to listen for trains and didn't hear any, so we started across. The bridge wasn't much wider than the tracks, so we walked down the center between the tracks, stepping from one crossbeam to the next. We got across okay and then had to go back. We listened again and started out. When we got just past the middle, we heard a train coming ahead of us. It was too far to run back, and there wasn't anywhere to step aside, so we ended up grabbing hold of the side of the boards

and dropping down the side, hanging on tight as the train went by and then we pulled ourselves back up. Somehow we managed to get back to the other side. Edna and I were always special friends after that because we had survived that adventure together.

Let's take a look at the story to see how it passes muster with our checklist.

- Who: We know that Scooter, Buzz, Edgar, and Edna were involved.
- What: We know that Scooter dared the others to walk across the bridge, Edgar and Edna did it, and encountered a train, but lived to tell about it. We don't know why Buzz didn't join them or what his involvement was.
- When: When this story is read in context, we know which summer Edgar was fourteen.
- Where: The story took place in Edgar's hometown, on the railroad bridge above Larimore Creek.
- Why: Edgar's desire to save face and protect a girl.

The story checks out okay on the basics, but classmates wanted to know more about the following:

- What were you thinking?
- How did you get down and back up?
- Were your knees shaking after you got back up on the track?
- Weren't you afraid of falling?
- Did you and Edna talk to each other while you crossed?
- What did the others say after you got back across?

In addition to adding detail, Edgar decided to work on paragraph structure and add some dialogue during the rewrite.

The summer I was fourteen was a red letter one. Scooter, Buzz and I hung around with Edna most days. Edna just seemed like one of the guys, not a girl, and we did everything together. We weren't romantically interested in girls yet, but we were struck with the urge to wander and explore and put our strength and cunning to constant test.

One day we set out for Evergreen Park on a lark, with nothing particular in mind. On the way we passed the train bridge over Larimore Creek. Scooter dared us to walk across it. That was a pretty scary thought. The bridge was half a block long, and high above the creek below in the middle. The bridge wasn't much wider than the tracks, and there was no railing. Nobody in his right mind would ever walk across it. But we were young and full of vinegar and Edna decided we should do it. She started toward the bridge. I wasn't so sure, but Edna's daring was contagious. Besides, I wasn't about to let some girl show me up, and I couldn't let her do it alone. I sped after her.

When we got to the track we looked around for Scooter and Buzz. They stood several feet behind us, watching.

"Aren't you guys coming?" Edna hollered.

"You go first!" Buzz shouted back.

"You guys are just chickens!" Edna retorted. "Edgar and I will show you, won't we Edgar?" With that, she continued on.

I gulped and nodded. Before we stepped onto the span, we put our ears to a rail to listen for trains and didn't hear any, so we started across. We walked down the center between the tracks, stepping from one crossbeam to the next, being careful not to get a foot caught in the spaces. I tried not to think of the distance below us, and the fact that if I fell to the side, I could tumble over. I concentrated on the thrill of the adventure. It really was exciting to be up there, doing something nobody else dared to do. It was more exciting than my first time on the high diving board. I felt like I could do anything.

We got across okay and then had to go back. We listened again and started out. When we got just past the middle, we heard a train coming toward us. It was too far to run back, and the bridge had no extra room to step aside.

"Quick! Grab hold. We'll have to hang over the edge," I shouted to Edna. The train was coming around the bend. The driver saw us and clanged the bell like a fire alarm. It was too late for him to stop. Thinking back, I'm sure he was absolutely sick, certain he'd either run over us or we'd drop to certain death below. We did neither. We were young and strong and in terrific shape. We dropped over the edge with a death grip on two planks and hung on for dear life, bracing our feet against a truss below. The train was a short one, so it passed quickly. As soon as the last car passed, we pulled ourselves up, threw a leg up on the track and hauled ourselves back up on the track. Our legs were shaking so badly it was hard to stand up right away, but we didn't dare dawdle.

"Let's get out of here!" Edna whispered, her voice shaking slightly. I didn't need urging.

We clambered to our feet and began to gain speed as we went the rest of the way across. As soon as we got to the other side, we leapt from the track and fell to the ground in a heap.

"Hot dog! We did it! We really did it!" Edna finally gasped.

Scooter and Buzz were there waiting. "We thought you were goners for sure," they shouted.

"There was nothing to it. You cowards missed all the fun," I retorted. "I'd do it again in a minute." None of that was true. I thought I was a goner too, and wild horses couldn't drag me out on that bridge again, but never in a million years would I admit that to them.

They slunk off, and we didn't see them again for the rest of the day. Edna and I sat there for a few more minutes, not talking. My respect for her had gone through the roof. She had more guts than any of the other guys. She had more guts than me. If she hadn't gone first, the rest of us would have spent five minutes daring each other to go first and calling each other cowards, and then gone on down the road.

"I still can't believe we did it!" she exulted as we finally stood up. We fell together in a big hug of celebration, then turned to walk home, talking about the experience. We didn't even care about getting even with Scooter and Buzz because we were so glad we'd had this thrilling escapade. Edna and I always had a special bond from having shared this adventure.

Before You Print

Once you finish all those edits and rewrites, you may want to hit print and start mailing or e-mailing copies of your story, but before you do, be sure to check spelling and grammar one last time in case any rewrites went astray. Some writers prefer to leave these details until the end anyway. That's your call. Just don't forget to do it. Then print copies and share with everyone you know. But unless these are bound copies, you don't have to consider that your final draft.

Let your story age

Writing is an intense experience, and after you invest as much mental muscle as it takes to get those first words on paper, your brain may feel like mush. You may think this is the best you can do, that it sounds "pretty good." Initial edits can be good, even excellent, but they are seldom your best. Set it aside and take a break. A week may be long enough, but longer is better. Work on other stories while it ages. Even after a couple of edits, further improvements often pop out like magic in a well-aged story. Eventually it will reach the point where you can read it months or years later and feel satisfied. You may even smile broadly to yourself and think, "Wow! *I* wrote that!" Then you'll know it's as good as it can get.

Read your story aloud

Even if you feel corny doing it, read your story aloud. You don't have to have an audience. It works fine to read it quietly to yourself. This step ensures that the words flow smoothly and that they sound like you're just talking, not reading. If you find your eyes seeing one thing and your tongue saying another, match the words on paper to the ones your tongue uses.

After you've read your stories to yourself a few times, you'll be able to read them with drama and flair. Not everyone enjoys reading their work aloud, and not everyone wants to listen, but if you are willing to share, reading stories may become the best part of family gatherings. Even if they don't want to hear everything you've written, friends and family members will want to hear what you wrote about them. Young grandchildren especially enjoy hearing stories that include them.

Know When to Stop

People who ponder details so obsessively they can't make a decision are said to suffer from "Paralysis by Analysis." Writers are vulnerable to this malady when they begin revising. Unless your purpose in writing is to produce a polished work of litera-

The best part about writing is stopping.
— Colin Walters

ture, revise a time or three, then place your story in the finished file and move on to the next one. A good process flow is to write drafts of three or more stories before you even think about revisions. Then write a new story for each one that you finish revising. If you are still not satisfied with a story after three revisions, set it aside and work on something else for a time.

Lest you feel a bit discouraged with all this talk about dead wood, details, and the time required for serious edits, please keep these points in mind:

- Everything beyond writing that initial draft is optional.
- Your decisions about editing and polish are as personal as your story.
- There are no right answers.
- Your progeny would rather have raw drafts of a hundred stories than three polished pieces of prose.

Chapter 7:
Stories from the Shadows

Writing gives you the illusion of control, and then you realize it's just an illusion, that people are going to bring their own stuff into it.

— *David Sedaris*

Sometimes students come to class discouraged. "I tried to write, and I just don't know how to say what I'm thinking," they groan. Without fail, the stories jamming them up are linked to painful memories involving embarrassment, rejection, guilt, shame, trauma, or family secrets. They try to write these haunting stories, but the words get stuck. They won't come out at all, or they go in circles. A voice whispers in one ear, *Go ahead and write the story. People deserve to know, and you'll feel better if you get things out in the open. Speak your truth!* Another voice whispers in the other ear, *You don't have the right to tell this secret! ... Have you no respect for your father? ... Nobody in the family will ever speak to you again! ... Just what the world needs—another whining victim story!*

That's a heavy load. No wonder they're stuck. Writing about secrets and stories from the shadows of life is complex. Your thoughts swim in a sea of confusion. Do you dare expose your intimate memories to the world? How much should you tell? Should you even try to write about painful memories?

Looking beyond your personal confusion and reticence, lifestory writing, like journalism, involves certain ethical considerations. Since you purport to be writing a true version of your experience, questions of accurate representation may arise. Are you really telling it like it was? James Frey's creatively embellished memoir *A Million Little Pieces* generated a firestorm of controversy when word of his exaggeration hit the news. Oprah had endorsed and recommended his book. She publicly flayed him, he lost his agent and contracts for future books, and the public clamored for honesty in all memoirs.

Honesty about your own experiences is one thing, but there is also the matter of honesty and openness where personal information about other people is involved. Do you have the right to disclose things that may be an invasion of someone else's privacy? Should you name names and tell it all like it really was? Will your family or friends disown you?

The process of writing stories from the dark side of life is no different from writing other stories as far as the actual writing goes. What makes it more challenging is the soup of emotions the story swims in. The ingredients of that soup are complex. In this chapter, we'll look at the ingredients one at a time.

Why Write These Stories?

Before we go any further with this topic, one thing must be clear: writing a story is one thing, sharing it is another. Although any story may be written, some are best kept private. At this point we are considering only writing. We'll get to the part about sharing later in the chapter.

The unexamined life is not worth living.

—Socrates

If your mind keeps returning to a memory like your tongue goes to a mouth sore, it's unfinished business. One of the best ways to conclude unfinished business is to write about it. When in doubt, write in secret and decide about sharing later. Read on for various ways that this sort of writing can benefit you. Some, but not all, of these benefits depend on sharing the story.

To learn new things about yourself

In 1970, Joseph Luft and Harry Ingram introduced a concept called the Johari Window, shown in Figure 14, which illustrates this concept of hidden self-truths. The Public Area includes things about us that both we and others know. Some, like nose size, are obvious. Others are things we tell people. The Hidden Area includes things we know about ourselves that we don't tell people. Some of these hidden things are stuff that simply hasn't come up. Others are secrets by design.

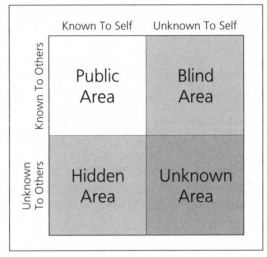

Figure 14: Johari Window

The Blind Area includes things others see but you don't, like a tag poking above the neck of your shirt, that you always grin when you criticize someone, or the slump you may be developing. Finally, the Unknown Area includes things that nobody—not even you—knows about you. This may include undiscovered abilities, courage under pressure you haven't faced, or an undiagnosed disease or chemical imbalance. Most information in the Unknown Area can only be known in the future, but some of it could be known sooner if you put known pieces of information together in new ways. Writing stories is one way to do this, as Paula tells us.

My parents never encouraged my interest in going on to college. "We can't afford it. You can get a job in the plant like your mother. If it's good enough for her, it's good enough for you!" my dad growled the few times I brought it up. Mom would just sigh and say, "I know," and change the subject.

I did go to work at Valley Foods, like Mom, but I also took night classes at the Community College. The counselor there helped me get a scholarship to State. I took out loans for the rest, carried more than twenty hours each term, and finished in two years, graduating at the top of my class. I had no trouble finding a job teaching high school English, which I continue to find challenging and rewarding, even after twenty-three years.

Two years ago I tried an experiment with my juniors. I asked them to write six stories about things that happened in their lives before they entered their teens. They enjoyed the project, and the results were amazing. I decided to do the project myself, but I didn't stop at six. I wrote stacks and piles of stories about all sorts of things.

As I read back through my stories, I realized an amazing thing. Those limits my parents placed on me, the way they didn't support me or believe in me, those things chafed like coarse sandpaper when I was young, and that never really went away. I've always gotten mad again when I thought about it. But finally I realized that my determination to do it anyway, in spite of them, to show them I could, was rooted in that chafing. It pushed me extra hard to do well, and it has helped me understand my students better than a lot of the other teachers.

Once I realized this, my resentment disappeared. Dad and Mom were doing the best they knew how. I'm glad I discovered this. Dad has cancer now, and won't be around much longer. I'm glad that I can openly tell him how much I love and appreciate him. He acts embarrassed, but I can tell he likes it. None of this would have happened if I hadn't written those stories. My life is much richer now.

Paula explained that she threw out several stories. "There was a lot of anger in many stories, and nothing good would have come of sharing them. I wrote for myself, not for them. It was like therapy and a lot less expensive."

To heal raw memories

Paula's story is an example of healing that resulted from writing about angry memories. Sharon Eakes, an executive coach, told me a story about the power of putting secrets in writing. She spent much of her career working as a therapist in an alcohol rehabilitation facility. In one therapy group exercise they asked members to write down their deepest secret, "The secret they drink to keep hidden. We didn't ask them to tell these secrets to anyone. On the contrary, they burned them. The amazing thing is that as soon as they burned them, most of them immediately told what they'd written. We didn't ask; they just did it." Writing it down was powerful, and freed most of them to disclose that awful secret, at least within the group.

She explained that this exercise was an important step in their recovery. The secret wasn't a whole story in the typical sense, but nobody would question that the whole story played through their minds as they wrote down those secrets and held them until they were thrown in the fire. In some mystical sense, the power of those secrets melted in the fire.

This healing element of lifestory writing is especially powerful for people who endured physical or emotional abuse at any age, those who grew up with substance abuse in the family, or those who are grieving over the loss of loved ones, but it also dispels smaller clouds. Writing about how specific incidents affected you can break their power to control your life, even if you never show or tell the stories to anyone.

Caveat: As Paula noted, this sort of writing is a form of therapy. Unfortunately, no form of therapy is perfect for every individual. If you suffer from serious depression or anxiety, it may not be enough. Medication and/or counseling should remain an option when writing fails to lift your spirits in a reasonable time.

To give your story depth

Lifestories based strictly on facts, events, and neutral or happy thoughts may seem flat, lacking some key element. Just as a pencil sketch comes to life with the addition of shadows, a lifestory seems more honest, complete, and credible with shadowy moments to set off the highlights. You don't need lengthy stories of tragedy. Salting your stories with a few mentions of disappointment, embarrassment, or other discomfort will generally suffice. All of your experiences work together to make you the person you are today, for better or worse. Neither you nor anyone else can fully appreciate who you are without recognizing some of these elements.

Lifestory writing classes bond quickly as they read stories to each other, providing a safe place to air questions. In one class, Rudy shared a concern about a story he was having trouble writing. In his early twenties, he had gone through considerable agony deciding whether he truly wanted to get married, and he almost broke his engagement. Then things settled down and he went ahead with the wedding. He's been married to that woman for nearly fifty years and he had never told anyone about his doubts. "Do you think I should write about them at this late date?" he wondered.

A lively debate ensued. The group consensus was that he should write the story, but keep it to himself for the moment. He agreed. After reading the story to the class at the next meeting, he decided that his hesitation was quite human. His wife could handle the revelation, and some grandson in the future might take heart by reading his story. Until then, Rudy's stories had lacked that shadowy human side that we sense in live relationships. This story snapped Rudy's life into three dimensions, disclosing human frailty to his readers. The class's enthusiastic reception of this story encouraged him to be more open about doubts and mistakes in other stories.

To build bridges

Explaining your point of view to someone else can be especially difficult when the situation is emotional and the person you're dealing with tends to tune you out or discount what you're saying. Michelle wrote a number of stories from her childhood in which her mother played a major role.

> ... I realized that I needed to have a discussion with Mama about the way she'd turned a deaf ear to my problems as a kid. Her way of dealing with things taught me to avoid problems myself. But how does one avoider talk to another about avoidance? I knew that if I even tried to start a discussion, one or the other of us would change the subject within seconds. So, I wrote a story about a couple of times when she ignored me and how bad I felt. I also included a part at the end where I explained that I knew she hadn't meant to be hurtful, and that I knew Nana had been the same way with her. I ended with "I love you Mama."
>
> The next time I was there for a visit, one afternoon I gave her the story, and I went out for a walk. When I got back, she had tears in her eyes. "I'm sorry," she said. "That's all I knew how to do."
>
> "I know and that's okay," I told her and then I gave her a hug. She's not much on hugging, but this time she hugged me back instead of stiffening up like she usually does. We didn't discuss it, and never will. It's enough that I was able to tell her and she knew.

You can use stories to let people know you were angry, sad, confused, or whatever. Stories have a huge advantage. Readers can't interrupt you or sidetrack you. The whole message is there, in black and white, and it can be read any number of times. The story may be an end in itself, or it may lead to further discussion. In either case, you can refer back to what you said if the need arises, and there's no question what you said. There could be a question about what you meant, but that would also be the case in conversations. Give careful thought to these stories and make them as clear as you possibly can. Lest we overlook the obvious, you can also use stories to let people know how much you care about them.

To inspire or teach

You never know what another person will find inspiring. One particular story in our family history continues to inspire me in an unexpected way. It wasn't written as a story—it was recorded as the testimony of my great-great-grandmother in New Mexico in 1894 during divorce proceedings against her husband of twenty years—but it reads like a story. The picture she paints of this Scottish coal miner's drunken abuse and failure to support his family is horrifying. Her efforts to keep her children fed, clothed, and sheltered were remarkable. Her determination to end the abuse by leaving was especially courageous in that era. She had backbone. I find this account and the odd notes my mother and grandmother wrote about her further life and adventures encouraging, and I'm proud to have such strong determination and persistence in my background. I'll never encounter the specific conditions she faced, but her example of resourcefulness and finding a way to make the best of a situation is powerful.

Indirectly her story also documents the genetic predisposition toward alcohol abuse that runs in the family. Sadly, her son also fell into alcoholism and non-support early in his life, exacting a high price in living conditions for his wife and children. Dozens of cousins have told the story of the drunken grandpas to their offspring to teach them about the effects of alcoholism and their own possible vulnerability.

If you write stories about overcoming adversity of one sort or another perhaps they will encourage and inspire your own descendants. You can't know which story might do that.

Writing On

Writing about past events reconnects you with them. Writing about emotionally charged memories may pour fuel on smoldering embers, flaming the situation back to life with a fierceness that can take you by surprise. Something about writing, and seeing the words in black and white, makes them seem tangible and durable, and it's harder to shove them back in the closet, but your Inner Critic will keep trying. Read on to learn about tools for dealing with difficult stories.

Getting clear

Even when no secrets are involved, the primary reason people have trouble with some stories is that they aren't clear what the story is, how they feel about it, or what it means. Who hasn't experienced the turmoil of thoughts spinning like a top during a trying time? Usually things settle down before too long, and we move on to other things. We may think we have come to terms with the matter and let it go. In one sense, this may be true—you have moved on to other things. Nevertheless, if you can't write easily about it, you haven't made sense of it. Now's your chance.

Freewriting

Freewriting, the warm-up exercise described on page 68 in Chapter Four, is a blockbuster for unjamming mixed mental messages. Write as rapidly as you can, without stopping. You write whatever comes to mind. Don't worry if it isn't relevant or grammatical. Just let the words flow as in this example:

> ... Sandy from diff planet—plastic smile—barf! Talked & talked & talked & asked few ?s. Hated answers & then she'd start lecturing me. Talked 90% of time—weird!!! job interview—gut said cut & run. But—needed job—8 month gap hard 2 xplain —broke— CAN'T move home. Shoulda stayed w/Al—never thot she'd call back. That smile! Urp! Just think about get'g next interview!! ...

Notice the use of dashes, abbreviations and symbols in this sample to speed hand writing. This author wrote sparingly, indicating most detail by exclamation points, underlining and caps. If this were to be turned into a story, the detail would be added later, along with grammatical trimmings.

When you finish a session of freewriting, read back over what you wrote. You may be surprised by what tumbled out. Use a highlighter, or cut and paste relevant highlights to use later. You may recognize a connection to the right brain here, the seat of emotions and unarticulated impressions. Freewriting is a way of giving words to the unstated.

Generic freewriting may get words flowing when you're stuck, and a focused version may be especially helpful for sorting out skidding thoughts. For this version, start with a specific topic and write. Much freewriting belongs in the wastebasket, or maybe the fireplace. You aren't writing for keeps, you're simply making word doodles. Eventually one of those doodles will jump out at you, prompting an "Aha!" moment. Take that one and run with it. Repeat this process as many times as needed until things begin to fall in place and make sense.

Lists

Lists are another valuable tool for plowing through confusion. Make lists of thoughts you have about your story or the memory that sparked it. This list idea is another version of freewriting, but without the structure of sentences. It records key concepts neatly and cleanly. You add context and association later. Don't give a thought to order. You can add order to a working list later if you wish. You can use a timer or not. Some people respond well to the pressure of a timer, others need to drift in a relaxed state, waiting for thoughts to come. Try it both ways.

Mindmaps

Mindmaps are described on page 44 in the planning chapter. Aside from their value in planning projects, they are useful for sorting loose thoughts. They may also help retrieve dormant memories relating to your current topic. Mindmaps can show relationships between ideas more clearly than ordinary lists, and they are an especially strong tool for right-brain thinkers.

Exercise

Do focused freewriting, make a list, and draw a mindmap on a single specific topic. See which feels the most natural. Since the first tool will yield the freshest results, repeat the exercise with several topics, varying the order until you settle into a preference.

Talk to a friend

Telling your story to a trusted friend, actual or imaginary, may help. An actual friend will ask questions to help you sort things out. Useful questions dig for details and establish order. Examples include:

- Then what happened?
- How did you feel about that?
- Who was that?
- What did that mean to you?
- How did things change after that?
- What did you do about it?

An imaginary friend can be a powerful resource. Visualize someone you admire sitting in a chair and asking you questions. Answer these questions the same way you would answer a flesh-and-blood person. As arcane as this may sound, this technique has led to major breakthroughs for lots of people.

If you belong to a writing group, you have a golden resource. Tammy came to a group meeting one day lamenting, "I started writing, but I couldn't get beyond the first page. I kept trying, but I couldn't sit there more than five minutes." She was trying to write a sad story that involved discord between her parents, her father's frequent bursts of rage, and squabbling siblings. She felt the story had valuable information for her children, but, although she experienced no trouble writing ordinary stories, she couldn't get this one out. Tammy's group helped her realize that she had mixed feelings about things that happened in her story, and about her father. When she explored these mixed feelings further, she was able to write her story and it unfolded rather differently than she'd first expected. You'll find more information on writing groups in Chapter Eight.

Visualizations

It's entirely possible to experience insight and healing without ever setting pencil to paper. Any library has stacks and piles of self-help books and CDs with visualizations and exercises to help you understand where the claws of past entanglements enter your mind, and how to rid yourself of them. Beth tells of one that worked for her:

> There were several snotty girls in my class in grade school who made my life miserable. They would cluster around at recess telling secrets, playing jacks and things like that. If I even walked near them, they'd look out at me and taunt me by saying "You can't play with us!" I knew it was because I was Jewish. It wasn't fair. It hurt like heck, and there was nothing I could do about it but hate them.
>
> Much later, after I was grown and started looking for answers, I found a book that suggested visualizing each one of those girls very clearly. I was supposed to surround them with white light and tell them I forgave them. Then I was to blow them each a kiss and watch them shrink and blow away into nothingness on the wind of my breath.
>
> It sounded pretty eerie, but I tried it, and to my astonishment, it worked! I have seldom thought about those girls since, and when I do, it's just a memory of something that happened. The pain is gone.

You might find it helpful to try a similar visualization when you feel stuck with your writing. The advantage of writing about your insight is that it makes the situation more concrete, and you have a record of the resolution that will reinforce your enlightenment each time you read it.

Rewrites

Please note that you could possibly rewrite some stories a dozen times over a period of several years and change your perspective a time or few before you hit pay dirt. I say this not to discourage you, but to keep you from becoming discouraged if you don't experience results in hours or days. We aren't talking magic here, we're solving the puzzle of life, and that requires time and patience. About half my life ago, a senior colleague mused that life was like peeling an onion. "Every time I think I finally know who I am, I discover another layer inside," she told me. "I wonder how many more layers I'll eventually find?" I remember her words when I reread some of my own stories, such as *Rocking Chair* (page 213) and discover further layers of meaning. This story began as a simple memory. As the memory deepened, I added layers and the epilogue.

Be creatively honest

While people may question the accuracy of your memory and even your honesty in any story, stories about crisis and trauma are lightning rods for criticism because they tend to arouse defensiveness in readers as well as authors. But don't let fear of being called into question force you into writing a dull police report of a story.

Think about the incident and the people involved, then pretend you are writing a movie script. What would these people say in a movie? Though you are unlikely to recapture a verbatim transcript, whatever comes to mind will reflect the sense of what was really said. Likewise, you can reconstruct how you reacted or felt, whether bad or good. How do you *think* you felt when you were the last one chosen for the softball team, or the time in junior high when you heard people whispering in the seats behind you and then they smiled nastily when you turned around? What about the time you were passed over for that promotion? How do you *think* you felt when you managed to play your whole recital piece without forgetting a single note, or when you got an 'A' in history when you hated the class and nobody thought you could hack it? When you project back into the moment to relive the event, you will remember the feeling, to the extent you were ever aware of it at all, and you may experience it more strongly now than you did then.

The key question is whether it's more important to document facts with clinical accuracy, or to give current or future readers the sense and feel of what things were like back then. Chances are good that the slight edge of creativity will make the story come alive for them in a way that cold facts never will. After all, which is more real to you? The weight of the turkey Grandma fixed for Thanksgiving dinner in 1946 and the number of people who came, or the memory of merry laughter, bumping elbows with relatives crowded around the table, suffering from groaning satiation, the fragrance of the mincemeat pie, and Cousin Pete puking from eating too much?

Exercise

Close your eyes and recall the experience you're writing about. Focus on the scene and the people until they are vividly in mind. Replay the words and actions like a mental video, concentrating on your feelings. When you have a clear sense of your reaction, open your eyes and write about it. You may go into detail, or simply add a word or two, depending on the story.

Write into the fireplace

As long as you have doubts about sharing your story, or your thoughts are still jumbled and subject to misinterpretation, keep your writing private. The most secure way to avoid any risk from having others scorched by the flames of passionate outpourings is to write it, read it over, and burn it. As I worked through the inner turmoil involved in completing my master's degree in counseling psychology, I wrote reams of pages, by hand. Not one of those pages survived a single hour beyond the time of its writing.

When I tell this story to classes, students ask, "Don't you wish you'd saved them? Don't you wish you could look back at them now?" Absolutely not! The writing served its purpose. Whatever insights I derived back then were updated long ago. I don't recall specifics, but one reason I burned them was their potential to be misunderstood. I didn't want to have to explain things I didn't understand myself. Besides, why would I want to reread crazed ramblings? They weren't stories. They were freewriting, the raw gushing of a churning mind. Had I been trying to write a story or report of my experience, I might have pulled a few key points into notes before the folio hit the flames, but the purpose of the initial writing was to settle my mind, not to record history. That mission was accomplished.

There is a primal satisfaction in seeing distressing words go up in flames. Some religious groups hold burning bowl ceremonies on New Year's Eve. Attendees write grudges, hurts, bad habits, obsessions, or anything they want to be free of on slips of paper. Then they burn the folded slips in a bowl, symbolically purging the soul to make room for spiritual progress and blessings in the coming year. Usually they write blessings and other things they desire on a second slip and place them in a sealed envelope to be read a year later. People are often astonished how many of these hopes are fulfilled.

From both a metaphysical and biblical point of view, the process of writing and releasing is potent. According to the Law of Attraction, whatever you think about will become manifest in your life. You can replace negative circumstances with more positive ones by replacing negative thoughts with positive ones. Following this line of thought, it makes sense to write freely about sadness, grief, and other bad things. When you reach clarity, record the insight, burn the rest, and move on to writing happier things, including your hopes and dreams.

For some, keeping toxic stories around maintains their grip. For others it may be the opposite. John Kotre, author of *Make It Count*, explains, "Usually it's by telling the toxic story that you begin to stop the transmission of damage between generations. As those who speak of the Holocaust say, 'Never again.' " Victims who have the courage to speak could be saying the same thing. When you achieve clarity of mind and purpose, you'll be able to speak out with power and conviction.

This idea of writing into the fireplace sounds drastic, and not everyone will have the desire or need to indulge in it. I recommend it for two specific situations. The first is for a symbolic clearing of old baggage and confusion, as discussed above. In these cases, you don't plan to revisit the issue.

The other application is similar, but the secrecy serves a different purpose. Sometimes, like Janine, you need privacy to sort your thoughts before you share them. Janine is haunted by memories of her previous husband, and wants to feel more resolved about that part of her life. Because her thoughts are so muddled, she doesn't feel ready or able to discuss these feelings with her current husband. It's not that she's afraid to tell him, but she wants to be clear in her own mind before she talks with him or writes openly about it. Meanwhile, she doesn't want him inadvertently picking up a notebook that would raise questions she isn't ready to answer.

Don't despair if you lack a fireplace or privacy to burn in secret—shredders work. Alternatively, you can stash pages in a safe place until you can spirit them off for secure disposal. Do whatever you need to do to safeguard your privacy, whether your words are on paper or a computer.

Whew! All that talk about secrecy has me feeling like this is a manual for spies. The warnings are critical for certain people, but relatively few readers fall into that category. More often than not, the people at issue live elsewhere and won't be digging through your notebooks or computer files.

Use humor

Humor keeps you from sounding like a drama queen, and it can offset the sting others may feel when they read words that seem embarrassing or harsh. You don't need to tell every gory detail, just enough to get the idea across, and often you can poke some fun at yourself in the process. Frank McCourt uses folk tales to inject humor into *Angela's Ashes*, as Mary Carr does in *The Liar's Club*. Both of these authors grew up in abject poverty and abuse. Their use of humor demonstrates that they not only survived, but they prevailed.

Humor may come naturally to you, and be part of your heritage. Not all families are defensive about their quirks and aberrations. Some revel in them. As one woman put it, "My stories are the main attraction at holiday gatherings. They hoot with laughter at the ways I poke fun at our craziness and roundly roast a few. Maybe that's because we all love each other, and take pride in our uniqueness." Her family members would feel hurt if they weren't included!

A matter of respect

Shadowy stories often present extra challenges for portraying characters in a respectful and honest way while minimizing repercussions. You can't assume responsibility for the reaction of every reader and still write your own deepest truth, but there are some ways to work around obvious land mines. A few tools for meeting these challenges follow.

Recast what you say

There's usually more than one way to say things. Thelly Rheam shares this story taken from the website for the Association of Personal Historians:

> The Smiths were proud of their family tradition. Their ancestors had come to America on the Mayflower. They had included Senators and Wall Street wizards. They decided to compile a family history, a legacy for their children and grandchildren. They hired a fine author. Only one problem arose— how to handle great-uncle George, who was executed in the electric chair.
>
> The author said he could handle the story tactfully. The book appeared. It said "Great-uncle George occupied a chair of applied electronics at an important government institution, was attached to his position by the strongest of ties, and his death came as a great shock."

While we can admire the creativity of that author's ability to please clients, that degree of recasting is misleading. My father claims that his grandmother excelled at this sort of optimism, and that the obituary she wrote when his grandfather died was a masterpiece of creativity, with little basis in fact. That obituary lives on, nearly a century later, and genealogists today must dig deep to document the discrepancies.

A more productive form of recasting is to refocus the story on relationships rather than problems or irritations. Stories exploring relationships are enlightening, and often helpful to others. They respect the fact that others do the best they know how at any given time, and that they are the products of their own upbringing and environment.

In her book *I Am My Mother's Daughter*, Iris Krasnow explores stories of relationships between eighteen daughters and their mothers, drawn from interviews with over one hundred middle-aged daughters. She uses the story of her relationship with her own mother as a thread to weave the others together. In every case but one, the daughters had thorny relationships with mothers who ranged from aloof or smothering to one who beat her daughter with chains. These daughters share their stories of how they came to terms with their mothers, before or after the mothers died.

The stories are raw and real. These mothers caused their daughters pain, but one of the noteworthy features of the book is that each story is told with respect and compassion. Each daughter realizes that her mother was a fallible human being who did the best she knew how to do, and that she was the product of her own mother's limitations. The women came to realize that they'd been yearning for a fantasy mom who never existed, so they came to love and appreciate their mothers for who and what they truly are.

"How noble," you may growl. "But you don't know about *my* mother." Or father, or Uncle Jake, or Boss From Hell, or ... the list goes on. How do you handle things when you are still seething with anger or licking your wounds? Read on.

Writing as witness

The first thing you can do is write into the fireplace until you come to grips with your feelings. Quite aside from the possibility of offense, you won't do yourself any favors in the long run by distributing a pile of stories that sound vengeful or spiteful, nor do you want to come across as a whiner or victim.

When you begin writing, focus on writing as a witness. Stick with what happened, how you reacted, what you learned as a result, and how this experience affected you and helped shape you into the person you are today. As you write, the safest way to convey truths about a person is to show them in action. For example, take the following excerpt:

> ... A few minutes later the verbal storm breaks. I don't register her words, just the tone. Her face reddens darkly as she erupts with a gushing torrent of criticism about the way Joe and I manage our family finances. It's all I can do to hang onto the paintbrush. I feel like flinging it across the room, maybe even in her face, and hollering, "What right do you have to criticize me about that? After all, that's the way you've always done things and the way you raised me to do them! Besides, it's none of your business!" But I don't say a thing. I never do. We never do. I swallow my anger, keep painting, and the moment passes. I sulk in silence, wondering why I've bothered to give up a perfectly good day to come over here and help her get her house fixed up when she obviously doesn't appreciate it.

The mother's actual words aren't used, just a description of the message. The author's reaction speaks for itself. No labels or analyses are required. Likewise, a description of your grandfather giving you a nickel while handing your cousin a silver dollar is self-explanatory.

Responsible Writing

When family members and close friends hear about your project, they wonder what you'll say about them. They hope they'll sound like heroes and fear you'll show all their warts and wrinkles. The potential for delighting people you care about is

Use your freedom to choose what to tell whom responsibly.

there, but so is the potential for hurt and anger, and strained relationships could become worse. Ostracism and retaliation are not fun. Moving beyond the family, friends and colleagues may have secrets they aren't eager for you to divulge. Old bones of your own may be dug up in revenge. Things could get ugly. Responsible writing strives to benefit all concerned—or at least avoid (further) damage to feelings and relationships.

The good news is that few stories are that traumatic, and when they do smart a little, most people are resilient enough to handle it. The Blind Area in their Johari Window shrinks and life goes on.

How can you reap the benefits of this type of writing without creating problems? The first step is to decide whether you are writing for yourself or to share with others. If you have a single doubt, keep your work private until that doubt is dispelled. Just as spoken words can never be unsaid, shared stories can never be unread. If you know a story could hurt or anger someone, or cause any grief for them or you, don't share it unless you are fully prepared to deal with the consequences.

Some writers like Larry Retzack are comfortable hanging all the family linen on the line. In a Yahoo! Group post, he wrote:

> As for not writing about family members who are less than per-fect characters, my father was an alcoholic most of his life and that sure didn't block my writing. If anything, it prompted it as a way to get back at an undeserving parent. I wouldn't worry a whole lot about revealing personal facts about relatives either ... unless there were an iron-clad case of libel. Ultimately writers, like most people, pretty much have to do what they have to do and if that's blocked, well, there are worse things in life, right?

Your situation may be more like Jana's. She is a world-class tender heart who would shrink from openly criticizing Hitler. For example, she hesitated to let her family read a story that mentions she was irritated by a relative's late arrival at a party. That may sound petty to some, but it's a big deal to Jana. Per-ceptions of propriety and risk are entirely personal.

Delay release

Parents pose an emotional land mine for many people. You may be concerned that no matter how tenderly you write, some of your stories could hurt your parents. You may be overly sen-sitive, but the concern is valid. Seeing your own shortcomings in print, even when it all worked out in the end, can be uncomfortable, and some disclosures could be downright mean. Edgar told a story about youthful exploits that would have caused serious family turmoil had they come to light. The fact that he had done such things did not reflect well on his parents, and the ruse he used to get away with them made it worse. He'd kept the secret for nearly forty years and considered making a clean breast of it in his lifestory. But his parents are still living. He decided that telling them now would be pointless and hurtful. "Why make them feel like bad parents at this late date when basically they weren't?" he finally concluded.

If your thoughts are more like Jana's than Larry's, you could hang onto your stories until the people you worry about are out of the picture. Edgar decided to go ahead and write his story, but it will remain private until his parents are gone. That strategy is feasible with parents. If you're concerned about a sibling or someone who will probably live as long as you or longer, it's not that simple. You may be able to show the stories to them privately and talk through their reaction. You may decide to write around the matter or take Larry's approach and brave the storm. No single answer suits everyone.

The ultimate delayed release is to arrange for your stories to be found and read after your own demise as Francesca did in Robert Waller's novel and movie, *The Bridges of Madison County*. In this powerful example of delayed disclosure, Francesca kept the secret of her brief and passionate affair with Robert Kincaid for the rest of her life. She wrote her story, presumably after her husband died, and arranged for her children to find it after her death. A lively debate can be held on whether she should have told the story at all, handled it as she did, or whether she should have told her children sooner. Would her children have had an easier time understanding if they had been able to discuss it with her? How would it have affected their view of her and their relationship with her? Though this book is fiction, the issues it raises are real and relevant, and there are no right answers.

Limit distribution

You don't have to give copies of your finished project to the whole world. For example, you could limit distribution to your children and ask them to keep the whole thing quiet. The risk in this approach is that you may have a bigger mess on your hands if word leaks out, which could happen sooner or later. If it does, you'll have the double-trouble opportunity to tell Aunt Gertie or brother Joe why she or he didn't get a copy while also dealing with their reactions to the stories.

Privacy matters

Since most experiences involve other people, indirectly you are also writing about them. Your stories may involve matters they'd prefer to keep secret. For example, Maria has vivid memories of taking her younger sister to get an abortion. This was a watershed memory for Maria, laden with guilt and fear. She wants to write about this, but nobody else in the family knows of the abortion. Likewise, few people know the history of Ted's lifelong friend and golf buddy, who spent time in prison years ago for fraud. Ted stood by him when he got out, and their relationship has been significant in Ted's life. Ted wants to write about his experience of standing by him, but doing so will reopen old wounds for his friend.

Do you have the right to tell a story that will disclose other people's secrets or things they would rather have forgotten? Do you have the right to tell stories that may embarrass them or hurt their feelings? In the United States, you are constitutionally entitled to write about anything you want, short of libel. It is not always good judgment to exercise this freedom. There are several questions to consider:

- What impact did this experience have on your life?
- What lessons can others learn through your disclosure?
- Is the benefit to you and/or your readers sufficient to justify turmoil for those you are writing about?
- Can you tell the story without naming names?
- Can you disclose this information without casting yourself in a victim role?
- Does it matter if people think of you as a victim?
- How are you likely to feel about discussing this if asked to explain?
- Are you writing out of vengeance or spite?
- Do you want people's memory of you to include this sensational material?

There are no formula answers to these questions. You must always decide for yourself about your specific situation. Your challenge is to understand the questions clearly enough to make responsible decisions.

A good rule of thumb is the old maxim: Do no harm. If you happen to know that your sister's husband had a torrid affair that she never found out about, why tell her now, seventeen years later, by including the information in one of your stories? What would be gained? Think carefully before disclosing things like criminal records, embarrassing health details, personal indiscretions, sexual orientation of people still in the closet, and similar material. Compassion is commendable. If the material doesn't play a key role in your story,

Above all else, strive for compassion.

think of it as sensationally distracting background clutter and review the section on focus and pruning. Let your purpose in writing—the purpose you defined as part of your preparation, and/or the purpose for this specific story—be your guide.

If you have a compelling reason to include questionable information, ask the person if they mind having their name used. In some cases it would work to change the name and enough details to hide the identity from all but those who already know. There's also the option of delaying release until the situation changes.

Ultimately, if someone played a major role in your life, you have the right to tell about that in your story, regardless of their feelings about the matter. Once again, guard against vendettas and casting yourself as a victim, and stick to the role of reporting as described above. Name-calling is especially dangerous in volatile situations. When you do decide to tackle a controversial topic, don't skirt the issues. If you start cleaning things up or bending things a little to accommodate people, you cross the line from memoir to fiction. Fiction is fine—just be clear on what you are writing, to yourself and to your reader.

A royal example

Memoir is the hottest literary genre today, and it sometimes seems that this genre is becoming a print version of the *Survivor*-type television series with authors believing that the more sordid and raunchy their story, the better the work will sell. Many decry this situation while others spend fortunes keeping up with the latest sensations.

Britain's Royal Family has often been in the center of this storm of controversy. The family has always been in the public eye, and biographies, authorized and otherwise, are nothing new. As fatal cracks began to spread in the Princes' marriages in the 1990s, authorized biographies (the royal equivalent of memoir) scandalized the whole nation with graphic and wanton disclosures of parental abuse (mostly in the form of emotional abandonment), eating disorders, emotional instability, and flagrant adultery. Kitty Kelly surveys the resulting carnage in *The Royals*, an in-depth saga of the House of Windsor. The already falling currency of the Monarchy took a nosedive when the take-no-prisoners memoirs began to appear. The British public was in an uproar of disapproval after the televised BBC interview, *Charles: The Private Man, The Public Role,* based on *The Prince of Wales*, the biography Charles collaborated on with Jonathan Dimbleby.

Your stories aren't likely to cause the downfall of a dynasty, but the results could be equally devastating on a personal scale. Group discussions about the topic of what to write and what to hide are always lively. Some people opt for total honesty, claiming that it's better and more healing to get the truth out, while others advocate compassion and quote 1 Peter 4:8, "Love covers a multitude of sins." Ultimately, it's a personal decision, to be made by each writer.

Chapter 8:
Other Challenging Topics

If writers stopped writing about what happened to them, then there would be a lot of empty pages.

— *Elaine Liner*

This chapter includes a potpourri of additional challenges you may face with certain topics. They each relate to other sections, but don't fit smoothly elsewhere. Just as memories jump all over without regard to a timeline, writing topics jump all around without fitting smoothly into a coherent topic flow.

Embarrassing Memories

We all have embarrassing or shameful memories we'd prefer to keep in a dark corner in the closets of our mind. Why would we write a story about the time we showed up a day late for a job interview? Or the time we sat through half a day of classes with the back of our dress unbuttoned? Or the time we struck out with the bases loaded and cost our team the game? We aren't eager to brag about speeding tickets, or copying in math class. It's not easy to write about the agonies of being too fat or too skinny, or having pimples or ... the list could go on for pages.

What do you do with these stories? That's entirely up to you. Nobody will know the difference if you don't write them. Perhaps they don't deserve whole stories. Perhaps they can fit into a couple of sentences or a paragraph in another story. Remember that reason for including shadows? To give depth to your story? This is one place you may find that depth material.

Sometimes there's a fine line between embarrassing and shameful memories. People may hesitate to write about youthful pranks and similar indiscretions. "I wouldn't want my grandkids to think I condone behavior like that," said one man during a class.

Laughter at our own foibles is the privilege of age and the elixir of youth.

"What if you heard your grandson had done something similar?" asked a classmate.

"If he wasn't in the room, I'd probably laugh. Then I'd probably give him a little lecture."

"So, grandkids tend to think their grandparents are stuffy old fogies. Why not let them know we had fun, too. It might build a sort of bond with them. Heck, it might even make them proud of you! You can still tell him why it wasn't a good idea."

Some memories of events that were mortifying at the time mellow and become humorous over time, like this example:

I hopped in the car without thinking and pulled into the street to get out of Beth's way while she left for work. Only as I pulled back in the drive did it dawn on me that I'd only picked up my car key. The house key, which is generally in my pocket, was in fact in my pocket. But my pocket was in the pants hanging on my clothes tree in the bedroom. Beth always locks the door when she leaves, and today was no exception.

I sat in the car hyperventilating while I considered the options. Then, thankful from the bottom of my heart for the automatic opener we'd installed on the gates across the drive, I pulled back out into the street and headed for our daughter's house, twelve miles across town. Ellen has a key to our house. Ellen and her husband are not early risers like us, and they live in the center of a row of townhouses. When I pulled up in front, I honked my horn. A minute later, I honked again. Then again. After five honks, several neighbors looked out to see what the early morning commotion was. Fortunately, Ellen also looked and came dashing out to the curb.

"Dad! What on earth?!" she shrieked when she looked in and saw me sitting there, wearing only my BVDs.

"Don't even ask. Just get me my house key," I growled.

If you did something you are ashamed of, or something that hurt somebody else, telling about it at this late date may show how you overcame the results and "became a better person because of it." You aren't merely bragging or tooting your own horn with a message like this. You may inspire someone else who struggles with something similar. Many people in recovery write lifestories for this very reason. They use their stories to gain perspective on their own past, to purify their souls, and to inspire others to avoid the same lifestyle land mines.

Boastful Memories

It's easy to come across as a braggart when writing of personal success. There isn't much danger when you tell of winning the fifth-grade spelling bee, or scoring the winning touchdown, especially if you include an account of the hard work that went into preparing. The occasional victory is great, and readers rejoice with you. When you write of these victories, it's appropriate to mention your jubilation, i.e., "My feet hardly touched the ground for the next several days," and to be generous about sharing credit with those who helped you along the way.

The challenge is greater for those who achieve long-term success in business or other venues. A running account of how you beat the socks off your competitors time after time, won every case you litigated, hung around with one celebrity after another, and so forth can quickly sound boastful or arrogant. I've set several celebrity memoirs aside halfway through after becoming irritated by their arrogance. No doubt the authors considered themselves genuinely humble, but their attempts at modesty rang false to my ear. I've also read gripping celebrity memoirs that I could hardly put down. The gripping ones included more action and discussion of issues.

To avoid the arrogance factor, include plenty of action to balance the victories, show the roles others played in your success, and don't shy away from mentioning the price of success. If you worked eighty-hour weeks, your family paid a price. If you had children, you missed Little League games, ballet recitals, and more daily encounters than any book can hold. If you never married, or didn't remain married, was that a price? Honesty about cost interjects a note of sincere humility and brings your story closer to ground level.

Gratitude is another expression of humility that warms readers' hearts. Everyone has much to be grateful for, and those who acknowledge this, often and consistently, win the hearts of both those around them and their readers.

A special form of lifestory—I call them "self-help memoirs"—celebrates accomplishments by using the author's lifestory as a base for explaining how others can achieve the same or similar results. Zig Ziglar was an early master of this form, and other books of this sort abound.

One of my personal favorites is *Liberating Greatness: The Whole Brain Guide to an Extraordinary Life*, written by Hal Williamson with his wife, Sharon Eakes. Hal uses his own lifestory, beginning with his diagnosis as a seriously retarded schoolboy, through his career as lead patent attorney in two major corporations, and ultimately the creator of the widely acclaimed *Pathways to Greatness* seminars. His life has had more ups and downs than a roller coaster ride, but he always bounces back. In his book, Hal teaches readers how they can apply the scientific principles he intuitively discovered that allowed him to transcend his early diagnosis. The book would be as appealing as a bowl of dry bran flakes without the milk and sweetness of Hal's own stories that breathe life into theory. His stunning successes don't sound arrogant because they are set in the context of a wide range of events, learning from the experiences, and above all, *gratitude.*

Conflicting Memories within Families

Many of our most challenging stories are based on the fact that family members may perceive each other in widely differing ways. For example, Laura is incredulous that her cousin describes their mutual grandmother as a kind and loving woman. "The grandmother I knew was a total witch. She was absolutely hateful to my sister and me. But since she clearly played favorites among her own children, why not our generation?"

While it's true that people do have varying relationships, time blurs memory of facts about who did what, and when and where they did it. Aside from memory, many aspects of any situation are a matter of personal perception and strongly colored by our own mindset and beliefs. You can read a compelling example of the impact of personal perception in the story *Mayhem at Camp RYLA* on page 229. This story illustrates the variability among people who witnessed a staged event. Several years ago, I wrote the following essay to illustrate my experience and understanding of how my own memories evolved.

The Art and Science of Memory

Memory: the space in which a thing happens for the second time.
— Paul Auster

Some philosophers and psychologists believe that each time a memory is invoked, it becomes embellished by the circumstances under which it is remembered. Over time, memories evolve into memories of memories more than memories of the original event.

I remember a day when I was barely two years old. My mother and grandmother (Rene) were talking about a train trip Mother and I had made. I listened to the conversation with interest. "I remember that!" I proudly exclaimed, because I knew

143

what they were talking about. Mother and Rene talked about remembering things all the time, and now I could, too. Or so I thought.

Rene corrected me. "No, you don't. You were just a baby. You remember hearing us talk about it."

Her explanation made sense. In a flash of insight, I realized remembering is more than just knowing what someone is talking about. When you remember something, it's like being there again; "seeing" the place, "hearing" things that were said, and so forth. Obviously, I didn't have the experience to articulate all this insight, but it was there—complete, permanent, and instant.

"Okay," I told her, delighted that now I really understood what remembering was. I went to my room and lay on my bed savoring this delicious new dimension I'd just entered. I lay there, wearing my red and white striped seersucker overalls, with no shirt underneath, my sandaled right foot propped on my raised left knee. I slowly stroked the fingers of my left hand to help me think while I practiced remembering all sorts of things to learn how all this new stuff worked.

Today, as I write about this experience more than fifty years later, the core memory forms a small vignette. I can still experience the feeling of being very small and close to the floor, and I can almost reach out and touch the ivory-enameled plaster on the living room wall I faced as the conversation took place. I remember sunlight in the room and the sharp angle formed by the inside of the archway opening into the cool, dark hallway that led to my bedroom beyond. I remember hearing the conversation about the train ride over my right shoulder from the kitchen table where they were sitting. Once again I feel the spark of recognition as that flash of insight lit up the biochemical soup of my developing neural system.

That core part of the memory, the part before I went to my room, is, I think, still clear and pure. I don't remember when and where we went on the train, or the specific words of the conversation. I don't remember what I did after that. I believe that it happened as written above. That's how I want to remember the conclusion to this scene, and I believe it is possible that it happened just that way. I do remember those overalls and the new pair of sandals that hurt my feet the first couple of days each summer until they toughened up. I recall lying on my bed, with my foot propped up, playing with my hand and thinking. I just don't actually remember doing it at that exact point in time, and I don't remember what I was thinking in the memory of lying on the bed. It's convenient to tag these memories together. They make a consistent and seemingly accurate package, and I always add this part in my own recollection of the occasion. The memory has become embellished and enlarged by the countless times I've remembered it this larger way until I can hardly separate the core content from the package that has grown around it.

There is more to this memory than walls, words, and clothing. Each time I recall it, I relive the thrill of discovery. I watch the image of the tiny child who was the seed of my current being with as much detachment as if she were my own grandchild. I remember my own discovery and think to myself, *How amazing that I learned so quickly and easily!* That joy of learning and discovery has become part of the memory for me now, and recently another part has begun creeping in—a part that reminds me that I am remembering a very personal experience, and that I have nothing to compare it with. I have no idea how other people learn things. I realize that everything every child learns is amazing. Life is amazing. And so is memory.

What is real, the core memory of the event, or the embellished and enlarged memory? I'd say they are both real and both serve a purpose. The core memory is historically accurate; scientific, or left-brained, if you will. The embellished one showcases my developing self, a sense of the path I've traveled, the insight I've acquired, and the sort of person I've become—an analytical introspector, among other things. This version of memory is a right-brain art form.

So which is the more accurate account, art or science? You be the judge. Both are real, both are honest, and both are valid. Your choice should conform to your purpose in writing. Are you striving for clinical documentation of detail, or to convey a sense of the person you understand yourself to be? In the latter case, don't be too much of a stickler for facts. Let your imagination run free to fill in the penciled outline of core memories with color and texture that flow from related ones. Call it life fiction if that feels more honest. Whatever you call it and write, be true to yourself and your finished picture will capture your spirit as well as events.

Many years ago, my sister and I spent a quiet evening talking about our childhood. There were only two incidents where we closely agreed. Both occasions required elaborate collaboration beyond the norm, so it isn't surprising we'd remember them the same way. We remembered mundane matters as differently as black and white. Somehow, we were able to avoid arguing about this, and finally stumbled into the conclusion that we were both right. We agreed on basics like names of relatives, dates, and addresses, but that was about the extent of our shared memories. Her descriptions of the people she remembered as her father and mother were dramatically different from the parents I knew. We realized that we grew up in different families! With that understanding, I can tell my stories, she can tell hers, and if they don't match, that's why. We each have our own reality—separate, but equal.

You may be deluged with corrections and disagreements as well as accusations of having a creative memory. Accept the input with good humor, then stick to your own story, written from your own experience, with a clear conscience. If you wish, you can include their input or comments with the attributing phrase, "In Sally's version of this story ... ." The contrast of memories can be useful, enlightening, or even entertaining. The discussion of story integrity on page 60 provides guidance on including comments from others.

Faith Matters

For many people, religious faith, beliefs, and experiences are so much part of who they are that these matters will naturally be woven into their stories. Others find it more difficult to write of intensely personal convictions. Many people attend church on a regular basis, and have personal beliefs at considerable odds with others in their congregations, yet few may know of these discrepancies. Others never set foot in a house of worship, but hold and live by deeply spiritual beliefs.

Whatever your beliefs, religion and faith are deeply personal, and your thoughts on the matter are relevant. You may find it challenging to write of faith if it isn't something you generally discuss. Perhaps you'll find it easiest to write about it as an essay, or in the form of a letter to a friend. Make a list of questions you would ask someone if you wanted to know more about what they believe and weren't too polite or restrained to ask, then write your answers to each question.

You might write about prayers that have been answered, or moments you've felt especially close to God. You could tell of times when your faith has given you strength, courage, or comfort. Other topics include how you came to hold the faith you have now, and what your childhood experience was. Perhaps you've gone through times of doubting. If your family shares your faith, it may be easier to write about; if they don't, it could be more challenging. Many churches have begun sponsoring groups that write spiritual autobiographies on topics such as these, and many books exist to guide you in this direction.

Caveat: The one thing you are well-advised to avoid doing as you write of your faith is using a judgmental, preachy, or evangelizing tone. Those who appreciate evangelistic messages are already in the choir. The rest will probably stop reading and write you off as a fanatic if you preach.

Medical Matters

Healthy people may not think to include medical reports in their stories. It's not something they often think about. But anyone who has filled out a questionnaire in a doctor's office lately knows that they all ask about family medical history. Whether you have enjoyed glowingly good health or suffered any number of ailments and afflictions, your descendants will benefit from knowing.

For those less fortunate health-wise, writing about ailments, afflictions, chronic conditions, or acute episodes without coming across as a whiner or hypochondriac presents a special challenge. There are several angles to consider:

- What is your purpose in discussing your condition—what sort of reaction do you want to elicit in your readers? Sympathy? Understanding? Admiration of your ability to overcome obstacles? Inspiration to take care of their own health?
- Is your story about the illness itself, or about relationships centered around the illness?
- How much overall emphasis should this have?

Another aspect of medical matters is experience you may have had as a care-giver for relatives or friends who had debilitating conditions, and other ways these situations impacted you. Don't hesitate to include these stories. They'll have value one way or another as examples for others, and future readers may be intrigued to learn how you and others "back then" handled these situations. In a few decades, today's various rehab, long-term care, and similar support facilities may seem as primitive as the sanitariums or leper colonies of past eras.

Writing about Your Ancestors

Including background information and stories you've heard or remember about previous generations places your own life within the context of the larger family. It gives depth and per-haps more meaning to your own lifestory.

As you write, you may refer to documents and other re-sources to check dates, locations, and other specific data. You may be able to describe visual details from pictures you find. Mention or include the picture to preserve your own credibility with readers. If you're lucky enough to find old letters or jour-nals that record your ancestor's personal thoughts, use that person's own words, in the form of quotations.

You'll always write about these other people in the third person, and you must guard against the temptation to attribute thoughts and feelings to them. You can share your own obser-vations, or record the general impressions shared by family members through the years, but always make it clear that you are reporting second hand or stating assumptions, not speak-ing from inside the other person's head.

The years were not kind to my great-grandmother Matilda. Al-though she had been a stunning beauty, healthy and strong in her early years, after she caught the flu in November 1918 while nursing a sick relative, she was never fully well again. The doctor advised a warmer climate, so the family moved from Oklahoma to Tempe, Arizona. They stayed in that area for two years. My grandmother and her sister dropped out of school for months at a time to stay home and care for their ailing mother. Twenty years later she died of tuberculosis, the disease that killed her father fifty years earlier.

Later pictures show Matilda looking haggard and dismally sad. Her disease would have constantly drained her strength, making their incessant moves difficult—my great-grandfather spent his whole life chasing pots of gold without ever touching one. I can only imagine how grim and gray her life must have seemed in later years, especially as the Great Depression set in. Did she ever regret marrying the man who must have seemed a godsend to a young widow with seven children? Did she give up hope that he'd ever make a steady living? Was she bitter, or merely tired? Did she look back on her years with Governor Roberts' son as an unreal dream? When I visit her lovely grave in Austin, right behind Miss Ima Pigg, the renowned Texas philanthropist, I ask these questions, but I have yet to hear an answer.

Writing Someone Else's Story

You may have an elderly relative or know someone else who has lived a fascinating and meaningful life, but is unable or unwilling to write about it. There are many fine books to guide you through what is often referred to as the story-catching process. Basically you interview these people, encouraging them to talk about the relevant areas of their lives. Ask questions to bring out details, opinions, and feelings about events. Verify facts such as birth dates, addresses, and names from other sources when possible. Use the same sort of memory grabbers and trigger questions to prepare for this project that you would use for writing your own lifestory.

Recording your interviews frees you to listen to nuances of speech and capture the non-verbal aspects of the story without taking notes, which often miss key points. Ask permission before you record. Some people are leery of talking to recorders. Take a little time at the beginning to experiment with microphone placement, to ensure that you can make sense of the recording later. This step will help both of you get comfortable talking with a recorder running. Tape will work; newer digital recorders are great, and video is awesome. Use what you have.

Write these stories the same way you write your own, preferably in past tense. Depending on the preference of your subject, you may even write in the first person, making any additions, corrections or changes that the person specifies. Generally it will feel and sound more natural to write in the third person. It's difficult to write credibly in someone else's voice.

Editing Someone Else's Story

When word gets out that you are writing your lifestory, other people may ask you for help in writing their own. They may ask you to read their work and suggest improvements, or to simply make the changes. This can be a challenge. My recommendation is to listen carefully to determine whether the person actually wants constructive feedback, or merely wants to be assured that he or she is a talented writer. In the latter case, respond with compassion. Even when you have difficulty being honestly positive about the writing or story content, you can always say something like "Iris, I know your descendants are going to be simply thrilled to have this story."

If the person is serious about wanting constructive feedback, take it easy. Don't overwhelm anyone with a long list of faults. Pick out two or three key elements, and make sure to find strong points to mention at the same time. Your suggestions may take the form of pointing out information gaps, or places where the story doesn't flow well. You may mention consistent grammatical errors. You may proof-read for spelling and grammar errors. Or, you may do all of the above. It largely depends on your sense of the situation and your own comfort with pointing out errors in someone else's work.

Whatever sort of assistance you offer, never lose sight of the fact that this is not your story. The story belongs to the person who wrote it. You can suggest changes, you can point out flaws, but you should never pressure others to be untrue to their own memory or personal interpretation.

Preserving and Expanding the Work of Others

In the first chapter, I mentioned that I pieced my mother's notes and stories into an organized account of her early life. I also transcribed the story my husband's grandmother wrote about her life. At times I was tempted to reword sentences, fix grammar, or otherwise spruce up their stories. I resisted these temptations. I intuitively knew that if I tinkered with their words, I would hijack their voices and their truth. I capitalized a few names, added missing periods, and fixed spelling errors that were obvious mistakes rather than personal aberrations. Otherwise I left them as they were. I intervened only to minimize confusion.

In my mother's story, I found documents showing that she had a couple of facts wrong. In those cases, I added a short explanation at the end of the paragraph to explain and correct the error. A few times I inserted material from my own observations. I italicized these additions and corrections, initialing each one. I added forewords to each story, explaining the history of the manuscript, how I came to have and work with it, and the system I used to protect their integrity.

Other additions to Mother's story consisted of comments contributed by one of her cousins. Their mothers were sisters, and Helen had many additional points to add about the early years. As with my own, I put Helen's remarks in italics, with her initials.

Chapter 9:
Maintaining Momentum

Keep writing. Keep doing it and doing it. Even in the moments when it's so hurtful to think about writing.

—Heather Armstrong

Whether they draw up a plan or simply start writing, most people finish half a dozen stories or so, and run out of steam. Other priorities distract them, they lose interest, they lose sight of what they set out to do, or they begin to feel overwhelmed. This section includes suggestions for maintaining momentum and staying on track.

Make an appointment to write

Make your writing a priority, but keep the size of your commitment manageable and honest. Don't delude yourself that you are going to spend two hours a day on this project when your work fills ten hours a day. Whether you can afford one hour a week, or a certain amount of time each day, schedule regular times to write and stick to it.

Now, having given you the "eat your spinach" line about scheduling your writing time, I'd be remiss if I didn't admit that I don't strictly follow that advice. I do write nearly every day, but the truth is that I'm a binge writer and an impulse writer. Two stories came to mind as I wrote those two sentences, and if I weren't working toward a deadline to finish this chapter, I'd open new documents and write two stories in a row, *Confessions of a Binge Writer* and *I Feel a Story Coming On*. That's how I write most of my stories. I feel them "coming on," something like a cold. As it is, today I'll have to add the ideas to my list, and write the stories later. *My Write Hand,* on page 238, is a typical story of the sort I'm likely to write when I feel one "coming on."

In case you wonder how I can give you this advice about scheduling and then not follow it, I'll refer you to the earlier discussion of brain structure. Just as no two fingerprints are the same, no two brains are the same, in function, in work style, or in any other respect. We're more alike than not, but the world would be an easier, happier place to live if everyone realized the extent of our personal uniqueness and respected and celebrated our differences rather than becoming irritated by them. Fortunately human beings have the option of overriding natural inclinations.

Write when you can if you can't write when you plan.

If you can arrange to write at regular times and stick to that commitment, your writing will benefit in the same way your body benefits if you treat it to regular exercise. If that isn't the case, don't beat yourself up, and do not give up.

Chain your writing

Don't end a writing session with a finished story. Write at least a few sentences on your next story before you quit. This will help you pick up your train of thought the next time you sit down to write. Editing can be as demanding as writing, sometimes more so. The same trick, of editing a few lines of the next story or section, can help keep you on track with editing.

Find writing buddies

In her book *Wild Mind*, Natalie Goldberg explains the value of a writing buddy. Natalie meets her writing buddies in places like cafes where they sit and write together for an hour or two. They don't visit—they write. Before they leave, they often read to each other from what they wrote and share feedback.

You may benefit from writing with a buddy, but you can't do all your writing this way. You'll need other time for planning and revising. If you do find a buddy, you don't need to actually meet. Just making an appointment to write, at the same time, or by a certain specified date, can be enormously helpful. If you get stuck, your buddy can help you get back on track. You and your buddy can read each other's stories, and provide feedback for each other. You can meet in person, talk on the phone after writing separately, or e-mail stories back and forth.

The best place to find a writing buddy is in a writing group. You may also find other writers by hanging around coffee shops where people go to write. Talk to librarians, who may know writers, or post a notice on bulletin boards or in the personals announcing your interest in finding a writing buddy.

Join a writing group

Writing groups are another buddy system. Some meet as often as once a week, others once a month. However often yours meets, you'll have the challenge of writing something new to share at the meeting. As a rule, these groups remain small, and members make copies of their work for the others to read and comment on. It works best to distribute copies ahead of time to give the others time to prepare for the discussion. Having a range of comments can do wonders to help you increase your skill and find fresh new ways of expressing yourself.

To find a writing group, check at your library or bookstore. You may be able to take a class at a local university or community college to meet other aspiring writers and form your own group after the class ends. The best groups have enough diversity of interest to keep each other challenged, but enough in common to understand each other's genre, and you should feel comfortable with all the members. Although almost any group can be helpful, you may find that general writing groups focus more on publication and polish than you care about. The ideal group for your purpose is a lifestory writing group. If you can't find one, post a notice at the library, bookstore, or other public bulletin board announcing your interest in starting a lifestory writing group. Most public libraries are eager to cooperate with groups like this. Use this book to work through planning and writing together, learning from each other as you go.

Writing groups need a few ground rules to be successful. Recommended examples include:

- Regularly scheduled meetings, at least once a month. Twice a month is better. Weekly is ideal, but often too fast-paced for many to keep up with over an extended period of time.
- Enough members to maintain momentum if one or two are out of town, but few enough for everyone to read each time. Specify the length of the meeting and stick to it.
- Keep track of time so discussion is divided fairly and not dominated by one or two members. Members can rotate turns as timekeeper from meeting to meeting.
- All writing and discussion is confidential within the group.
- No socializing during the meeting. Keep the focus on writing.

Internet writing groups offer yet another form of support. You can find hundreds of these by searching Yahoo! Groups, Google Groups and MSN Groups for starters. I have been involved with several excellent groups. Many fill your inbox with idle chatter, so it's a good idea to look through the archives to get a feel for the group before you start posting. I use a Yahoo!

e-mail address with an alias to scout a group before I make a decision about participating. If I like it enough to jump in, I join with my real name and active e-mail address. With Yahoo! Groups, you'll find a link to edit your membership and specify how you receive messages. You can receive them all as individual e-mails, clustered into a maximum of one per day, or read them all on the website rather than receiving any e-mails. I belong to a large number that I check only occasionally on the website. One productive way to use these groups is to hang around for a few weeks and post a few messages, then find a person or two whose writing and ideas you admire, and get acquainted by private e-mail, if they are so inclined. This can lead to trading work by e-mail for valuable critiques and ideas.

Still another type of support group is to keep family members and friends posted on your progress. You don't need to promise a finished product by any particular time, although you may do this if you wish. Talking about your progress can keep your interest and energy high, similar to self-affirmations made out loud in public.

Curing Writer's Block

You know the feeling. You sit at your desk, or the kitchen table, or in the bookstore coffee shop, you have a pad of paper and a couple of pens, and a story idea. You pick up that pen, and place it on the line at the top of the paper, but that's as far as you get. Your fingers freeze. They simply won't move. Just to make sure, you scribble a tiny spot at the bottom of the page, and verify that there is ink in the pen. You scratch your head, yawn, stretch, and try again. Still nothing. You get up and fetch a fresh cup of coffee. That's it. Coffee, strong and black. That's what fuels writers, right? That or whiskey, à la Hemingway. Wrong. Neither coffee nor whiskey is a reliable crutch. Caffeine can intensify anxiety about being stuck; alcohol makes you quit caring. The words are still stuck.

Suddenly doubt sets in. What was it that made you think you could write? Just why is it that writing these stories seemed so all-fired important? *I'm not a writer*, you tell yourself. *This is nuts!* Then it dawns on you. This is the fabled writer's block.

Writer's block can occur at any point in a project from the very beginning to the last phases of editing. Fortunately, the affliction is not fatal, and prescriptions for recovery abound. Many books, like *Overcoming Writer's Block* by Karin Mack and Eric Skjei, or *Anybody Can Write*, by Roberta Jean Bryant, are full of ways of overcoming it (her book has lots of other great tips). Short of reading a whole book, some suggestions for overcoming writer's block follow. Think of the items on the list as resources on folded scraps of paper inside a jar, rather than a ladder. There is no order to the list, so use whichever one seems right for your situation.

Review your purpose

When you feel bogged down, pull out your purpose statement and review it carefully. Perhaps you need to redefine your purpose. Some factors are unclear at the beginning of a project. Some people need to write a few stories before they really understand where they are going.

Review your story list and other material

Whenever you need new inspiration, go back to your story list or your collection of memory material. Two minutes with a photo album, old e-mails, or my timeline is always enough to get my fingers flying again. Ditto with my bulging folder of unfinished stories.

Change your venue

Back in Chapter Two you read about the importance of having a spot to write that suits your style. When you feel blocked, it often helps to write in a different spot for variety. If you always write at the same desk, on your computer, try taking a tablet and pen to a comfy chair in another room. Go to the library or a coffee shop. If you are a wandering soul to begin with, wander to a new location.

Change your tools

In the suggestion above you may have noticed the suggestion that you move from your computer to a chair—with a tablet and pen. Nobody can clearly explain why, but writing by hand is quite different from writing on a keyboard. This observation is most relevant to those who are fluent on a keyboard, but it's true even if you hunt and peck. My personal hunch is that different clusters of muscles are involved, controlled by different brain centers. We learn to write by hand as young children, so writing by hand may resurrect earlier memories. It has a more personal feel. You generally write slower by hand, giving your brain more time to process the information. On the other hand, typing fast allows words to gush forth more fluently.

Whatever the reason, changing to another writing tool will often shift your mind to a new, looser place and liberate locked-up words.

Write a letter

Set your writing project aside and write a letter (or an e-mail) to a friend or relative. You can write about your project and current case of writer's block or about anything at all. Write the letter to get words flowing, and then turn back to your story and keep writing.

Use scrap paper

Whether you are writing longhand or on a computer, use scrap paper to jot down thoughts and ideas about the story that's giving you trouble. Make a list of points you want to include. Make a list of three or four ways to start the story. Or, you could just start writing the story. This is scrap paper, and you expect to throw it away anyhow, so just write. Total nonsense is okay.

Doodle

Sometimes it's enough to just begin moving your hand. Doodle, sketch, or whatever your hand feels like doing. This loosens up the creative right side of your brain and helps it throw off the domination of that left-brain-residing Inner Critic.

Move around

Sometimes physical movement loosens your mind. Although you run the risk of becoming sidetracked by distractions, get up and move around the room. Put on some music and dance around. Do some yoga. Go for a walk.

Do some cleaning

Creating physical order by sorting a mess can work wonders in ordering mental chaos. You may not even realize your mind is working on your story ideas, but suddenly the words you needed will pop into your mind. When that happens, drop what you're doing and go write them down.

Work on a craft project

Redirecting your creative juices to a sewing, craft, woodworking, or similar project may help get the words flowing again. So can working jigsaw puzzles.

Listen to music

Some people find background music helpful, others consider it a distraction. If you have music on, turn it off. If you are in a quiet room, pop in a CD, plug in your iPod, or turn on the radio—if you can find a continuous music station. Talk stations and programs are likely to distract you.

Take a shower

Running water is notorious for unleashing creativity and problem-solving powers. Baths can also help, but the votes generally go to showers. Keep paper and pencil handy. Some bestselling authors keep waterproof writing materials or voice recorders in their showers. Inspiration, when it hits, is fragile. Don't let it escape.

Freewrite

This all-purpose tool is a great blockbuster. Refer back to the section on warming up on page 68 for a refresher.

Write around the block

When you feel terminally stuck, instead of trying to write the first sentence or headline, begin with your ending and write backward. Write some dialogue. Write something that makes fun of your topic. Write anything at all, just to start the flow of words on paper and "write around the block."

Have a chat with your Inner Critic

Visualize that Inner Critic sitting on a chair across from you. Let him have his say, then respond with words like: "I am *not* going to let you get away with this. You are *not* going to keep me from writing this story. You have a six-week time out! Now go to your room and stay there!" Say these words fiercely. Say them out loud if there's nobody around to call the men in white coats, and watch your Critic slither away.

Have a chat with a friend

Especially a writer friend. Pity parties are useful, if you keep them short.

Write about why it's hard for you to write this story

Exploring your feelings about the story may uncover the reason for feeling blocked. There may be aspects of the story you haven't thought about that you aren't quite ready to write about. Perhaps you feel disloyal about disclosing personal information about someone else. Maybe the memory still makes you too sad, anxious, or helpless. Knowing what the problem is may disclose a solution.

Then again, it may not. If that's the case, set the story aside and write about something else. You can come back to this one later when your perspective clears or you feel stronger.

Sometimes you just aren't ready to write about some specific topic. Sometimes the topic comes to mind, and you try to write about it, but it simply doesn't work. If the words flow at all, they don't seem "right" to you. You aren't happy with it. That's usually a signal that the topic is premature. You need to let it develop and grow in the inner workings of your mind. Don't push it. Think about the topic now and then, but in a light, idle way. Rest assured that when the time is right, you will know.

Chapter 10:
Finishing Touches

Keep writing. Keep doing it and doing it. Even in the moments when it's so hurtful to think about writing.
— *Heather Armstrong*

You keep reading that "any lifestory you write, anything at all, is better than writing nothing. If all you leave behind are some chicken scratch notes, some descendant is going to be pleased to find those." The lists and notes that my mother didn't use in her story are valuable as family history. Chicken scratch notes are fine, if that's as far as you get. Don't get rid of those scribbles—save them in a special folder.

On the other hand, once you've gone to the trouble of writing a pile of nice stories, isn't it worth some thought and effort to make them easy to read, attractive, and error-free? Whether you are using a clone of James Michener's Remington, or the latest in desktop publishing software, this chapter is a tool kit to answer common questions about punctuation and grammar. You'll find answers to basic questions, with references listed for additional resources.

There's an important reason that you find this information near the end. Writing drafts requires a measure of courage and latitude in expression. If you aren't an experienced writer, the onus of complex punctuation and grammar rules could be fatally discouraging. Style rules are similar to rules for basketball. You can shoot hoops without rules, and all the rules in the world are useless until you can get the ball through the hoop. Ditto with dribbling the ball. Once you master those skills, you're ready to play the game of basketball with other people, and then you need rules to keep the game moving smoothly.

It works the same way with writing. First you must get words on paper, then concern yourself with meeting readers' needs. Punctuation and grammar are the rules that facilitate reading and understanding. If you ignore too many conventions, readers may be distracted or have trouble understanding. You want to strike a balance between standard usage and the charming quirks that stamp your personality into your writing. Your choice of words, the rhythm of your sentence lengths, and your overall outlook on life will shine through to display your uniqueness, whether or not you completely standardize punctuation, grammar, and style.

Punctuation Guidelines

Punctuation works like stop signs and traffic lights to regulate the flow of words. It helps them work well together and make sense. A defined set of rules increases the odds that readers will derive a common understanding. Unfortunately, we don't learn punctuation by speaking the language. People who graduated from high school before 1970 probably learned punctuation and grammar fairly well, then forgot most of what they learned. Those who graduated more recently may not have received a solid grounding at all. We all recognize it as we read, but when it comes time to use it, beyond a simple period and a comma or two, and maybe the odd quotation mark, we are out to sea. What's a person to do?

Grammar check will catch most punctuation errors, and punctuation rules are easy to find on the Internet. The following guidelines will be sufficient for nearly any punctuation question you'll come across in writing lifestories.

Apostrophe

An apostrophe tells the reader the word is either possessive, a contraction, or a special type of plural. Use an apostrophe:

To replace missing letters in contractions	Don't, isn't, weren't
To form possessive nouns	Sally's book, readers' needs
To refer to the plural of letters and words that end in single vowels.	Do's, E's

Colon

The colon is used for the purpose of *introducing* the content that follows. You can use a colon in your story in any sentence where you directly introduce something. The colon gives special emphasis to the words following it by slowing the reader's eye. Use a colon:

To introduce a word or series of words	Gather the following equipment: pen, paper, eraser.
To emphasize a single word or series of words	Her decision could be summed up in one word: brilliant.

Colons and verbs both introduce the following words, so never place a colon directly after a verb, i.e. "The reasons are: ..."

Comma

Commas are the most commonly used punctuation mark in the English language. Commas tell a reader to pause, thus governing the rhythm of the sentence and clarifying meaning and avoiding ambiguity. If you read your sentences aloud, carefully and accurately, you can generally rely on your ear to tell you where commas are needed, but for precision, use a comma:

To separate items in a series	Common types of lifestories include vignettes, chronological accounts, and scrapbook collections.
Before conjunctions in compound sentences	I love to walk in the woods, but on snowy days I stay home.
To attach additional components to the beginning or end of a sentence	When it's cold outside, I wear a warm coat. I did well in history, although I hated it.
To set off a non-essential or explanatory component	Mr. Joyce, our school principal, was exceedingly strict.

Dash

Few people realize that there are two types of dashes: em-dashes are the width of a capital M, and en-dashes are the width of a capital N. You'll find both dashes on the Insert>symbol menu in your word processing program.

The em-dash—often typed as two hyphens side by side with no space between the dash and the words on either side of it—is used to connect groups of words to other groups. Generally, the dash does this in two ways: it separates words in the middle of a sentence from the rest of the sentence, or it leads to material at the end of a sentence. Use an em-dash:

For special emphasis, stronger than using commas	Sue Grafton—my very favorite mystery writer—is speaking here next month.
To indicate a break in thought	Conrad—did I mention yet how much I hated Conrad?—sat at the head of the table.

To add a new thought to the end of a sentence	We plan to go to Mexico for the winter—of course we may yet change our mind.

The en-dash is generally represented by a single hyphen. For precision, use an en-dash:

For numerical ranges	2003–2005
For phone numbers	888–777–0000
To link names that are not compounds (hyphenated words and names are always joined with a hyphen)	The Morely–Jones experiment

By default, auto-correct in word processing programs generally replaces a space followed by two hyphens and another space with an en-dash.

Ellipsis

Few people realize the ellipsis is an actual punctuation mark, not just a line of periods, varying arbitrarily in number to express the desired degree of emphasis. It is correctly formed with three periods, with spaces between the ellipsis and surrounding letters or other punctuation marks. Your word processing program may autocorrect a row of three periods into an ellipsis with narrow spaces between. If this is the case, use a standard space before and after. When an ellipsis occurs at the end of a sentence, insert the ellipsis after the correct ending punctuation as in the first example below. Use an ellipsis:

To show that words have been left out of a quotation	"... The reason ... to remain steadfast to our purpose. ... "
To convey an unfinished thought	"I never have been sure what happened that day ... ."

Exclamation Point

Exclamations express strong emotions. Because they are so strong, use them sparingly! And never use more than one!!! Use an exclamation point:

After an exclamatory sentence	I couldn't believe she actually went through with it!
After an interjection	Wow! That was really fast.
After a strong command	Let go of me!
To express irony, surprise. or disagreement	Well now, that was nothing I'd ever expect!

Hyphen

Hyphens appear to join things, but technically, they are separation devices. Use a hyphen:

To separate compound numbers	Forty-five, one hundred seventy-three
To separate some compound words	sister-in-law, ten-year-old
Between compound adjectives before a noun	Red-orange car, lemon-lime drink
To break a word at the end of a line	Hyphenation is generally controlled by activating it in your word processing program. Look under Tools>Language to find the options.

If you chose to use automatic hyphenation in your story, read the final copy carefully. Automatic hyphenation occasionally miscalculates.

Parentheses

Parentheses set information apart from the rest of the sentence. In most cases, parentheses, commas, and dashes are interchangeable. When the sentence is in heavy on commas, replacing some with parentheses or dashes can clarify meaning. Dashes are more dramatic and emphatic than parentheses.

When the closing parenthesis is at the end of the sentence, place the ending punctuation outside. When one or more complete sentences are included between the parentheses, place the final punctuation mark inside the ending parenthesis. If multiple sentences are inserted as an aside within a sentence, insert the appropriate punctuation between them, but omit the final one. Use parentheses:

To enclose extra information	They go to Spain (their favorite vacation place) every April.
Around the abbreviation or acronym that follows a full name when it is first introduced	Environmental Protection Agency (EPA)
Around one or more sentences inserted within a sentence	Sarah thought we should begin the project (assuming funding comes through) in January.

Period

The ubiquitous period was probably the first punctuation you learned to write. Everyone knows what they mean, and generally how to use them correctly. In case you need a refresher, use a period:

At the end of a sentence	This is an example.
After a mild command	Please bring me a tissue.
After initials	J. B. Lippincott is a publishing company in Philadelphia, no relation to us.

After most titles and abbreviations	Mr. Jones lives at 211 Oak St. in Podunk.

Quotation Marks

Quotations are used with dialogue and to set off short quotations, but they also have other uses. Use quotation marks:

To set off dialogue (but not indirect dialogue)	"Let's take a walk," Mary said.
To set off short, direct quotations	According to Albert Camus, "The purpose of a writer is to keep civilization from destroying itself."
To mark irony	Looters in New Orleans "liberated" the contents of many stores.
When defining a word or using an unfamiliar word for the first time	My shoes had "kilties," a fringed leather flap found on some shoes.

Combining quotation marks with other punctuation often becomes confusing.

- Periods and commas always come inside quotation marks.
- Semicolons and colons always go outside quotation marks.
- Question marks, exclamation marks and dashes go inside quotation marks when part of quote, but outside when not.

Since dialogue can be a little tricky, illustrations for punctuating dialogue follow. For all but internal dialogue (unspoken thoughts of a character), the words of the speaker are enclosed in quotation marks. Advice, suggestions, and indirect reference to things people have said are not considered dialogue and should not be enclosed in quotation marks.

Introductory Explanation

Concluding Explanation

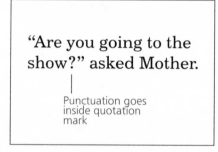

Capitalize first word
of dialogue

She said, "Let's go to town."

Comma separates
explanation from
dialogue

Ending dialogue
punctuation goes
inside closing quote

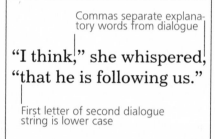

Comma separates explan-
ation from dialogue

"This is my wagon," he bragged.

First word after
dialogue not
capitalized

Questions and Exclamations
with Concluding Explanation

Interrupting Explanation

"Are you going to the show?" asked Mother.

Punctuation goes
inside quotation
mark

Commas separate explana-
tory words from dialogue

"I think," she whispered, "that he is following us."

First letter of second dialogue
string is lower case

Quotations within Quotations

Internal Dialogue

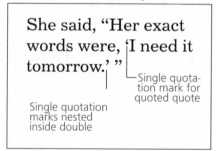

She said, "Her exact words were, 'I need it tomorrow.' "

Single quota-
tion mark for
quoted quote

Single quotation
marks nested
inside double

Unspoken thoughts are punctuated
like quotation, but without quotation marks (italics optional)

This is not a good idea, I told myself yet again.

Figure 15: Punctuating Dialogue

Using italics for internal dialogue or unspoken thoughts is optional and a recent convention. You'll find an example of this usage in *Topsy Turvy Attitudes* on page 235. It's entirely correct to punctuate internal dialogue like conversation, but without quotation marks. The explanatory words and sentence form make it clear that the words are thought, not spoken.

For dialogue passages spanning two or more paragraphs, put opening quotation marks at the beginning of each paragraph, but only place a closing mark at the end of the final sentence of the dialogue.

According to standard usage, you begin a new paragraph with each change of speaker. For extended passages of short dialogue, you can often omit speaker identification for a couple of rounds, but don't let it run too long without a marker. Have someone check it for clarity.

If you have a string of rapid, very short exchanges of words between two characters, it's becoming more common to include them in a single paragraph.

> Rosie insisted she found it first. I knew better. "I did, too!" she insisted. "You're nuts. You weren't even there," I countered. "You always try to get things your way." The argument was as old as sisters themselves. The words seemed to ooze from a primal ritual of sibling rivalry encoded in our DNA.

Your word processing program probably has the option of using curly "smart quotes" in place of the all-purpose straight ones (") used by typewriters. The AutoCorrect feature of your program controls the character used. You'll generally find the menu for controlling AutoCorrect functions under the Tools menu option at the top of your screen. Key words to look for, on the menu or in Help are: quotation marks, curly quotes, smart quotes. If you don't find the words you need in the main contents of Help, try asking the "wizard" or "expert."

Question Mark

Use a question mark:

At the end of a direct question	What are you going to do about that?
Multiple question marks can be used within the same sentence	"Was it blue? real? solid? imagined?" she asked.

Semicolon

Use a semicolon:

To link independent clauses closely related in meaning that are not joined by coordinating conjunction	I began working for Jones Construction; I liked it a lot.
In front of adverbial conjunctions joining simple sentences	He lacked imagination; therefore, the result was dull.
To separate a list or series of elements when one or more items contain an internal comma	On our trip we visited Santiago, Chile; Buenos Aires, Argentina; Montevideo, Uruguay; and Lima, Peru. We had several notable guests, including John White, CEO of Eximeter; Alberta Falavey, President of Sublima; and Chris Excello, Senator from Iowa. Their respective birth dates are Jan. 7, 1984; July 17, 1948; Mar. 27, 1938; and Apr. 17, 1974.

Slash

Use a slash:

To indicate alternate words or phrases	She/he, lifestory/memoir
For abbreviated dates	4/16/49

Style and Grammar Matters

Good grammar is seldom noticed—it blends into the story. Poor grammar sticks out like thorns on a rose, distracting the reader. Familiarity with the rules helps you know when it's okay to bend them.

Grammar peeves

Lifestory writers are not the only ones who commit grammar infractions. Mistakes detailed below are so ubiquitous that few people even realize they are wrong:

It's/its—It's is the contraction for "it is." "It's raining outside," is the same as "It is raining outside." Its is a third person, non-specific possessive pronoun. "The tire lost its tread." Confusion arises because nouns use 's to morph into possessive form. "That's Harry's book."

Hint: Pronouns do not use 's to become possessive—they take a new form: my, mine, your, yours, his, hers, its, our, ours, their, theirs. You can make your own hint by asking yourself: Am I trying to say "What is it is name?" Or, Does it make sense to say "It is raining?"

I/me—Few people make mistakes when the first person singular pronoun is used alone, but when it joins a pair or group, chaos reigns, and error prevails. "It's me" has bumped the more correct "It is I" in common usage, but it's still not okay to say, "Dad took Jan and I to the zoo." You wouldn't say "Dad took I to the zoo." Anyone knows Dad took *me*. On the other hand, few people ever say, "Jan and me are going to the zoo."

Hint: Remove the extra pronoun and it becomes clear. As in the above example, you wouldn't say "Dad took I to the zoo." So put Jan with me and off we go.

Myself—Many people think it's more polite, humble, or cultured to say, "Joshua and myself" instead of "Joshua and I" or "Joshua and me." You occasionally see sentences explaining that "Joshua and myself were given matching toy fire engines," or "Mother and Father gave Joshua and myself matching toy fire engines." The first example is subject to double weakness. Not only is the pronoun wrong, but it's a passive sentence. In the first example, correct usage is "Joshua and I ..." and the second is "... Joshua and me."

Hint: As stated above, take Joshua out of the picture and the correct pronoun choice is obvious.

All ... are not ... —The phrase "all ... are not ..." is in such common usage that few people realize what they are really saying or hearing. When you say "all men are not tall," the literal meaning is that there are no tall men. You've said *all* men are *not* tall. You probably mean that some men are tall and others aren't. The most precise way to convey your meaning in the first case is to say "Not all men are tall," or a variation such as "Some men are taller (or shorter) than others." State the inverse information precisely as "There are no tall men." Attention to precise meaning will get around this confusion.

Negative statements—It's not technically wrong to say, "She did not think skydiving was safe," but your writing will sound more polished if you restrict the use of "not" to negations or comparisons, not evasions. A smoother rephrase of the sentiment is, "She thought skydiving was dangerous."

Word bloopers

Several incorrect or imprecise words and expressions are in common use. You can find exhaustive lists in grammar books or Internet sites. A few flagrant offenders follow:

- All right—Often incorrectly written as alright.
- Already—Often written as all ready. Already means something has happened before now. All ready means everything is in order.
- Affect/Effect—These two words are often confused. Affect means to cause something to happen to someone or to move a person emotionally. Effect is the changed state that results from an action by somebody or something. When feelings are

involved, use affect. When results are involved, use effect. Better yet, use alternate words.

- Farther/Further—These two words are not interchangeable. Farther refers to distance; further refers to time or additions.
- She is a woman who is ... —Redundant. State it more simply as "she is ..."
- Interesting—Rather than telling that something is interesting, get to the point and tell what caught your attention.
- Irregardless—Incorrect form of regardless.
- Fewer/Less—These two words are not interchangeable. Fewer refers to number, as, "We sold fewer cookies this year than last." Less refers to amount, as in "The mattress had less air the second night we slept on it."
- Nauseous/Nauseated—Nauseous means sickening; nauseated is the feeling of needing to throw up. You only feel nauseous if you know you are making other people sick.

Overworked words

Some words have been over-used to the point of vagueness. When you use a word like nice, you have a mental image of the situation, including sensations and emotions. Readers will catch your pleasure, but infer their own meaning. You must be specific. Often a single descriptive word suffices. The following list includes a number of the most overworked words with alternative meanings. You'll find additional suggestions in the thesaurus included with your word processing program, but the most comprehensive thesauruses are on the Internet. Do a search for "online thesaurus" to find a selection.

about—approximately, nearly, almost, approaching, close to
affect—adjust, influence, transform, moderate, incline, motivate, prompt
amazing—overwhelming, astonishing, startling, unexpected, stunning, dazzling, remarkable

awesome—impressive, stupendous, fabulous, astonishing

bad—defective, inadequate, poor, unsatisfactory, disagreeable, offensive, repulsive, corrupt, wicked, naughty, harmful, injurious, unfavorable

basic—essential, necessary, indispensable, vital, fundamental, elementary

beautiful—attractive, appealing, alluring, exquisite, gorgeous, handsome, stunning

better—preferable, superior, worthier

big—large, enormous, extensive, gigantic, huge, immense, massive

certain—unquestionable, incontrovertible, unmistakable, indubitable, assured, confident

choose—select, elect, nominate, prefer, identify

decent—respectable, adequate, fair, suitable

definitely—unquestionably, clearly, precisely, positively, inescapably

easy—effortless, natural, comfortable, undemanding, pleasant, relaxed

enjoy—savor, relish, revel, benefit

entire—complete, inclusive, unbroken, integral

excellent—superior, remarkable, splendid, superb, magnificent, unsurpassed,

exciting—thrilling, stirring, rousing, dramatic

far—distant, remote

fast—swift, quick, fleet, hasty, accelerated

funny—amusing, comical, droll, entertaining, bizarre, uncommon, ludicrous, unusual

good—satisfactory, serviceable, functional, competent, virtuous, striking

great—tremendous, superior, remarkable, eminent, proficient, expert

happy—pleased, joyous, elated, jubilant, cheerful, delighted *hard*—arduous, difficult, formidable, complex, complicated, rigorous, harsh

hurt—injure, harm, damage, wound, impair

important—significant, substantial, weighty, meaningful, critical, vital, notable

incredible—astonishing, amazing, extraordinary, staggering, mind-blowing, fantastic, remarkable

interesting—absorbing, appealing, entertaining, fascinating, thought-provoking

like (adj)—similar, equivalent, parallel

like (verb)—enjoy, relish, appreciate

mean—plan, intend, suggest, propose, indicate

more—extra, additional, replenishment, supplementary

new—recent, modern, current, novel

next—subsequently, thereafter, successively

nice—pleasant, satisfying, gracious, charming

old—aged, mature, experienced, used, worn, former, previous

perfect—flawless, faultless, ideal, consummate

quick—brisk, prompt, responsive, rapid, nimble, hasty

really—truly, genuinely, extremely, undeniably

regular—standard, routine, customary, habitual

small—diminutive, miniature, minor, insignificant, slight,

sometimes—occasionally, intermittently, sporadically, periodically

take—grasp, capture, choose, select, tolerate, endure

terrific—extraordinary, magnificent, marvelous

think—conceive, imagine, ponder, reflect, contemplate

try—attempt, endeavor, venture, test

very—unusually, extremely, deeply, exceedingly, profoundly

want—desire, crave, yearn, long

You can see from this list that the English language offers a stunning number of word alternatives. Don't overwhelm readers with a plethora of unusual words, but do pop your head out of that staleness rut now and then.

By following tips on focus, pruning, and paragraph structure in Chapter Five, and the guidelines on punctuation, style, and grammar in this one, you'll produce a masterpiece.

Chapter 11:
Pulling the Project Together

The act of writing is the act of discovering what you believe.

— David Hare

If you begin with a clearly defined project plan at the outset, the vision of a finished volume will drive your efforts, perhaps for years. However long it takes, one day you will write the last story and finish editing. You will be ready to compile them, print final copies, and send them forth to delight your family.

On the spontaneous writing path, you begin without a clear idea of what you'll ultimately do with your collection, but eventually your scrapbook will bulge, you'll be inspired to organize your stories, or your family will clamor for copies of your stories. Whatever the case, it will be time to turn that pile of paper into a finished project showcasing your work.

Organize Your Material

The guidelines in this section represent the far end of the path begun with the preparation exercises described in Chapter Two. For the purpose of simplicity, I'll refer to your finished project as a story album, because it contains a collection of stories like a photo album contains photos. You can enhance the value of your story album by including a table of contents, list of main characters, maps, and similar items. The following descriptions will help you decide how to organize your album and which additional elements best suit your purpose.

Story order

If you wrote chronologically, you determined the order at the outset. If you took the scrapbook approach, you could simply print out your stories and pop them in a binder, but it's worth some thought to arrange them in a meaningful order. The two most common systems for scrapbook albums are chronological and topical. You may think of variations on these themes.

You may recall some discussion of themes back on page 31 in Chapter Two. Take a look at the theme-connected stories, *Crunchy Frosting, Fair Warning,* and *Can You Bring Your Gun to My Wedding?,* on pages 199–205. Notice how *Fair Warning* could go with either of the others. You'll have the same sort of challenge. Decisions are arbitrary.

Another theme-related decision is the method for tying your stories together. In *Adventures of a Chilihead,* on page 218, I added a short paragraph of introduction. This is similar to the way a musician or singer talks with the audience, telling short stories to introduce pieces in the performance. *Adventures of a Chilihead* is a chapter in a story album. In one sense, the individual stories in *Adventures of a Chilihead* follow the threaded story linking technique described on page 65, with a difference. Lori Jakiela's book, *Miss New York Has Everything,* was my example of this technique. Her stories flow together with mere paragraph breaks and a little intervening narrative. The Chilihead stories are distinctly separate, to the point of having titles. *Fall, Then and Now,* on page 222, links much shorter stories together into a single one, using the sequential technique described on page 65.

Like Jakiela, Annie Dillard threads short elements into chapter-length stories in her classic memoir, *An American Childhood.* Both authors follow a chronological story sequence through the books, with occasional flashback insets, and both leave time gaps between chapters. Each chapter is a self-contained story, and could be read independently without confusion. Continuity of characters and settings link the chapters.

The best way to get a firm grasp of structural options is to read stacks and piles of published memoirs to see how other people handle things. At the same time, you should realize that your structure is as unique as your story, and there is no specific "right way" to organize your work. Don't agonize.

Timeline

Just as your timeline helped identify story ideas, it may be the single most valuable tool for arranging your finished stories. Beyond its organizing value, it gives readers an overview of your life and helps them understand story events in the context of your life. The timeline is especially helpful in a topically arranged album. If you haven't made a timeline, it isn't too late. Refer back to page 47 for instructions. Place a copy of your finished timeline in the front of your story album, right after the Table of Contents, or as an appendix at the end.

List of characters

I'd like to see a list of characters included in every story I read, whether fiction or fact. Out of desperation, I once compiled my own list for a mystery novel that had more characters than the sea-crossing scene in *The Ten Commandments.* It was the only way I could make sense of the story. I strongly recommend that you include a list of the major players in your lifestory. Place it right after your timeline. If it isn't at the front, mention it in a foreword so readers know to look for it.

My list of characters includes categories for Family, Friends, Business Associates, Casual Acquaintances, Community Confederates, and Others. I recently added Virtual Friends—people I've come to know well through e-mail, but haven't met in person. I include a sentence or two for each person with a summary of who they are, how and when we were involved or acquainted, and other relevant information. The important point is to introduce continuing characters. You don't need to include every teacher, store clerk, and fellow bus rider you briefly mention in a single story.

Family tree

Your family tree makes a nice addition if you have the information and mention your family in many stories. You don't have to include all your ancestors back to Charlemagne. Only those you write about matter. The family tree doesn't take the place of the List of Characters, but it is a nice supplement. You could draw the tree by hand, have someone do it for you, or use one of the genealogy programs to generate a printable one.

Maps

If you have lived in various parts of your state or the country, or even in various parts of the world, add a map of places you have lived. To make my map, shown in Figure 16, I began with an outline map of the USA and colored in the seven states where I've lived. Then I labeled each of the towns where I lived, including the dates for each, and drew sweeping arrows from one to the next. Enhancements like this appeal to people with an inner artist. If you aren't an artist, a simple list will do.

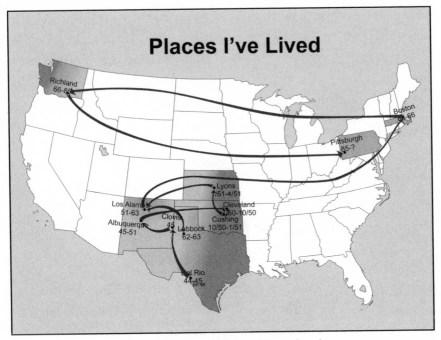

Figure 16: Map of places I have lived

Life overview

A one or two page overview of your life is a valuable addition to an album. This overview puts meat on the bones of your timeline and helps readers get a sense of your life as a whole. The overview has applications beyond your album, and is valuable even for those who chose the chronological approach. The document is easily shared with distant relatives who may not rate full copies of your album. It will be useful to future genealogists as they trade information with each other down the line. You may want to update this overview each year or two, when you update your timeline.

Your overview could have another use that may never occur to you. In recent years many people have begun pre-planning their funerals. In *Creating Your Own Funeral or Memorial Service*, Stephanie West Allen suggests incorporating an overview of your life into your funeral or memorial service. You can specify that copies be made, you can have someone read the story during the service, or you can record yourself reading it. You could even make a video of this. A video can include photos and other video clips. The possibilities are limited only by your imagination and desire to prepare the material.

Cover design

No matter how you choose to bind your album, you'll want to personalize the cover. Two simple lines of type would suffice:

MY LIFE
by John Jones

But with all the effort you are putting into writing the stories, perhaps you can come up with something a bit more imaginative. Has there been some sort of theme to your life? Have you triumphed over some obstacle? Are you well known for a particular skill? I've got to give my grandmother credit for her *Clara the Great* title. *My Patchwork Life* could be a theme title for a quilter. *Engineering a Future* was used by an engineer whose engineering perspective permeated his way of thinking about everything. Hal Williamson's title, *Liberating Greatness* refers equally well to his own life and the material he teaches. Don't hurry into a decision. Give it time and mull it over. Make a list of possibilities. One day a name will come to you and you'll *know*, this is *it*. That's the one to go with.

You may also want to put your picture, a montage of pictures, or some other graphic on the cover. Don't forget the spine. It's nice for people to be able to identify your album when it sits on a shelf. Whether you use binders or have it bound as a book, you'll need at least a strip of type with the title and your name for the spine.

Publishing Options

When you think of publishing your lifestory, most likely you'll think of printing it on paper. This is the most durable and long-lasting way to share your story, but today you have additional choices. You can put the source file on a CD for people to print or view onscreen. You can use photographs, video, and audio clips to create video stories by using multi-media software like Microsoft PowerPoint, PhotoStory, or any of the multitude of multimedia album management programs, then burn the finished creation to a CD. You can set up a website, send stories by e-mail, or ... Who knows what the future will bring?

Publishing choices are not an either/or decision. Written stories provide source material for producing other forms. The following information will help you explore options for print and multimedia publishing.

Print copies

This discussion of printing and copying is directed toward those who have been working with a computer. Once in a very long while, someone has such artistic handwriting they want to retain the appearance of the document. In this case, photocopies or scanned images are the obvious solution. The same approach works with typewritten stories. For more flexibility, seek help in getting your stories transferred to computer files.

You could print final copies on your home printer, but that would take a huge amount of time, and double-sided printing is difficult and slow on home printers. When you factor in the cost of ink, home printing is not a bargain for large quantities. Also, inkjet printers don't usually produce the sharpest print, and ink may run if spills occur.

The next option is to print a master at home and make photocopies at a copy shop. Use bright white paper specifically made for your printer to get the crispest type. Although you'll print a single-sided master, you'll surely want double-sided final copies, which is easily managed with photocopying.

One step up from printing your own master is to copy your document file onto a CD or memory stick, take it to a copy shop and have them print all copies from the file. (You may also be able to e-mail the file to them.) This option will give you the crispest, cleanest print and avoids the possibility of dust or smudges on the copier glass. It is surprisingly affordable, because the cost-per-page goes down dramatically when you print hundreds of pages in a single job. Print shops in office super stores offer this service, generally at the same price as copies, with a slight additional charge for printing from your file. Check with neighborhood print and copy shops as well as the office super store print departments to compare prices. Discuss your project with them and ask to see samples before making your decision.

Besides the printing method, you'll need to choose paper, decide about using color printing, and select a binding method. Read on for guidance on these decisions.

Paper

Ordinary copy paper is not your best choice for final copies. It isn't acid free, and it isn't sufficiently opaque to work well for double-sided printing. The process used to make utility copy paper, newsprint, and other consumable products leaves an acid residue. Over years or decades, the paper turns brown and becomes brittle, eventually crumbling. After all the effort you invested in writing, editing, and planning, it's worth a small additional investment to keep the result looking good for decades longer than ordinary paper would last.

For an album that will last a century or longer, invest in high quality, acid-free (archival quality) paper that is opaque enough to support print on both sides without showing through. The degree of whiteness is a matter of personal preference. Such paper is becoming more readily available, and most print shops can special order an appropriate product if you can't find it locally. Don't hesitate to order it from a website and take it to the copy or print shop. They should give you a slight price reduction for providing your own paper. If you use cover stock and acetate sheets, make sure they are also acid free. You can get acid-free cardstock and other products in the scrapbooking department of craft stores.

Black-and-white or color

No matter how you print, color escalates the cost of the project. You can include an occasional page with color photographs or other material and stick to black and white for text pages. Some commercially published books include inserts that cluster all photos, black-and-white or color, onto glossy pages of photo quality print. You could do the same thing by consolidating select photos onto a few pages for a color insert. Black-and-white photos can be incorporated with text since today's black-and-white printers and copiers print them well.

Binding

Depending on your budget, you can do anything from slipping copies into report covers as my grandmother did to having the whole project professionally printed and bound with your choice of hard or soft cover. Options for self-publishers include the following:

Three-ring binders. Choose binders with insert pockets on the covers and make inserts for front, back, and spine. The advantage of binders is that you can use divider tabs, you can add pages later, and they lie flat when open. You can move to larger binders or add additional ones as your collection expands, and the spine displays the title as it sits on a shelf.

Binders are an excellent choice if you plan to continue adding stories over time. Thelly Reahm, the friend who has written over 500 stories for her family members, uses binders and presents family members with update packets each year at Christmas. She has already set funds aside to have final copies bound in hard covers at the end of her life.

Comb binding. Comb binding is a solid plastic strip with what looks like curled comb teeth that loop through small rectangular holes spaced down the edge of the pages. This is the most affordable binding alternative. You will also need front and back cover pages of acid-free cover-weight paper or cardstock. Some self-service copy shops have comb-binding machines available for self-service use with binding strips you can purchase at office supply stores, and all copy shops will do this binding for you for a modest fee. If you choose comb binding, invest in acid-free protective vinyl outer cover sheets.

Coil binding. The advantage of plastic coil (spiral) binding over comb binding is that you can fold the cover all the way back. You won't find self-service spiral binding equipment at copy shops, and the price is somewhat higher, but with cardstock covers and vinyl sheets, it makes a handsome book.

Other options. Many print shops offer additional options such as glued cloth strip binding. Check with print shops in your area to learn what else is available.

Handmade covers. A visit to the scrapbooking section of a crafts store will give the arts-and-crafts person limitless inspiration for customized ways to make custom covers for post- or ribbon-bound albums. If you're handy, you could make hand-decorated fabric or leather covers for ring binders. Check the library for books on hand binding for additional ideas.

Perfect binding. This is the technical term for what we generally refer to as paperback binding. Perfect-bound books larger than 4.25" by 6.75" are called trade paperbacks. With the advent of electronic publishing, the cost of self-published trade paperbacks has plummeted. Today, depending on the page count, it's possible to have a single copy of a manuscript printed and bound with a soft cover for around $10.00, plus shipping, with no set-up fee, by uploading your file to a print-on-demand publishing site on the Internet. If you don't have cover art of your own, they have a selection of customizable templates available. Any details would be out-of-date almost before the ink in this book was dry, so if this publishing route interests you, do an Internet search for electronic or "print-on-demand" (POD) publishers and check it out.

Print-on-demand publishing for your album has an advantage some people will especially appreciate. It isn't uncommon to receive requests for copies of your album months or years later. Making additional copies is a nuisance. Aside from the time, you may be out of paper, and you may not want to spend the money to accommodate that particular request, but find it awkward to charge. Once your file is uploaded to a POD publisher, it will stay there for years on end, ready for making new copies anytime you want them. You can order as many or as few as you wish, and you can give the website address to other people and let them order (and pay for) their own.

Beyond getting your book printed and bound, you can find e-publishers who will provide an ISBN number, Library of Congress registration, and other elements needed to turn your publication into a volume you can sell in web stores. POD books are generally unwelcome in "the establishment," so this route may not be ideal if you have visions of seeing your book on the shelf in bookstores. If commercial distribution is your aim, there are many fine books that can steer you through the process of finding agents and publishers. A POD volume may be an effective way to produce demo copies to show commercial publishers.

Hard-cover binding. Hard-cover editions are more expensive, and generally harder for the self-publisher to arrange. Some POD sites do offer hard-cover options.

Preparing for printing

Your preparation depends on the way you saved material as you worked and the printing method you choose. Most people who write chronological accounts of their lives keep everything together in a single file, or maybe one file per chapter, and that makes printing easier. When you don't have a huge number of files, it's not difficult to set page numbers and headers separately for each file, printing each separately. See page 257 for instructions on adding page numbers.

Scrapbook-style writers are more likely to save each story as a single file and end up with dozens or hundreds of tiny files. If you decide to print a master copy of your finished project on your own printer, you can work from any number of files, adding page numbers and headers (if you want them) to each. Additional graphics and pictures are easily inserted where you want them. As a last step, type up a Table of Contents and take the whole pile to be copied.

If you want to have the whole project printed from disk by a copy shop or POD publisher, you'll need to consolidate everything into a single file. This isn't as daunting as it sounds, and it offers several advantages. Page numbers will flow smoothly. You can insert story files along with supplementary material like your timeline and various graphics, and arrange any headers you decide to use to flow along from one item to the next. Chapter Twelve explains why and how to use styles, headers, and section breaks for such a project.

To consolidate the stories, copy the contents from individual story files and paste them into a single new document. Apply any styles you need for titles and body text as you go. You can decide whether you want to begin a new page for each story, or simply leave an inch or so of space between. If you have various sections in your album, start a new page, with a section title for each. A couple of paragraphs or more that introduce and explain the section is a nice touch.

The POD route requires one more step. Ultimately your file needs to be in PDF format, the kind that opens in Adobe Acrobat. You may be able to upload a Word document to the publisher and have it converted there, but it's better if you can do your own. That way you can easily look through it to make sure it's just the way you want it before you send it off.

To do this, you need a conversion program. OpenOffice has a built-in PDF export function. Perhaps your version of Word or WordPerfect will have one that works well. Test it and see. If you don't have one built in, excellent freeware programs are available. Search the Internet for "Free PDF Writer" to find software, for example, the program, PDF Writer. Download and install it. It works like a virtual printer. With the external programs, you don't save the file, you "print" it by way of the Print menu, using PDF Writer (or whatever program you select) as your printer. This creates a PDF file that will open in Acrobat Reader. You can't edit the contents of PDF files, but you can edit your original word processing file, then reprint it to PDF format as many times as it takes to get it right.

Final copies

Once you finish the formatting, you are ready to make your copies. Head to the copy shop, armed with your acid-free, heavyweight paper—and the document file if you are having it printed on-site. You can have them print just the pages, or they can handle details like comb or coil binding, hole-punching, and copying covers, or you can provide covers yourself for them to use. Pick up your finished copies, insert them in binders if they aren't comb- or spiral-bound, and you're done.

If you choose the POD route, you'll use the link on the publisher's website to upload your file for printing. You'll also upload a file with your cover art if you have one, or you may be able to design a cover on-line with their standard template designs. Order a test copy for final inspection and read it carefully. If you need to make changes, edit your document, resave to PDF, and upload it again. Place your order, and that's it.

Multimedia options

Saving stories on a CD is the least expensive way to share your material with large numbers of people, and it also serves as a backup against computer failure. Since technology is advancing at warp speed, you should keep two important considerations in mind when going this route.

Advancing technology

In 1988 I made the switch from our first computer, an Apple II+, to the PC format. There was no way, short of printing copies and retyping things, to transfer my files from the original Apple format to PC. In less than ten years, all of my early work became technologically obsolete. My WordPerfect files are still accessible after nearly twenty years, but files older than eight or ten years require a lot of reformatting. If I don't resave them all soon, they could become unreadable.

Because of these known problems, archival experts suggest that saving a file in Rich Text Format (RTF) or Portable Document Format (PDF—think Acrobat Reader) is likely to help it remain accessible far longer than formats specific to individual word processing programs. I strongly recommend that when you finish editing a story you make a backup copy in both RTF and PDF format. These two formats are readable on any operating system in use today on home computers. You can save in the usual way to create an RTF file. Open the Save As menu, and select Rich Text Format from the File Type field below the file name.

The same obsolescence concerns apply for digital graphics, audio and video files. Think of 8-track tapes and Betamax videos. This is not a reason to avoid making multimedia albums. It is meant to remind you that these are made for today, to be enjoyed in the short term. Many of them can be kept viable, but somebody will need to open and resave the file every ten years or so to keep them current.

Fragility

Aside from concerns about advancing software, we can't be sure how long storage media will last. Some CDs and DVDs are guaranteed for one hundred years, but until hundreds have passed the test of actual (rather than simulated) aging, who knows? To put this concern in perspective, storage options are evolving so fast that like the old 3.5" floppies, one day the CDs and DVDs we use today will become obsolete, and somebody will need to update the material for newer software and newer storage media. Play it safe. Make at least two copies, and recopy every few years.

Applications

Going beyond the matter of storage media, you can take the stories you've written and use them as the basis for several other forms of publishing. For audio recordings, install a microphone on your computer and record yourself reading your stories. The simplest way to do this is to use the Sound Recorder included with Windows. You can find this utility in Windows, on any version from 95 through XP, by going to Start>All Programs>Accessories>Entertainment. With a little experimenting, you can make fine recordings. This utility only saves recordings as .wav files, which is the format used on commercial CDs. Your files will be quite large. You may wish to find a utility that will convert the .wav files to .mp3 or another compressed format that will play on iPods or one of the other tiny players. Don't get rid of the .wav files though. That file format is likely to be recognized for decades to come. Burn them to DVD for backup.

The Sound Recorder requires that you read the story straight through. There are programs available that will give you sophisticated editing capability. You can purchase programs, or do an Internet search for "free sound editing program" or "open source sound editing program." There is no charge for open source programs. The best currently available is Audacity. It is relatively easy to learn and use and produces excellent results. Regardless of the software you use, the key to great sound recordings is a good microphone.

Another idea is combining pictures with story recordings to create a narrated photo album. Use a program such as the free Photo Story 3 for Windows download from the Microsoft site. PowerPoint and many other slide show programs let you add or narrate a sound track. OpenOffice and WordPerfect have the equivalent of PowerPoint.

You can also post stories on your own website or blog, and several websites will save your stories indefinitely, some for free, some for a fee. For a nominal fee, most of these sites will also help you get your stories printed and bound. You may find this a convenience, though you can do the same thing yourself.

Celebrate!

Whatever method you've used to print and bind your final copies, plan a major celebration when you have them in hand. This is a huge accomplishment, attained by an elite few people. Many people start writing stories, but only the truly diligent and faithful complete the course to produce finished volumes. You deserve to be congratulated. Of course you'll want to sign each copy with an inscription to the recipient, and maybe wrap it nicely. Distribute them in person if you can, or mail them if you must, then sit back and wait for the rave reviews.

Chapter 12:
The Story Doesn't End Until You Do

*I never know what I think about something
until I read what I've written on it.*

— *William Faulkner*

Most lifestory writers who get to the point of publishing a collection of their stories feel a little lost after they hand out their finished volumes. For years they have been writing away, one story after another, and suddenly the urgency is gone. The project is finished. But they can't stop thinking about stories. It's become a habit. They think of all the stories they didn't write. They think of details they didn't include in stories they did write. Not only that, but new memories and adventures lead to new stories. Now what?

The answer is simple: Keep writing! You may enjoy writing more than ever without the pressure of a project waiting to be completed. There are many other things you can do, just for fun. Here are some ideas to get you started—or maybe I should say to keep things fresh—so you'll keep on writing.

Try New Media

Remember the section in the last chapter about recording CDs of your stories? Give it a try. Select your favorite, and sit down with a microphone. Whether you use an old audio recorder or try the computer doesn't matter as much as just doing it. If you want to use the computer, I recommend using a headset designed for use with PC video-conferencing or voice recognition software. You may not need the earphones, but in my experience, the microphone quality on these units is superior to free-standing mikes. You don't need the most expensive, but don't get the cheapest either.

Besides simple audio recordings, try narrating a slide show with a dozen or more old photos. PowerPoint or one of its companion products, OpenOffice Impress or Corel Presentations, gives you control over timing and a wide array of transition effects for fading from one slide to another. Check Insert>Sound on your program to tell whether you can record directly, or you must record a soundtrack and insert the file. Other slideshow programs may also allow you to record soundtracks.

Take Your Stories Public

As their writing matures, many people find it rewarding to share their work more widely in publications. Your friends may urge you to do this. Besides magazines, there are a growing number of anthologies, such as the *Chicken Soup* series, that accept submissions from the general public. There isn't room here to cover submission details, but a web search will turn up lots of information, and your local reference librarian will be happy to help you research the topic.

An easier way to share your stories with the public is to post them on websites. A search for "submit your life story" turns up millions of results. Many of these sites showcase stories on specific topics. Others are designed for anyone to post nearly anything. You can easily find several that would be happy to have your stories, along with many sites featuring writing contests for lifestory writers. Joining an online writing group is another way of sharing with a more limited audience.

Try a Little Fiction

Some stories from your life seem to beg for additional color and twists. Give yourself permission to color outside the lines by recasting a story as fiction to escape the need to adhere strictly to fact. This simple redefinition allows you to become any sort of hero you wish. You can climb tall mountains, and explore that road you've always wished you'd taken. You can add friends you never actually had, ace exams, bat homeruns, or do anything at all. Show your stories to friends if you wish. Post them on websites. Whether you share them or not, do have fun with it—just be sure you make it clear that they are fiction.

Keep Writing for Fun and Enlightenment

If you wrote your whole lifestory from beginning to end, now you can take time to go back and dig more deeply, exploring specific topics, and writing for fun or further self-discovery. Follow the lead of published memoir writers, many of whom have written several volumes. You don't have to stop with just one. You also don't have to do a second or third the same way you did the first. Branch out.

Keep writing to keep your brain growing and healthy. Keep writing to give your descendants more to think about. And most of all, keep writing to spread the contents of your heart around the world and through the ages.

Appendix 1:
Sharon's Stories

As I pointed out earlier, after my initial foray into lifestory writing with my *Albuquerque Years* project that focused on my preschool years, I became an avid scrapbook writer. Since then I've experimented, intuitively or by design, with a number of different writing styles, topics, and types of stories and amassed a collection of several hundred. Stories in this appendix include an assortment that illustrate points I make various places in the earlier part of the book. It's my fervent hope that you enjoy reading them while they deepen your understanding of the various styles, devices, and techniques they've been chosen to demonstrate. I further hope that you are inspired to write stacks and piles of your own stories, in your own distinct voice, about your unique experiences.

Crunchy Frosting

"Can I bake a cake?" I asked, calling up the stairs.

"I guess so," came the reply from the bedroom where Mother sat at her sewing machine. Actually, I can't remember her ever saying I couldn't cook something—asking was just an expected formality.

The cake I had in mind was one I had helped her make, and I had my own copy of the recipe. Now that I was ten, I had my own green metal recipe box, and I carefully copied recipes I liked onto white index cards. I used the typewriter, laboriously pecking out each word, so they would still look nice when I was grown and married and cooked all the time. I already had three cake and two cookie recipes in my file.

I took out the card for Walnut Chiffon Cake from behind the Cakes tab, and placed it on the counter. I especially liked to make chiffon cakes, because I didn't have to cream the butter and sugar for them. Adding Wesson oil was much easier! Recalling the first part of Mother's maxim, "Always get everything out before you begin, so you know you have everything you need and so you won't forget and leave something out, ..." I worked my way down the list of ingredients. I took each item from the cabinet shelf or the refrigerator and placed it on the stainless steel countertop, next to the Mixmaster.

When I had all the ingredients gathered, I began measuring, sifting, and mixing, according to the directions. I put each ingredient away as I used it, following the second half of the maxim, "... then put it away as soon as you use it, so you won't get distracted and leave it out or put it in twice." Soon the cake was in the oven, and a delicious spicy fragrance filled the air. Heeding yet another maxim, "Clean up your mess as you go, so it won't pile up and grow," I washed the dishes I'd used to make the cake. I was practicing to be a Perfect Housewife.

Then I got out my recipe for butter cream frosting. I took a cube of margarine from the refrigerator and placed it on the counter. Next I looked for powdered sugar. I couldn't find any. Oh well, I thought, I'll just use regular sugar. I don't think it will matter. I kept the Mixmaster going nearly forever, but that frosting looked funny. It didn't get fluffy like it was supposed to, and it was way too yellow. Sticking a finger in, I gave it a tentative taste. A bit crunchy, but not bad. I decided it would do. By this time the cake was cool enough, so I spread the frosting all over it and went out to play.

After dinner we had the cake for desert.

"What on earth did you put in this frosting?" asked Daddy.

"Sugar." I could hear his teeth crunching as he chewed the frosting.

"You don't use granulated sugar in cake frosting!" Mother told me.

"But we didn't have any powdered sugar," I explained.

"Why didn't you ask?"

"I thought this would work."

"Well, I guess it's okay, but don't do it again!"

Personally I thought it tasted just fine, and I liked the way it crunched. But nobody else seemed to share my opinion. After that I mostly made Cocoa Chiffon Cake, because it didn't need any icing.

— January 2002

This story tells so much more than just the story of that cake. You learn of my mother's methodical approach to cooking, and also to cleaning up the kitchen. The story barely hints that the third part of the mantra was more form than substance, and that dishes often did pile up in our kitchen. If you read between the lines, you'll discern the preoccupation common among young girls in those days about preparing for marriage and their own family. The custom of preparing a hope chest full of embroidered linens and such things was beginning to wane, but still a living memory.

I'm working my way down a list of theme stories about my favorite foods, recipes, and memories of making special foods. This is one of them. Some other stories include my maiden pizza baking adventure, the Awful, Terrible, Horribly Bad Chocolate Stew, as well as stories of my right-brain approach to cooking that produces Glop in seventeen different varieties.

Fair Warning

"How many eggs do you want?" I asked my soon-to-be hubby.

He had arrived in Los Alamos from Boston two nights ago and was staying with my parents for a few days until our apartment was vacated and he could move in. I'd stay here for another week until our wedding. Today, Monday morning, we had to report for the first day of our summer jobs at Los Alamos Scientific Laboratories. Wanting to practice my housewifely skills, I had gotten up extra early to fix him breakfast. Mother and Daddy were considerately sleeping in. Coffee was already perking and bread for toast was by the toaster.

"I'll have two," he said with a coy grin. He sat waiting at the table, watching me and instinctively assuming the air of entitlement appropriate for the main breadwinner.

I looked in the refrigerator for the jar of bacon grease Mother always kept for frying things like eggs. After shoving a few jars aside, I found it. At least I thought I did. The first spoonful didn't look quite right as it hit the pan, but I added a second for good measure anyway, and turned up the heat. Within seconds it began to bubble around the edges. There was no pool of grease—this glop was still white, and sitting in a puddle that increased in size, but not color.

"Oh no!" I wailed. "This isn't grease, it's white sauce!" Mother and Daddy had moved to a new house a few months earlier while I was away at school. This was my first time cooking in the new kitchen, and nothing was where I expected it to be. Not even the bacon grease. To this day I never have figured out what a jar of white sauce was doing in that refrigerator.

"That's okay. I'll just have cereal. What kind do you have?"

"But I wanted to fix you eggs."

"Don't worry about it."

I got out the cereal and a bowl. "How about toast?"

"Okay. I'll have a piece." You guessed it. The toast burned. At this point the electric percolator quieted down. I filled a cup and set it on the table.

"Oh. I don't drink coffee. Do you have some tea?"

I didn't know whether to laugh or cry. I poured him a glass of orange juice and myself a bowl of cereal. He convinced me to laugh, and he married me anyway. Now, whenever anything goes wrong in the kitchen, I remind him of that breakfast, and that he had fair warning.

This story would fit in my food collection—or it would fit with others like the following one in a theme about the early years of married life.

Can You Bring Your Gun to My Wedding?

Every young girl dreams of her wedding, complete with the billowing white dress, flowers, tears, music, vows, cake and gifts. None dream of asking guests to bring guns.

Parvin and I did most of our courting via the USPS, back in 1962 when we could mail a letter for four cents. We met in my hometown of Los Alamos where he was working as a summer grad student. After a glorious summer romance, he went back to MIT, and I began my freshman year at Texas Tech. That summer we had both met Wayne, who would begin grad school at MIT in the fall. Wayne shared an apartment with Parvin and another student the following winter, and letters in the ensuing months were full of Wayne's colorful adventures.

Sometime in May, shortly before finals, I ripped open another envelope from Boston. With growing horror I read that Wayne, who would serve as an usher at our wedding in mid-June, was planning to kidnap the bride. From experiences the previous summer and stories in those letters, I knew Wayne was a hard-core, hell-raising prankster from North Dakota. I didn't doubt for a single minute that he would actually try to pull this off. I was hysterical. With considerable trepidation, I finally worked up the courage to ask for help.

"Daddy, Parvin told me his friend Wayne is planning to kidnap me at the wedding,"

"Is that right?" he replied, grinning ear to ear.

"That's what he says."

"Well, I wouldn't worry about it if I were you," he said, intending to be reassuring. He wasn't. Since he wouldn't take me seriously and I was reluctant to press the issue, I turned elsewhere for assistance. A couple of days later my grandfathers arrived for the wedding.

"Pop, one of Parvin's friends is planning to kidnap me at the wedding. Could you bring a gun along, just in case?"

"Well, you should have asked me sooner. I didn't bring one with me." I could see his gut twitching as he continued with an almost straight face, "But I don't think you need to worry about it." I was running out of hope, with only one grandfather left to turn to.

"Cub, one of the ushers is going to kidnap me at the wedding. Will you bring a gun along?" Uncle Harry was standing nearby. He answered for both of them.

"Hell, Sugar, show us where he is! We'll help him out!" Both men doubled over, whooping with wild laughter. I ran from the room and burst into tears, wondering wildly where I could find a derringer to tuck in my garter.

By the time the Big Day rolled around, all I could think of was getting out of there before Wayne made his move. The wedding memories are a blur, mainly created from the photographs Pop was so busy taking. Today I joke that my vows weren't valid, because while the minister was asking the questions, I was double-checking door locations and planning a quick escape. In the reception line I paid little attention to the guests—I was too busy scanning the room to keep track of

Wayne's whereabouts. As I shoved the traditional piece of cake in Parvin's mouth, I was visualing the most direct route to duck into the small office where my going away outfit hung. I probably set a world speed record for ripping off that wedding dress and changing. Finally, holding my wide-brim straw hat tightly in place with one hand, and Parvin with the other, I dashed out the door. As a precaution to calm me down and foil the car decorators, we left in my father-in-law's car, which had been conveniently pulled up to the door.

When we finally drove out of town, I slowly began to relax. Then I realized I was maybe just a little disappointed that it hadn't happened.

Today I'd laugh as hard as my grandfathers did, and consider it a major adventure. I might even tease Wayne and dare him to do it. Today I dream of my daughter's wedding, complete with the billowing white dress, flowers, tears, music, vows, cake and gifts. I would not dream of asking guests to bring guns.

My daughter's wedding (which took place since I wrote this story) was perfect, with the flowing dress, flowers, and all the rest. I have every reason to believe that she was fully present during the ceremony, so her vows can be considered binding. There were no guns, and no kidnapping threats, but the guests at the Evil Table did ambush their room. But that's Susan's story to tell, not mine.

Donnie Becomes Real

As I think back through the years, I'm not surprised to realize that Donnie never seemed real. Only my memories were real.

I was so excited the afternoon Mother came home from the doctor's office, grinning from ear to ear and proudly proclaiming, "Guess what? I was right. There *were* two babies on the x-ray!" She'd already told everyone she knew that she was going to have twin boys on her birthday. Nobody had believed her. Even if it was twins, they reminded her, her birthday was six weeks before the baby was due. She was right about twins. Now I figured she probably would have them on her birthday.

When we climbed into our bunk beds that night, Robin and I started talking about the twins. We talked for quite awhile before I told her to be quiet so I could go to sleep. She finally did, and then I spent another hour thinking about it some more. Having two babies around would be perfect. I couldn't hold more than one baby at a time, so Robin could hold the other one, and we wouldn't have to argue about turns.

Then I thought about telling everyone at school. I practiced what I'd say the next morning. We didn't call it "Telling Time" in fifth grade. That name was okay when you were little, but we were fifth graders, way beyond that kid stuff. Now we had "news" first thing in the morning. I carefully rehearsed how I'd hold my hand up real casual—not frantically waving it like a show-off. I'd keep my elbow a little below my shoulder and sort of look down at the back of the chair in front of me while I waited to be called on. Then when it was my turn, I would say, ever so calmly, "My mother found out yesterday that she's going to have twins." Boy, nobody would have anything to top that news! I went to sleep thinking about what to wear.

I waited longer than usual to leave for school the next morning. I stalled around in the bathroom for half an hour, getting my hair just right, because I knew I'd spill the beans if I hung around the playground before the bell rang. I wanted to save it for the formal announcement. Robin kept bugging me to leave, so I told her to just go on without me. I practiced my announcement all the way to school, and got there at the exact moment that Mr. Patri opened the door. Just about the time I got to my desk, he boomed out, loud enough for the whole school to hear, "Well, Sharon, I guess you're pretty excited about those twins, aren't you?"

Sometimes it just wasn't fair that my mother was the school secretary and sometimes it seemed like the teachers knew more about my business than I did. Actually it turned out okay that way though, because the boys pretended like they didn't hear, and the girls all flocked around, buzzing with questions and giggles before Mr. Patri made us all sit down.

After that morning, nobody at school thought much more about it. But I sure did. Mother's belly kept getting bigger and bigger. I didn't see how she could keep from popping. She'd made some skirts and a pair of pants with U-shaped holes in the front and strings to tie the skirt around her growing tummy. She wore huge, long maternity smocks over them. After a while the strings were barely long enough. By Valentine's Day she'd let us put our hand on her belly and feel the little guys wiggling around in there. We always thought of them as "the little guys," because we never doubted that it would be the two boys she told people she'd have.

In April, about a week before my birthday, she had to go to bed and stay there so the babies wouldn't be born. It was way too early. She wasn't worried and kept reminding us, "They won't come until my birthday on the twenty-third." While she waited in bed, we sewed piles of little flannel nightgowns for the babies—tiny nightgowns that fit my large baby doll. It was hard to believe that real babies could be that small.

Grandmother Rene and Granddaddy Cub, Mother's parents, came for her birthday, which happened to be on Saturday that year. After breakfast, Daddy took Robin and me to town to buy birthday presents for Mother. I got her a nifty butter dish. It was pale green on the bottom and the top looked like an ear of corn. There were six sets of tiny corn ears with it that had little prongs on one end to stick in an ear of corn so you could eat it without getting your fingers messy. After we got our presents, Daddy said, "I guess we'd better go home so I can take your mama to the hospital." I was amazed that he'd taken us to town if he knew she needed to go to the hospital.

Sure enough, when we got back to the house, Mother was ready to go. Daddy put her suitcase in the car, and then he and Rene gently helped her down the fourteen stairs in the house, the three porch steps, and the sixteen concrete front steps down to the car. Off they went.

Cub stayed at the house with Robin and me. We were so excited we couldn't see straight. Cub made us eat baloney sandwiches for lunch, and then I felt like I'd explode if I had to stay in the house another minute. Robin and I ran around like maniacs, ringing doorbells and telling whoever answered, "I just thought you'd like to know that my mother just went to the hospital." I was so excited I went to houses where I didn't even know the people.

Then we ran back inside to wait for the phone to ring. It seemed like it took forever, but it was really just a couple of hours. Cub was grinning when he hung up. "The first one's a boy. Three pounds, thirteen ounces." We were off like skyrockets, ringing those bells again. "The first one's a boy!" we yelled, hardly waiting to finish before we were off to the next house, then home for the rest of the news.

Cub was waiting for us at the door. "Two brothers," he said. "This one was three pounds fourteen ounces." A little breathlessly, we were off yet again for a third round of knocking.

Later on, when Daddy and Rene got home, we found out their names were Donald Alan and Ronald Benjamin. Donald had been named for Cub—Donald was his middle name. Mother's baby brother, who died of flu when he was just nine months old, was also named Donald. Alan was just a name Mother liked. Ronald rhymed with Donald, and of course Benjamin was for Daddy and his father.

Since the babies were so tiny, they had to stay in incubators. Robin and I were dying to see them, and the next day we did. Usually kids younger than twelve weren't allowed on the hospital wards, but since Donnie and Ronnie wouldn't be coming home for a long time, the nurses rolled the incubators over to the glass window in the nursery and let us peer at them from the hall. Sure enough, they were the same size as my baby doll. They were red and wrinkly and sort of ugly. They just lay there with their eyes closed. They seemed like dolls, not real babies.

Mother came home in a couple of days. It seemed strange having her come home without the babies. But she wasn't home all that much. She kept running to the hospital to pump her breasts so the babies could drink her milk instead of formula. Donnie was already gaining weight and everyone was pretty excited. But then he upchucked and they found out all of it had been in his stomach. All of a sudden everything changed. The grownups all got funny squinty looks on their faces and whispered a lot. I overheard Mother tell someone that Donny had something called pyloric stenosis, which meant he didn't have an opening between his stomach and intestines. Food was going into a dead-end.

That evening I'd been in bed awhile, and Robin was asleep. Daddy was at a meeting, and I heard Mother talking on the telephone. I slid out of bed and tiptoed out to the head of the stairs. I crouched down and listened real hard. I didn't know who she was talking to, but I heard her say that the doctor had thought about operating on Donnie to open his stomach, but decided not to. She said something about his pancreas and cystic fibrosis. I could tell that Mother knew he was going to die. Man, that was creepy! I snuck back to bed and lay there with that horrifying secret, wishing I'd never heard. I felt like one shoe had dropped, and now I had to wait to hear the rest of the dreadful news. Then I remembered that Ronnie was okay. We'd still have one baby. Things could be worse.

Finally, on Friday, when the babies were almost two weeks old, Daddy was already there when Robin and I got home from school. He and Mother met us in the hall by the front door. In an oddly quiet and gentle voice Daddy said, "Your little brother Donnie died today." The other shoe had fallen.

"Oh," I said solemnly, at a loss for words. All I felt was relief that it was over, but I knew I was supposed to be sad. Daddy put one arm around me and one around Robin, and Mother did the same, and we all stood there in a quiet little circle for a minute or two. That felt good. We ought to do this more often I thought. Then we stepped back—no point in overdoing things. Our family didn't go in for that mushy, huggy stuff.

"Do you have any questions?" Mother asked.

"Can Robin and I go to the funeral?" I was afraid they'd think kids didn't belong at funerals, and I didn't want to miss it. I'd only been to one funeral, and that was old Mrs. Will's. We got there late because we'd had to drive all the way to Albuquerque. It seemed like it was over before it started, so I thought I might have missed something. I didn't need to worry. They assured us we could go. It would be on Monday.

The weekend was busy. Rene and Cub came back, and so did Pop and Clara, our other grandparents. On Monday morning Uncle Dudley showed up, and Robin and I got to ride down to Santa Fe with him in his MG convertible. That was exciting, because he drove so fast he nearly skidded around the curves on the side of the cliff going down from town. I wanted him to put the top down, but he said it wasn't warm enough.

I barely remember the funeral. I think it was in some chapel that was sort of dark, and I think maybe Mr. Rayburn was the minister who said a few words. I kind of remember seeing a teeny-bitsy baby lying like a prune in a blue satin-lined casket, not much bigger than a man's shoe box. I don't remember going out to the cemetery, but I always remembered he was there when we drove by it. After the funeral, we all went to lunch at a restaurant. I ordered a grilled cheese sandwich.

I was surprised when nobody at school asked me the next day where I'd been. I'd sort of wanted to tell people about the funeral. Since it had been a weekend, I hadn't even been to school since he died. But nobody asked, and I didn't know how to bring it up. I mean, it would seem seriously weird to hold your hand up for news time and say, "Guess what—My baby brother died last Friday." One day at recess a few weeks later, Sondra, the class creep, told me that Mr. Patri had told the class about Donnie dying, and told them not to talk to me about it, because it might make me feel bad. I thought that was stupid, but I understood why he'd done it.

Before long, Ronnie was big and strong enough to come home, and immediately moved into the center of my reality, pushing Donnie out of mind, but not out of memory. Though he had never seemed real, he was never quite forgotten. Years later, when Ron (who soon outgrew the childish name Ronnie) did something outrageous, Mother or I would jokingly ask, "What ever would we have done with two of him!" But the idea of having two of him never seemed real to me.

ℰᏜℭᏜ

Forty-five years after the twins were born, Parvin and I returned to Santa Fe for a couple of days. This was my first visit to Santa Fe in nearly twenty years. As we drove into town along Cerrillos Road, we passed a cemetery.

"I think that's where Donnie's grave is!" I exclaimed. "Maybe we should go in and see if we can find it." Several people in the family had gotten into genealogical research, and nobody knew exactly where Donnie was buried. This was a golden opportunity to track down the information and document it for them.

The next day we set out to find him. Parvin thought he should be in the Veteran's Cemetery, since Daddy was a veteran and entitled to a plot for him. I agreed to try it, even though I was sure it was the wrong one. Sure enough, he wasn't listed, so I went into the office to ask about the cemetery on Cerrillos Road. The man there put me in touch with the caretaker at Fairview. She checked their records, found Donnie's plot number, confirmed that there was a marker and gave me directions for finding it.

After we left the Veteran's Cemetery, I began telling Parvin about the day Donnie died. Suddenly I couldn't continue. Remembering how Daddy had told us, and how we'd stood in that circle. I choked up. After forty-five years, tears I'd never shed began to flow. In a flash, I understood that I really had had another brother, if only for a few days. He had breathed and cried. I couldn't bear to imagine Mother standing by the incubator with her precious little boy in her arms, knowing each breath was numbered. Though I never noticed their grief and hadn't shared it, Mother and Daddy must have been devastated at the loss of this child. How proud they had been to have twins! It had become clear over the years how much they valued having even one son.

Suddenly I didn't want to find his grave after all. I've never been one to visit graves. After all, the occupants aren't actually there, so why bother, I've always thought. The next morning, as we neared the cemetery on our way out of town, I changed my mind.

"I do want to stop!" I exclaimed.

The cemetery was badly overgrown. We wandered along several rows, poking in the grass without finding Donnie. I had given up when Parvin nudged some overgrown grass aside, and there it was, a tiny bronze marker stamped with a small lamb, Donnie's name, and the year, 1955. I gasped, and quickly pulled away as much of the grass as I could, brushing soil aside with my hands. I found a twig and scraped around the letters. This much I could do for my brother's memory.

As I worked, I experienced déjà vu. I remembered a sunny summer day forty-five years earlier when we came here to make sure the marker had been properly placed. I remembered feeling sad, and relieved that we didn't stay long. When the little marker was as clean as I could get it, I snapped a picture to give Ron a tangible memento of his twin brother.

It was time to leave. Returning to the car, I sank into my seat, suffused with the peace of completing long unfinished business. I had found a long-lost brother and put him properly to rest. Donnie had finally become real.

This is one of my longest stories, partly because it's two stories rolled into one, with a gap of forty-five years between. In the earlier section, I'm a fifth grader, and totally self-absorbed. Notice the extensive use of dialogue. Also notice the detail about fixing my hair and planning my performance. Admitting to such egotistical behavior is a little embarrassing, but I'm telling it like I remember it.

The earlier part could stand on its own, but the second part would have less meaning without the first. The voice of the second part is entirely different, as it had to be. The first part describes a self-centered child. The second part describes a mature adult in search of family roots, connection, and meaning.

Rocking Chair

"Betsy told me that David told Jay he's going to ask Sally to go to Prom with him." I'm sitting in the rocking chair by the window in Mother and Daddy's room, talking to Mother's back as she sits at her sewing machine a few feet away. I stitch away as I talk, busily hemming a skirt. Mother doesn't say anything, so I continue. "I guess if he's going to do it, he'd better hurry up.

She doesn't have any idea what she'll wear if he does ask her, and it's only two weeks away."

Still no response from Mother, who doesn't seem interested in prom talk. I switch topics. "Jackie did something funny this morning in orchestra. She decided to challenge me for first chair." I pause and hear nothing. "Mr. Pinkerton said I should stay in first chair, and she got so mad she nearly walked out. After class I told him I didn't care if I was first chair or not, and he should let her have it. He said she had to earn it first. I think she's really mad. She wouldn't talk to me the rest of the day."

Mother still says nothing.

Dadgum! I hate when she does this. She acts like I'm not even here. Doesn't she read those articles in her magazines about how mothers are supposed to listen to their daughters and help them understand things and stuff like that? Heaven knows I try hard enough to give her the chance, but she's not doing her part. It just isn't fair!

My mind drifts back to the summer six years ago when we spent the day visiting Mother's Cousin Lucy at their farm out in the country near Clovis. Lucy had a new baby, and while she and Mother sat around the kitchen talking and feeding the baby, I sat in the living room reading *The Better Homes and Gardens Baby Book*. With the instincts of a homing pigeon I went straight for the good stuff—the part about how to tell your child the facts of life. I was in for a rude shock. The word was that if your child hadn't asked this question by the age of ten, you should assume she's already found out some other way and initiate the conversation yourself to make sure she has accurate information.

Pangs of guilty shock shot through me. I was already ten, and hadn't asked. In fact, I didn't even know I was supposed to ask. I had indeed found out about that stuff some other way one Saturday morning a year earlier when Mother, Daddy, and

Robin went to town. They had been cleaning out an old foot-locker, and I stayed home with the specific intention of exploring it while they were gone. I hit the jackpot and found the marriage manual the Army gave to newlyweds in 1942. It explained the technical details of the "act of coitus," and I got the picture. I was jubilant to finally learn how the father's "seed" got into the mother's tummy to find her egg and make a baby. I had figured that kissing was involved, but was pretty sure that simply kissing wasn't enough. I'd known it had something to do with Tom Loomis's Dirtiest Word, but wasn't clear on just what the "F word" was all about. Now, reading that book, the last piece of the puzzle had fallen into place.

My elation had been short-lived. As glad as I was to master the mystery, the whole process sounded utterly revolting. It certainly wasn't anything I wanted to ask about or even have anyone know I knew about! I carefully put the book back where I found it and went outside to play and didn't think too much more about it until that day at Lucy's. Then, learning that I was not only supposed to ask, but that I was behind schedule in doing it, I determined not to shirk my duty, and to get the matter over with. The most urgent question was how!

Not long after our visit with Lucy, Mother announced that she was going to have another baby, twin babies in fact. For several months I pondered how to use her condition to ask The Question that I now knew Good Daughters were supposed to ask. It seemed like it should be a little easier since she was expecting twins, but that definitely didn't turn out to be the case. Many nights I lay awake, plotting ways to ask The Question.

A few days before the babies were born, I sat at the sewing machine in her room making tiny flannel nightgowns while she lay in bed, trying to keep from going into labor as long as possible. I realized my window of opportunity was closing fast—so fast my head felt caught against the sill. The only way out of this stranglehold was to ask—ask now! I held my breath for about five minutes trying to build up courage and enough saliva to allow my tongue to come unstuck from the roof of my mouth. I pretended to be pinning pieces of flannel to look busy and hide my shaking hands.

When the words finally came, I hardly recognized my own voice blurting out, "How do babies get in there?" My tension (and I think hers, too) burst like a water balloon. I'd done it! I'd asked! I sagged into the chair, limp with relief.

Mother was ready. Maybe she knew that Good Mothers were supposed to bring this subject up, and she hadn't known how. There was a book, *The Wonderful Story of How You Were Born*, in the bottom drawer of her dresser. I had no idea how long it had been there, but she told me to read it and ask her if I had any questions. She also told me not to say anything about it to Robin, who was "too young to understand these things."

The book had lots of fascinating pictures. I learned quite a bit, and I was especially intrigued to learn about testicles. When I finished, I put the book back in her room and left without a word. There was no way I was going to ask her any questions, and she didn't bring it up again either.

My thoughts reconnect with the present. It wasn't easy playing the role of Good Daughter then, and it sure as heck isn't any easier now. I give it one last shot.

"Lynne wants to have a party Saturday night at her house. She wants to make pizza, but they don't have a recipe. Do you still have that one you made awhile back?"

"Yes."

So she can hear me! She's obviously been ignoring me on purpose. What on earth is this all about? What in the world am I supposed to do now?

"Can I make a copy for her?" I ask, swallowing my anger. I don't know what else to do with it.

"I guess so."

A few more stitches and my hem is finished. I gather thread, scissors, and pincushion and put them away.

"I guess I'll go down and find that recipe. Is it in your box?"

"I think so."

I sigh in resignation as I walk down the stairs. I sure wish my mother would give me good advice like the mothers in the articles do. But for heaven's sake, if she ignores me when I talk about Sally and Jackie, I'm sure as heck not going to talk about anything that actually matters, like "How can I get Michael to ask me to prom?" That's at least twenty times harder than asking where babies came from. Maybe next time I'll get it right.

I find the recipe and call Lynne.

❧ ❦

Fast forwarding a whole generation, I recall this scene as I listen to my own daughter relate endless details of people, places, and events that I don't recognize or relate to, and I wonder, is this how Mother felt that afternoon? My daughter doesn't seem to be expecting or even wanting any response from me—is that what Mother thought? That I didn't care what she thought or that I didn't want to hear it? Maybe, like I am now, she was preoccupied and only half listening. Or, maybe she just didn't have any answers to give me if she had wanted to.

I'll never know the answers to these questions. Even if Mother were still living, I doubt she'd remember. Not wanting history to repeat itself too precisely, I do listen a bit more intently, and murmur, "Mm-hmm," now and then, to make sure she knows I do hear, and that I am scanning for relevance. Then I remember how hard it is to reply to people who never ask questions about what you think or toss the conversational ball back to you. I ask a question, hoping she'll understand that I care about her, even if I get lost in her details.

My mother may not have been a first-rate conversationalist, but today I know that she cared about me, and that she did the best job of listening and advising that she knew how. Maybe I did a little better, and hopefully my daughter will find the missing pieces of the puzzle.

This main story has a complex structure, with two layers nested in the main one. The second layer is a flashback with a third inserted as a flashback within the flashback. It's not often that I have the chance to use such a technique. I could have turned the epilogue into another full layer by beginning with a scene where I sat listening to my daughter and flashing back to my own memories. The layer would be completed by returning to the present at the end, as written.

This story uses a combination of dialogue and self-talk. I began it in the present tense to add contrast to the flashback material, and switched to simple past for the flashbacks. The choice of tense was deliberate. This story began as a simple memory of sitting in that rocking chair. The embedded memories were part of the original story, but when I first began, it wasn't obvious how to work them in.

Adventures of a Chilihead

Whenever the subject of chili arises, I explain to people that where I grew up, jalapeño peppers are used as pacifiers. That isn't quite true, but it is true that I grew up on red-hot enchiladas and frijoles with tomatoes and green chili. I've written a number of stories about the insanity around my love of fiery peppers. These are two of my favorites.

Breathing Fire

For two summers after high school, I worked in the technical library at the Los Alamos Scientific Laboratory. The second summer I was a married woman, so I brown-bagged it and ate lunch in the office with the secretaries instead of heading over to the cafeteria to enjoy the company of the handsome and eligible grad students as I'd done the year before.

Both the secretaries I worked and ate with were of Hispanic heritage and lived "down in the valley." Later in the summer, they brought fresh green chili from their gardens to eat with lunch. My family was also "Old New Mexico," though of Anglo descent, and I'd been eating and enjoying hot chili peppers as long as I could remember. I cast lustful glances at the crunchy green goodies they were enjoying. One day Vera had at least half a dozen spread out.

"Could I have one of your chilies?" I asked.

"Oh, you can't eat these. They're hot!" Both Vera and Bertha began to snicker.

"I can eat anything you can eat—the hotter, the better. I'll show you!"

"Okay. You asked for it." Vera tossed me a succulent green chili pepper, about eight inches long, tapering from a gentle point to a fat two inches at the shoulder. I bravely bit a huge hunk off the bottom. To my amazement, it was cool as a bell pepper, totally tame. I realized I'd been dealt a winning hand here, but didn't want to tip it, so I played it cool.

"Is this the hottest you have?" I taunted.

They looked surprised. I kept eating. They kept watching. I smugly crunched my way up the pepper, feeling just a tiny bit fraudulent. Maybe I'll tell them when I'm finished ... or maybe not, I thought.

In no time, I was up to the last bite. I bit it off with relish, knowing I'd won the no-stakes bet. Then—all bets were off. That last bite neared habanero strength. It had enough capsaicin for a bushel of New Mexico green chili peppers concentrated in one tiny spot. I was a human blow torch! I couldn't even scream. I set a speed record dashing for the water fountain. Water didn't help a bit. I would have given the Devil my soul just then for cheese or milk, but he was standing around the corner with Vera and Bertha, wiping tears of laughter from his eyes. After several minutes I was finally able to return to the desks where we were eating, my own eyes red and wet, but not from laughing.

I confessed what had happened, and they didn't let me forget it the rest of the summer. I still love hot pepper, but I'm always cautious about that last bite near the top!

Esstrah Spicy!

The odds that I would suggest going to a Chinese restaurant are slim to none, but I'm generally agreeable if someone else suggests it. One Sunday afternoon a few years ago, my mother-in-law suggested that the three of us have dinner at a Chinese restaurant one of her friends highly recommended. We arrived somewhat early for dinner, and found the beautifully appointed dining room nearly empty. The native Chinese owner greeted us, seated us, and handed us the menus, bowing and backing away to give us time to consider our choices.

Several minutes later he returned to take our orders. My husband and his mother ordered mild-flavored dishes. I felt daring and chose Kung Pao Chicken, or perhaps it was General Tso's. Whatever it was, it had that little warning chili pepper beside it on the menu. In my limited experience with Chinese restaurants, I had never found one that made hot food hot enough to be worth mentioning, so I tried something new.

"Extra spicy, please," I asked, hoping the result would liven up the meal.

"Esstrah spicy! Oh, yes. We give you esstrah spicy!" His ear-to-ear grin and the gleam in his eye set off inner alarms. What have I done? I wondered, briefly tempted to withdraw the request. But no, he had thrown down a gauntlet, and I wasn't about to back off. I bravely returned the smile and nodded my appreciation. I'd swear I saw him rub his hands in glee as he hurried back to the kitchen. I imagined the dialogue back in there. "Hey, lady wants esstrah spicy. You fix her up!"

Fifteen or twenty minutes later our dinners arrived, steaming hot on the platters. He set mine in place with a flourish. "Esstrah spicy for the lady!" he announced with a bow, showing all his teeth.

I looked in astonishment at the abundance of thin red cayenne peppers in my sauce. I gave up counting after eight. With trepidation, I tried a taste. Fiery! This dish was indeed esstrah spicy! Memories of an enchilada eat-off my father had with a friend of his in a small Mexican cafe in Albuquerque a few decades earlier flashed before my eyes. I saw him sitting there with sweat pouring off his forehead, enthusiastically forking in those enchiladas. I don't think he would have accepted the challenge unless he planned to prevail. Of course Daddy won the bet. Alex couldn't finish his. This was my touchstone. I'm my father's daughter. I'd ordered this dish, and I would eat this dish, come hell or high water. I didn't need to prove anything to my husband, and his mother thinks black pepper on her eggs is living dangerously. No, they wouldn't think less of me for putting down my fork early. But I would not, could not, wouldn't even think of walking out of that restaurant without consuming a respectable portion of that dinner.

I began eating, one small bite after another. It wasn't as hot as I thought, I decided. The procession of bites continued. Then I began to feel steam emerging from my nostrils and ears. Yes, it was as hot as I thought. The inside of my mouth was lined with fire. Fire flowed down my throat, into my gullet. And yet, the feeling was sublime. The endorphins had kicked in. It felt so good to hurt so bad.

As I ate, I occasionally glanced in the direction of the kitchen. A lattice-type divider was placed next to our table, so I couldn't be sure, but I frequently sensed eyes in the background. Well, let them watch. I was giving them a performance they would have to admire.

Almost before I realized it, I had finished my meal, except for half the rice and the peppers, which were neatly shoved into a pile to the side of the plate.

"Is enough spicy?" The owner's eyebrows were raised as he came to clear the plates. Whether his expression was one of concern or astonishment wasn't clear.

"Oh, yes!" I replied, nodding sagely and forming an "O" with forefinger and thumb. "Perfect!" I answered, with absolute sincerity. Did I glimpse a fleeting look of disappointment on his face? If so, it vanished instantly, replaced by respect. He bowed with a flourish.

"So, you come back. We make you more esstrah spicy!"

One of these days, when I'm ready for another endorphin rush, I just may take him up on the offer.

These are two examples of stories written on a theme. I have others on this theme, but these get the point across. After the brief introduction used to set the stage for the stories, they proceed smoothly from one to the next, without intervening commentary.

Some may consider my use of dialect in the second story insensitive. The whole experience hinges around the delightful personality of the restaurant owner/waiter. Sanitizing his speech would dilute the truth of his uniqueness and compromise the truth of my experience. His accent lent authenticity to the restaurant.

Fall, Then and Now

Walking along the road, the arrival of fall assaults all my senses. I can no longer ignore the red and gold leaves on the trees. These are fall in full glory, not some anachronism, colored ahead of their time. The air smells different today, spicier, earthier, filled with scents of ripeness and decay. The sun comes from a lower angle, its gentle warmth welcome after the oppressive blaze of summer. As my feet scuff through piles of blazing tree scraps on the ground, my mind rustles through a colorful collage of memory scraps.

Flashback, 1947: Our front yard was covered with leaves this morning. Daddy has raked them all into a huge pile in the middle of the lawn. Now he picks me up by my hands and feet and swings me back and forth as he's often done. My blood freezes as he swings me even farther to his left and puts extra force into the next swing toward the pile. A split second before he does, I realize he's going to turn me loose. I scream with terror as I hurtle through the air and land in that pile of leaves. Oh! That didn't hurt at all! That was fun! I'm elated as I brush leaves from my face and scramble up. "Do that again, Daddy!" But once was enough. I've scattered the leaves too much to catch me safely a second time. I splash around in the leaves for a few minutes, then he rakes them up again and piles them into the cart. Before long they're in the middle of the vegetable garden, where he lights a match and starts a huge bonfire that fills the air with acrid smoke. Mother comes out of the house with a package of marshmallows while Daddy whittles a couple of willow sticks from a bush along the ditch bank. We roast marshmallows over the embers of the leaves. I can still taste their smoky, sweetly toasty shells, full of oozy goo in the middle.

Flashback, 1954: Our family is up in the Valle Grande forest, high above Los Alamos, cutting wood for the fireplace. Before we start, we eat a picnic lunch of fried chicken, potato salad, apples, and cookies. This day, this fall, is especially great, because I'm wearing an embroidered red wool Mexican jacket. I've wanted one of these for ages. It's even better than new. It's the one Cynthia, the girl next door, outgrew. Cynthia is two years older than I am, and I've always felt lucky that I could play with her, so this is extra special. I have the jacket I always wanted, and it forms an extra link with Cynthia. I walk through the blazing aspens, kicking their leaves underfoot and feeling as golden inside as the leaves and the autumn sun.

Flashback, 1959: Daddy is on a business trip, and Saturday morning Mother has a great idea. "Let's go for a ride up in the Santa Fe forest to look at leaves." She quickly gathers sandwiches and large, juicy apples, and piles Robin, Ronnie, and me into the car. The mountain sides are ablaze, and when Mother finds an especially nice spot, she pulls off the road. We hike around a little and eat our lunch, sitting on rocks where we can look out at the leaves. This day is memorable, because it's "just us girls." Ronnie doesn't count, because he's still a tot. Some of our best times are the ones when Mother decides to do something fun while Daddy's out of town.

Flashback, 1960: The mountains behind town are dotted with groves of fiery gold aspens. Their blazing color matches my mood as I walk home from school, carrying my spotless new zipper binder with the orange plaid pattern printed on the cover, thinking of crisp apples in my lunch bag, my new wool skirts and sweaters, new teachers, the excitement of working on the new Olion's play, football games to be won, and (hopefully) new romances about to begin. Fall is my favorite time of year, at least until the first real snowfall, when winter gains the favorite position until the leaves get green again in the spring, and my preference changes again when the sun is high and warm in the sky and school is out for the summer. There's something wonderful about each season, and I always look forward to the next, stretching endlessly ahead, clear into my college years and who knows what beyond that.

Flashback, 1974: I stand stock still in the family room of our house. I can't believe how quiet it is. I can't believe how large and empty the house feels. Today is the first time I have ever been alone in this particular house on a weekday. My baby is in nursery school, and the couple of hours of solitude that buys me is precious at this point. Fall takes on new meaning to me now. It is no longer the time when I go back to school, but the time when my children go back to school and my days become my own, uncluttered by the constant interruptions of motherhood. I revel in the thought of copper chrysanthemums, raking leaves, crisp apples, and spicy fragrances, but just as much, I revel in the idea that I can begin new projects, renew memberships in organizations and forge ahead with fresh energy and anticipation. I'll stay busy through the coldness and dark of winter until it gives way to the sweet softness of spring and the sun-filled glory of summer again. The cycle stretches ahead in endless promise.

Back to the Present, 2002: Now, as my mind returns to the present, I notice that fall looks and smells as beautiful as ever, but something is missing. Maybe, just maybe, that something is the sense that fall is a beginning, a marker in an endless cycle, and that time will go on forever. Youth is missing, replaced in the overall scheme of things by the autumn of life, with its own colorful perspectives. The cycle no longer seems endless. Now fall brings with it a sense of endings, not beginnings. and it holds a strong sense of mystery as the future approaches a dimly veiled passage.

Well, now! I love a good mystery. Perhaps this evolution of fall is less macabre than I imagined. Kicking the last leaves aside, I return to our driveway and head into the house to resume my current mystery selection, looking forward to the coziness of reading beside a fire with a mug of hot spiced cider. Yes, fall is still a wonderful time of year.

This piece is an example of a reflective story using flashbacks arranged along a timeline. Some may describe this as an essay because it is about my interpretations as much or more than describing conditions and events. For publication these distinctions may matter. For your own work, they don't.

Mother Goes Gaga

"Let's go down to Southcenter this morning," Mother suggests at breakfast. I leap at the idea. George, Susan, and I have come over from Richland to pick up John, who has spent the past week with Mother and Daddy at their new house in Seattle. Trying to keep the kids occupied at her house here is no easy task. They aren't used to the house and don't know where things are. When they're bored, they fight. When they fight, Mother gets crazy, and I get a headache from it all. Tomorrow we'll go home, but today we need to keep busy. A trip down to this major mall should at least kill the morning.

We don't stay at Southcenter long. The kids each want to run off in a different direction, and shopping for things Mother and I would enjoy is out of the question.

"Let's go home," she announces after twenty minutes. This isn't a suggestion or request. It's an order. We head out to the car and climb in. While the kids renegotiate seating arrangements, Mother digs in her purse for her keys. Suddenly her head jerks up and she peers intently out the windshield. I follow her gaze and notice two men getting in the car parked to the right, diagonally in front of us. The driver is a nicely dressed young man, and an elegantly attractive older man with wavy snow-white hair opens the door on the passenger side.

Noticing that their headlights are on, I roll my window halfway down and holler helpfully to the younger man. "If the car won't start, it's because you left the lights on."

"Oh! Thanks. Can you wait just a minute?" he asks, lowering himself into his seat.

I look over at Mother. Her eyes are practically bulging out of their sockets. Her mouth hangs slack, and her knuckles are white from her death grip on the wheel. She gives a weak nod. Sure enough, their car won't start. The older man slowly unfolds his trim body from the car and saunters in Mother's direction. She fumbles with the crank in a frenzied attempt to roll her window down. He casually leans on the door.

"Do you happen to have any jumper cables we could use?" The words rumble forth, slow, sweet, and mellow as well-aged sherry, his smile exposing a few dozen perfect pearly whites.

"Oh, yes! I'm sure I do. We always carry them!" Mother stammers. What's come over her? I wonder. I've never seen her in such a state. I get out when she does and walk around to the trunk. She has trouble getting the key in the lock. Again, I'm baffled by her behavior. She's always had great hand-eye coordination. She finally gets the trunk open and rummages through it. She tosses a blanket aside, and moves a couple of small boxes and a mini-cooler. No jumper cables appear. She goes through them all again.

"I … I guess I don't have them today," she croaks in dismay. "I can't imagine why they aren't here. We always carry them." She's repeating herself. That's not like her. Neither is her shrill, quavering voice. She's acting like a moonstruck teenager. Who is this man, and what has he done to my mother?

"Well, no problem. Thank you so much for checking." Mystery Man flashes another yard of teeth directly at Mother and bows slightly toward her. I wait for him to kiss her hand, but he turns to leave.

"No trouble at all. My pleasure," she squeaks at his back.

"Try Mall Security. They should be able to help," I suggest. I don't want this stranger to think I'm as ditzy as my mother!

"Thank you. Thank you so much. We'll do that." He smiles and waves to me over the top of the door as he gets back in. I wait for him to blow us a kiss, but the moment passes.

Mother sits quietly for a whole minute, breathing deeply. Her hand begins to steady as she puts the key in the ignition, starts the car and backs out. A this point, I'm relieved that she can manage to drive at all!

"That was Caesar Romero!" she finally gasps as she shifts out of reverse. "I'll never wash my car door again!" she says in a misty tone. Now things make sense. I recognize the name of the classic movie star, and he certainly acted the part, but I'd had no idea what he looked like. She said she knew he was in town, but of course she never expected to actually meet him.

He hasn't lost the magic that makes women swoon, I thought, especially those who recognize him.

"No kidding? He really is a hunk! ... Good thing I noticed the lights," I observe with a wry grin. She nods, lost in a euphoric daze as she heads up the ramp onto I-5. I'm a little awestruck myself, and wonder if I would have been quite so nonchalant if I'd known who he was.

෫෨ඥ

A few months later, Mother is in Richland for a visit. I'm busy packing the kids' lunches, while she eats breakfast.

"It really was him!" she announces, out of the blue.

"Who, what?" I'm baffled.

"Him! Caesar Romero!"

"Oh. How do you know? I thought you were sure then."

"I was. But he was in Seattle again at the Dinner Theater last week. We went and sat right by the stage, so, now I'm really sure."

"That's great! Maybe someday I'll get lucky and run into Sean Connery." I turn back to the dishwasher with a smile, wondering if I'd go gaga, and embarrass my own daughter if the time comes. Why not? Mother deserved it, and so do I.

Besides being a fun memory that reflects my mother's personality in ordinary circumstances and an unusual encounter, this story begged for the use of lots of description and dialogue.

Mayhem at Camp RYLA

People flew in every direction as the jeep screeched to a halt amidst clouds of dust, frighteningly close to the spot where the crowd had been gathered. For a moment it had looked as if someone would be hit. I couldn't tell who was yelling louder, outraged campers or the junior staffers jumping out of the jeep, waving beer bottles and belligerently holding angry campers at bay. Arms flew in every direction. The situation would obviously break into a riot at any moment.

Just then Roger stepped forth from the crowd to confront the offenders. The other campers drew back at the sight of him, and became quiet. "As designated Constable of this camp, I hereby place all five of you under arrest for the crime of committing mayhem in the Land of RYLA! You have the right to remain silent, and the right to an attorney. Joe, will you and Carolyn please escort the prisoners to the administrative office and keep them there until court is in session?"

Joe and Carolyn stepped forward. "Do we need handcuffs or anything? Do we have any rope?" They both spoke at once.

"I don't think that will be necessary," answered William, a member of the senior staff. He turned to the prisoners and asked, "I think we can safely accept your word that you will make no attempt to escape from your guards while the investigation is being conducted. Can we count on your cooperation?"

"You can," they answered in unison, looking a bit subdued.

Joe and Carolyn led the five across the road and volleyball field, into the cabin that served as the camp office.

William turned to the rest of the campers. "Obviously, from the looks of things, a serious crime has just been committed. A trial will be held this afternoon with Judge Leo Nimsick from Cranbrook presiding. Court will convene at 2:00 p.m. It's now 12:43. We need two detectives to conduct interviews of the witnesses. Who will volunteer?"

Several hands shot up in unison. "Okay, I only need two. I'm thinking of a number between one and one hundred. The two of you closest get the job." Sandie and Q won the spots. "Now, I want the rest of you to answer any questions you may be asked as truthfully as you can. It's up to Sandie and Q to decide what to ask and who to interview. I'll see you in court at 2:00."

William Mitchell-Banks (a family physician in Creston, BC) turned to George Diana (a Spokane attorney) and the two of them walked back toward the cafeteria where they were joined by the rest of the staff: Ray Grout (a justice of the peace in Creston, BC), Gary Lemaster (Ass't Postmaster in Spokane), Leo Nimsick (a Provincial Court Judge in British Columbia) and me (a freelance writer and trainer). Once safely behind closed doors, our jubilation burst forth. "Awesome! Great show! Those kids did a fantastic job. If they didn't actually drink the beer in those bottles, they sure did a great job of faking it!" We whooped with laughter as we recalled specifics of the event. We hadn't told the junior staffers what to do, just that they should discretely disappear during lunch and be prepared to stage a crime of their own choosing shortly after 12:30, when everyone would be gathered in the assembly area after lunch. We made the assignment with full faith we would not be disappointed, but even so, we now realized we had underestimated the extent of their resourcefulness.

George went off to perform his appointed role of preparing the defense. Ray, the appointed District Attorney for the trial, went out to oversee the gathering of the evidence.

When Judge Leo Nimsick strode into the chapel-turned-courtroom on the stroke of two, attired with all solemnity in official judicial robes, all campers were present and seated. "Oh yay, oh yay, the court of the Sovereign Land of RYLA will now convene with Judge Leo Nimsick presiding." Albert's hair looked as if he'd hit the flour barrel in the kitchen in an attempt to look authentic for his role as distaff. A couple of campers snickered. The giggles were cut short by a healthy whack of the gavel.

"You may bring the prisoners forth."

Roger came through the door, leading the five accused junior staffers, who stood facing the judge.

"Will the district attorney please read the charges?"

"Mary, Steve, Linda, Alan, and Jennifer, you stand accused this day of committing mayhem in the Land of RYLA, endangering the welfare and even the lives of residents. How do you plead?" intoned Ray, maximizing his British accent.

"Not guilty!" they exclaimed with one voice. This plea met with an immediate chorus of boo's from the audience.

"Order in the court!" thundered Judge Nimsick, his words punctuated by vigorous gavel thumps. "The bailiff will escort anyone from the courtroom who is unable to maintain an attitude of proper respect." After a few startled glances, the campers settled back to watch. Obviously this was not intended as a ribald comedy.

"The Attorney for the Land of RYLA will present his case."

Ray stepped solemnly to the center of the room, standing sideways so as to speak to both the judge and audience. "Your Honor, and fellow Rylarians, this very afternoon, at precisely 12:41, a time when all of us, including the accused, were scheduled to be gathered on the assembly ground, the accused roared into camp in an open-top Jeep vehicle at a high rate of speed, headed straight for the center of the campers who were complying with the designated activity of the camp, causing the foresaid campers to run for cover in fright and hysteria. When the before mentioned jeep screeched to a stop, mere centimeters from the footprints of campers who had been previously standing there, the accused staffers jumped merrily forth from the vehicle, waving beer bottles, staggering as if intoxicated, shouting obscenities, and generally behaving in an obnoxious manner designed to provoke a fight. Indeed one person, Miss Mary Diana, was actually seen to be waving a gun! Your Honor, these staff members have violated numerous Rylarian ordinances, including the prohibition of alcoholic beverages on the premises, leaving the premises during camp sessions, behaving in a disorderly fashion, and endangering the well-being of their fellow Rylarians. I urge that they be found *guilty!*"

"You may call your first witness."

"The prosecution calls Roger Woodward." Roger strode to the front of the room and was quickly sworn in. "Please tell the court what you saw."

"Well, I was really surprised. I hadn't noticed that these guys were missing, so when they came roaring up like that, I was just, well, surprised."

"Could you tell the court what you saw that caused you to be surprised?"

"Oh. Yes. The five people sitting over there were piled in Steve's Jeep, which came roaring into camp, headed straight into the middle of the crowd. It looked like they were going to run right over us."

"And, Mr. Woodward, what did you do then?"

"I jumped back, trying to get out of the way, and knocked Cathy flat on the ground. She was standing behind me." Roger continued by stating that at least Linda, Alan, and Jennifer were taking swigs from bottles of beer.

"Thank you, Mr. Woodward. You may step down."

The next witness was Sally Johnson. "Miss Johnson, please tell the court what you saw."

"Well, I saw pretty much what Roger told you."

"But you also saw something he didn't mention. What was that?"

"Oh, the gun," her voice was quavering. She seemed about to break down in tears. "Mary had a gun. She was waving it around, and I saw her aim it directly at me."

"What did you do then?"

"I hit the ground!"

"Did you hear anything out of the ordinary?"

"Yes ... I heard a gunshot." At this point, tears were streaming down Sally's cheeks. "I just couldn't believe that Mary, of all people, would be shooting a gun. Especially not around people like that."

"Thank you, Sally. You can take your seat."

The next witness was Greg. He saw Alan point a finger right at him and say something to Steve, who aimed the car directly toward him. The final witness was Beth. She saw Steve looking over his shoulder talking to the girls in back as the Jeep raced toward the group.

"Your Honor, the prosecution rests its case."

George began the defense. He called Roger back to the stand. "Mr. Woodward, how close would you say that the Jeep came to the spot where people were standing?"

"Oh, I don't know. It looked like it probably would have run over someone if we hadn't moved so fast. I know it wasn't far."

"Thank you Mr. Woodward." He then called Sandie to the stand. Sandie testified that she had measured the distance from the foot prints closest to the Jeep, which had been left standing where Steve stopped. The actual distance was six feet, eight inches.

The next witness was Alan, who verified a piece of evidence as the bottle he'd been holding in his hand when the Jeep returned to camp. It was a root beer bottle. Mary came next. The evidence she identified was a silver-colored water pistol. This evidence had been collected from the defendants in the office immediately after they were escorted there.

A buzz arose among the campers.

"Order in the court!" Judge Nimsick gaveled them to attention. "On the basis of the evidence and testimony, it is the finding of this court that the defendants are innocent. It is also the finding of the court that the whole lot of you is guilty of interpreting what you saw and heard through the filters of fear, personal experience, and assumptions, to mention a few. I sentence you to an additional session of listening training to be conducted by Ms. Lippincott. Court adjourned!"

I was thrilled. When we planned this mock court as part of the curriculum for the Rotary Youth Leadership Awards in 1983, our intention had been to illustrate the workings of the legal system in the two countries represented. It did that quite well. As an added bonus, it illustrated better than anything I could have planned the extent to which personal variation affects human perception. All of the campers were equally surprised. None of them expected this "surprise attack" and no two of them had experienced the event the same way.

The most striking difference was the addition of the gunshot that Sally testified in utter sincerity, under oath, that she had "heard." None of us had previously known that Sally had been involved in an armed robbery a few months earlier. An innocent bystander in the bank where she worked as a teller was wounded during a holdup. The mere sight of a gun sent Sally into a frenzy! Today she had heard what she expected—and feared—to hear: A gunshot.

The final session of the communication skills module I'd been leading all week was the most energetic of the week, and made the strongest impression of any I've ever taught. If they never remember anything else, not one of those campers will ever again think of eye witness reports as infallible.

This story is a prime example of a personal story that has wider potential. My *purpose* in writing it was to document the experience for myself and for whatever purpose the District 509 RYLA committee found for it in the future. To ensure as much accuracy as possible (an ironic undertaking, considering the subject matter), I relied on my own notes, and had the story reviewed by Leo Nimsick and Ray Grout. The story has enough inherent drama of its own that there was no temptation to enhance a thing.

A story of this sort requires the use of dialogue. To keep the dialogue credible, I left personal linguistic quirks and idioms intact to emphasize the individuality of the speakers.

For our purpose as lifestory writers, this story demonstrates the plasticity of both initial perception and memory. Each of those witnesses was one hundred percent accurate. They reported precisely what they observed, understood, and believed to be true. No two agreed. In this case, indisputable evidence was available to demonstrate the empirical truth. Every person involved left camp with a changed understanding of Truth.

Topsy Turvy Attitudes

What on earth is her problem? I wondered, watching my aunt shove leftovers into a recycled bread bag before putting them in the refrigerator. *She can afford new bags or plastic wrap. Why is she being so chintzy?* To me, these minor frugalities were a symptom of poverty, an oppressive condition and mentality that had afflicted our family since before The Great Depression, and one I was determined to transcend. Why would anyone act like they still were poor? To my way of thinking, plastic bags didn't take enough room in landfills to be worth mentioning. It was my considered opinion that she should definitely splurge on new plastic wrap, for convenience, for possible hygiene reasons, and to safeguard the quality of her leftovers.

That memory dates back to 1986. At that point, the only things I personally recycled were returnable bottles, an increasingly scarce commodity. I did pick up aluminum cans, and ran them by the recycling center every few months to collect the few cents per pound offered by Warhola Brothers on the north side. Even though it was hardly enough to buy a cup of coffee, I appreciated the cash, but even more, I felt I was doing my part to preserve space in our landfills.

My awareness of landfill problems began much earlier. In 1969 the League of Women Voters (LWV) adopted landfill capacity as a national study item and I served on our local study committee. Our recommendation was that strong steps should be taken to curtail extravagant waste. At the rate of disposal in 1970, it was clear that the nation as a whole would be running out of landfill capacity within twenty years or so. I felt complacent at the time, because I used cloth diapers, rather than filling the earth with damp Pampers. Time flew by, and by the mid-1980s it was clear that the LWV study had been accurate.

Shortly after my visit with my aunt, the Commonwealth of Pennsylvania mandated neighborhood recycling programs. Monroeville distributed recycling barrels and instructed us to fill them with aluminum and steel, glass of all colors, and #1 and #2 plastics. Recycling bins for used plastic bags appeared in all the grocery stores. Paper products could be recycled behind the Senior Citizen Center. My husband and I got into recycling in a big way, faithfully filling our bin. We were already composting yard waste to maintain the quality of our soil and to keep the waste out of the landfill.

As I stuffed those ubiquitous shopping bags into bundles for recycling, their sheer volume amazed me. In a year's time, I estimated my discards would melt down to well over a cubic foot of solid plastic. If every household discarded the same quantity, we would create a sizeable hill of pure plastic. We'd fill the mall in a few years. I looked at those bags with new respect. I began to find new uses for them. In a moment of inspiration, I devised a method of cutting them into strips, joining the strips, and crocheting sunhats, tote bags and other ecologically correct accessories. I even began recycling bread bags to store leftovers. I looked at my aunt in a new light, realizing that whatever the reason, she had been ahead of her time.

What is his problem? I wondered, watching my father take a brand-new Ziploc™ bag out of the box. I suggested that one of the grocery bags still sitting on the table nearby would serve his purpose quite nicely.

"I can afford to use new bags," he stated with definitive authority.

"But what about the landfill? Don't you recycle?"

"I save newspaper for the boys. Their school recycles them."

I knew it was pointless to argue the matter. His mind was made up. I also recognized that he looked at recycling grocery bags as a sign of poverty, the same way I had earlier. To him it was a privilege and a sign of personal success that he could afford to use new Ziploc™ bags whenever he wanted.

It's true, I thought. He doesn't use that many. I silently chuckled at my topsy turvy attitudes, and wondered if his would ever flip around the corner.

This story is an example of an essay that uses personal experience as a vehicle for discussing beliefs and attitudes. The story chronicles the development of an opinion and how it shapes my evolving attitude. Stories like this are an effective way of presenting opinions and beliefs without preaching, and as I wrote the story, my own thoughts on the matter became more clear.

Notice that I used italics to set off self-talk, or internal dialogue. In *Mother Goes Gaga*, I left self-talk in normal type. This is a matter of choice. This story seemed confusing, and my eye stumbled as I read those lines until I added the italics. That wasn't the case in the other one. If I planned to link the two stories into a single unit or collection, I'd select one style, italics or plain, and use it consistently throughout.

My Write Hand

"Use your right hand." I remember feeling confused when I was four or five years old and heard this mandate. Which is my right hand? I'd wonder. I recall reminding myself that my right hand is the one I use to write. It is my "write" hand. I think even then, before I knew how to spell, I knew the difference, as well as the connection, between "right" and "write." I remember physically moving my hands, practicing the feel of a phantom pencil in each, to establish once again which one was my "write" hand.

Today I still have some confusion between right and left. Perhaps it's because I'm somewhat ambidextrous, but I think it's a bit different. My right hand is the one I use to do things. My identification of dominance with "right" generalizes to other body parts.

Usually this passes unnoticed, but I once participated in a study for TMJ pain. I was in the group that received biofeedback treatment. When asked to identify the jaw that gave me the most trouble, I said "my right one." On my last day of treatment, somehow the therapist and I stumbled on the discovery that when I pointed to my "right" jaw, it was located on the left side of my face. She always applied sensor pads to both jaws, and was monitoring physical right jaw results, while I was focusing on relaxing my functional right jaw, located on the left side of my mouth. All I could say to explain this was that I primarily chew on that side, so I think of it as my "right" side because it is dominant. We had a good laugh, especially because I'd gotten good results in spite of the confusion. Obviously my one-sided focus was generalizing to both sides, and in this case, that was a good thing.

The other place where I have significant left/right confusion is with a computer mouse. As long as I have a mouse in my hand, I'm fine. I have trained my fingers to respond appropriately to left-click and right-click cues. But if I stop to think about it, or use another device like a touchpad, I'm likely to mix the two up. Why? Because the pointer finger on my right hand is my "right" finger. So I'm actually left-clicking with my "right" finger.

I don't suppose it will catch on, but I'm proposing some new mouse terminology for the benefit of confused people like myself, as well as all the southpaws in the world. Instead of left-click and right-click, we could "main-click" and "alt-click." That way none of us will be confused. Maybe I still will, because sometimes I use my left hand, and on my left hand, my main finger is on the wrong side of the hand. I'd still need to reset things, or adapt on the fly, as I do now. I give up. I might solve things for southpaws, but we ambidextrous folks better keep our wits about us, and keep track of our write hands!

This is a typical type of story that results when I sit down to write because "I feel a story coming on," as mentioned on page 153. I occasionally teach classes in digital photo editing, and I often get the left and right mouse buttons confused when I give students directions. I was thinking of that confusion when I felt the urge to write, and the story spilled out, with little need for editing.

The Lifestory Circle

"By the way Mom, Tony's grandmother grew up in New Mexico, so you can talk to her about that." This is the first time I can recall my son giving me conversational cues, and I'm intrigued. We are on our way to a graduation party held in honor of a young man who just completed his master's degree in education. The reception is being held by his parents in their San Diego home, and we are told it will be informal. Lippy and Franz have multiple ties to this family.

We walk into a house filled with tantalizing fragrances and jam-packed with people holding plates piled high with food. Half a dozen apron-clad women cluster in the kitchen. This doesn't keep the hostess from rushing up with open arms to greet Franz, Lippy, and especially Tosh. "There you are. You must eat. There is plenty. We have lots more. It isn't all out yet." She turns to us with a smile as radiant as the southern California sun. "And you must be Lippy's parents. I'm so glad you could come. I'm Betty."

"My mom grew up in New Mexico," Lippy offers helpfully.

"Oh! New Mexico. So did my mother. You must talk with her." Betty turns to wave at a twinkly-eyed, white-haired woman standing nearby. "Mama, you must meet this woman."

Grandmother tells me she grew up in Albuquerque, and we awkwardly talk for a minute before Lippy walks up. "Come on out back and get something to drink." I assure Grandmother that I'll find her later, and follow him into the yard.

Soon we fill our plates and find seats in the yard. "By the way, Grandmother has read Granddad's stories about growing up in New Mexico and she really liked them."

"How did she get them?"

"I e-mailed them to Betty and she printed them for her."

"I guess I'll remind her of that. Tell her I'm his daughter."

"She'll know."

"Never hurts to connect the dots for people though." I chew in thoughtful silence for a few minutes. Over the last several months my father has written several stories, each describing some aspect of his childhood. As he finishes each story, he e-mails it around to more or less everyone he knows. The stories are indeed entertaining, even for those who have never been in New Mexico. I'm surprised that Grandmother saw them, but not that she enjoyed them. Lippy seldom calls home or answers e-mail, yet he took the trouble to send these stories to someone who would love them. The day is full of surprises.

After dinner I go back in the house and see Grandmother sitting at a table. I sit down beside her and mention the stories.

"Oh yes! I loved those stories. So that was your father who wrote them!" The ice is broken. We talk for half an hour. I learn that she and her husband moved out to Los Angeles from Albuquerque when I was three, right after the war. I had been living in Albuquerque myself for the last two of the years she was there. I learn that she is a year older than my father, and she tells me the intriguing story of her mother dying of tuberculosis and how her father brought their "new mother" to live with them right after the funeral. I hear about all her brothers and sisters, and how the family managed during trying times. We talk of growing old and giving up driving, and how proud we are of our respective families.

"Have you ever thought of writing down these stories you're telling me?" I ask, always the missionary for lifestory writing.

"My grandchildren are always after me to do that. Several of them have interviewed me for papers at school. But I don't always remember things right."

I grinned at that. "My goodness, what difference does that make? Are you going to let a few facts get in the way of passing these wonderful stories on to your grandchildren and their children?" We talked about the purpose of writing about our lives, and how we are trying to give an idea of what life was like, the "flavor" of the times and our families.

"So ... do you think you can start writing some of them down?"

"Yes, I think I can do that."

Betty joins us. "Your mother told me she is going to write down some of her stories," I say with a little wink.

"Well, it's about time. Your father set a good example for her! Now I want to see hers!" she says, patting her mother lovingly on the shoulder.

I hope Betty holds her to it, and I hope Lippy will e-mail those stories to me and to my father when they appear, to complete the arcane loop.

What better way to end than with a story about lifestory writing, the writing form for which I have such passion? This story brings this book full circle. Early in the first chapter I wrote about my father's stories, and this story shows how one person's stories rippled out farther than he would ever imagine. I'm delighted that my son appreciates the stories enough to share them. Just as I hope that particular Grandmother has gone on to write stories of her own, I hope that you will go on to write stacks and piles of your own stories, and that they ripple through the countryside and the ages, spreading wisdom, understanding and love to all who read them.

Appendix 2:
Memory Triggers

Tickler Questions

Background

Where did your ancestors come from?

What do you know about your family history?

Where were you born?

Do you have siblings?

Do ethnic roots affect family traditions or ways of doing things?

How did your parents meet?

Are they still living? If not, what were the circumstances of their death(s)?

Are there family anecdotes about colorful relatives?

Are there any stories you know about yourself from before you were old enough to remember?

Preschool years

What is your earliest memory?

What kind of clothes did you wear?

What was your sense of what you looked like?

Who did you play with?

What toys did you play with?

What is your most pleasant memory from this period?

What stories and songs do you remember?

What do you remember about learning things, like counting, reading, tying your shoes or making special things?

What was your house(s) like?

What was your bedroom like?

What inventions and technological advances have you benefited from? At home and at work?

What sort of relationship did you have with your parents? Grandparents? Siblings? Neighbors?

If you have younger siblings, what do you remember about their births? How did you feel about them?

What diseases did you get? How did they affect you?

What is the most frightening thing you remember?

Elementary school years

What was your first day/year of school like?

How did you feel about starting school?

Was school hard or easy for you?

Did you enjoy school?

What did you like best/least about school?

Who were your friends?

How did they treat you?

Did you have chores to do at home?

Were your parents involved with your school work and other activities?

How did you feel about that?

What kind of clothes did you wear to school?

What did you do at recess?

Were you good at athletics?

Who was your favorite teacher and why?

What were your favorite/least favorite things to study?

What were your teachers like?

What accomplishments did you have during this time, i.e. learning a musical instrument?

What organizations, i.e. Scouts, did you belong to?

What memories do you have of that?

Did you attend church? Which one? How did this affect your life?

Who was your least favorite teacher and why?

What are your memories of holidays during this time?

How did your family spend vacations?

Did you spend time away from home visiting relatives?

How did you get along with your siblings during this period?

Teenage years

What was school like during junior and senior high?

Did it change as you got older?

Were you more interested in your studies or social life?

What was your social life like?

Do you remember the first time you fell in love?

What was your first date like?

If you didn't date (much), why or why not?

What did you look like as a teenager?

What did you (people in general) do on dates?

What were boy/girl customs "back then"?

How and when did you learn to dance?

What was your favorite/least favorite subject at school?

Who were your favorite/least favorite teachers? Why?

How did you do in school academically?

Did you participate in sports?

What unpleasant memories do you have of school during your teenage years?

What kind of clothes were worn?

How did you feel about your appearance?

Did you have conflicts with your parents?

How did you resolve them?

What were they about?

How and when did you learn to drive?

How did your life change after you got your license?

Did you ever sneak a beer?

Did you smoke?

When and how and why did you drink or smoke?

Did you have a job?

How did you get around town?

What kids did you "hang around" with? What did you do together?

What do you remember about your first kiss?

Did you face any special challenges?

What organizations did you participate in, i.e. band, drama club, chess?

Did you earn any special honors?

What did you expect to do with your life?

What expectations did you have about your future mate?

College/Young Adult years

What college(s) did you attend?

What courses did you take?

How did you do academically?

What organizations did you belong to?

What did you do for fun?

What was going on romantically?

Military Service (if you served)

When, where, which one, etc.?

Were you overseas?

What adventures did you have there?

Adult, family

Did you marry? Who, when, where, etc. More than once? If not, why not?

Did you have children? How many? If none, why not?

Where have you lived?

Has family life been satisfying for you?

What would you do differently?

What have your relationships with your children been like? Have they changed over time?

What are some of the highs and lows with each child?

How have your relationships with your parents changed?

If your parents are no longer living, how did their deaths affect you?

Adult, work

What kind of work have you done?

How many jobs have you had?

How have you felt about work?

Who was the best/worst boss you ever had? Why?

Have you been affected by the changing corporate landscape?

Adult, other

What major historic/natural events (i.e. V-J Day, Kennedy Assassination, Space Walk, Desert Storm, Mt. St. Helen's, Total Solar Eclipse) have you experienced? Where were you? What happened? What did each mean to you?

What awards have you received? What major achievements (at any age)?

What major turning points (i.e. job change, going back to school, kids in school, retirement, divorce, remarriage) have occurred in your life? When did each occur? How did they affect you?

What technological advances (i.e. electric typewriters, electric shavers, microwaves, television, computers, call waiting) have you experienced? What has each meant to you? How did it change your life? When did it occur?

How has your philosophy of life evolved over the years? What major insights would you care to share?

What is missing now (i.e. milk delivery, farm-fresh eggs, family night playing canasta)?

Jump Starts

Pick a topic and write a paragraph

Hobbies you have had

Your first job

An early memory

A favorite relative

A neighbor you liked to visit as a child

Your earliest memory of a trip with your family

Care-giving for your parents

A life-changing decision

A teacher who was a problem

An accident you had or saw

Learning the value of work

Something you did that you wouldn't want your child to do

Pick a question and write for 15 minutes

What did you want to be when you were ten?

How important is trust in your life?

What do you like most about your father and why?

What contributes to making a good family?

When you were five, what made you feel happy and secure?

Who was your best friend in school and why?

What "house rules" did you live by as a teenager?

When was the last time you took time away from obligations, just for yourself?

What was your first thought when you found out you were going to be a parent?

When was the first time you can remember feeling loved?

What have your parents (or others) told you about the day you were born?

What war(s) affected your life? How?

Appendix 3:
Layout and Other Geek Stuff

I've given you a few tips along the way for managing your digital document, and in Chapter Eleven you learned about content and printing options. This chapter explains what you need to do to lay everything out nicely and prepare it for printing, whichever printing method you chose. This is where the real fun starts. RiterGeek (my favorite Internet techie forum username, but please don't tell) is coming out of the closet to share decades of hard-won expertise to help you make your project look slick. But have no fear. I'll keep it basic, and hold your hand as tightly as you wish. Things like styles, headers, section breaks, and that sort of thing aren't important for everyday purposes, so you probably haven't had a reason to learn them.

Now is a great time to remind you that research proves that continuing to learn, solve problems, and work with words, i.e., solving crossword puzzles and writing things, helps keep your brain young, healthy, flexible, and forming new neurons. Autopsies are showing cases of people with advanced Alzheimer's plaque who showed few or no symptoms of the disease. All these people were constantly active, solving puzzles and problems, learning new skills, and writing.

Age is no consideration. Many neophyte computer students in their seventies and eighties have become adept at adjusting margins, changing fonts, adding page numbers, inserting graphics, and using various other formatting features to produce polished-looking volumes. All that aside, if some or all of this stuff is too much for you, perhaps you could make it a team project and have a friend or relative help out. You can always stick to the default settings, or fall back on the old cut, paste, and photocopy method. Don't beat yourself up if this stuff is beyond where you want to go—hand it off.

The biggest challenge in writing this section is keeping it general enough to help a spectrum of people, ranging from readers who have older computers and software up to those who will be using dazzling new software packages in years to come. On occasion I have taught classes on word processing and photo editing, and I always emphasize to students that concepts are the single most important thing to learn. If you know the concept, you can use Help to find out how to do that function in any software program. That's the approach I take here as I give general instructions for Microsoft Word, OpenOffice Write, and WordPerfect. My apologies to Mac and Linux users. Your programs may vary slightly, but if you concentrate on concepts, you should be able to find your way.

To get the most out of this material, read the instructions in each section carefully, while sitting at your computer. Work through each procedure, following the instructions step-by-step. Repeat each procedure several times until you are comfortable with it. Before long, you'll be formatting like a pro and amazing all your friends and relatives.

Page Layout

Page layout determines the visual impact of your story. Layout elements include page size, page margins, font choice, line spacing, paragraph style, title and subtitle styles, and page numbering. More advanced elements include page headers, photographs or illustration graphics, and sidebar stories or explanations. Does that list sound discouraging? Be courageous. We'll take it a step at a time.

Page setup

This is the area where you set page size and margins, binding offset and certain other options, depending on your program. Look for these settings in:

Microsoft Word	OpenOffice	WordPerfect
File>Page Setup	Format>Page	Format>Page>Page Setup

Each page setup menu has multiple tabs. Explore all of them to discover the possibilities. Open a file with several pages and experiment with settings.

Page size

Unless you decide to use Print-On-Demand, you'll stick with the default 8.5" x 11" standard. For POD you may opt for a smaller page, for example 6" x 9". This is where you make those settings. Keep in mind that your own printer will still print on standard size paper, so your home-printed copies will have wide margins. This extra will disappear in the final .pdf file—check with the printing company for details.

Page margins

Margins for a standard 8.5" x 11" sheet of paper are typically 1" all around. This gives a printed line width of 6.5". This is a good balance between economical paper use and readability. Increasing the side margin to 1.25" makes it easier for the eye to track lines and makes the page look slightly less crowded. Illustrations of standard layouts are shown in Figure 17.

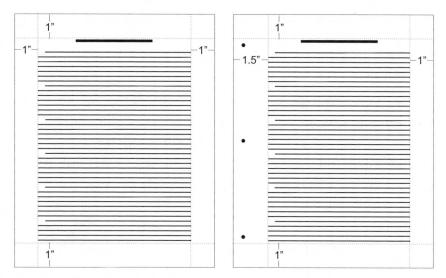

Figure 17: Common layouts

You may also decide to adjust the margin on the inside of the page to allow for binding. For example, a three-ring binder needs a margin of .5" to accommodate the holes. A margin of 1.5" gives breathing space between the holes and the edge of the text, as shown in the right figure above. Plastic comb binding and spiral binding only require an offset of .25" for a total margin of 1.25". If you plan to copy your finished pages on only one side of the paper, set the margins to make this adjustment.

If you plan to do double-sided copying and are meticulous about detail, you'll need different margins on odd (right) and even (left) pages. Word processing programs have a feature on the page setup menu for adjusting binding width.

Microsoft Word	OpenOffice	WordPerfect
File>Page Setup. Select Mirror Margins in Multiple Pages field.	Format>Page> Page tab. Select Mirrored in Page layout field.	Format>Page> Page Setup>Margins/Layout. Set binding margin increase and select Alternating.

If the margin selection changes to inner and outer, set them with the extra binding space on the inner margin.

Font choice

Times New Roman is the default font. This familiar, all-purpose font uses paper space economically, making it ideal for column-formatted periodicals. It is not used for typesetting commercially published books, although many self-publishers are beginning to do so. Wider fonts, such as Amerigo BT™, Garamond™, Bookman ITC Lt BT™, or Century 731 BT™ are good choices. All are serif fonts, meaning that they have tiny horizontal lines capping the vertical ones. The serifs in these fonts lead the eye along the page and work with the extra character width to ease extended reading on book-width pages.

Samples of a few serif fonts are given below. All are 11 point (pt.), but you'll notice that some are considerably bigger than others. Point size definition is an elusive topic and may have become an arbitrary decision by the font designer. Letters may vary in width from one font to another and the lower case letters may vary in height, along with default line spacing.

The fast gray fox chased the horrified hare right over the fence, with the hunter in hot pursuit. (Garamond™)

The fast gray fox chased the horrified hare right over the fence, with the hunter in hot pursuit. (Times New Roman™)

The fast gray fox chased the horrified hare right over the fence, with the hunter in hot pursuit. (Georgia™)

The fast gray fox chased the horrified hare right over the fence, with the hunter in hot pursuit. (Baskerville Win95BT™)

The fast gray fox chased the horrified hare right over the fence, with the hunter in hot pursuit. (Century 731 BT™)

The fast gray fox chased the horrified hare right over the fence, with the hunter in hot pursuit. (Bookman Old Style™)

You may not find these specific fonts in your collection, but you may be able to find one you really love by searching for "free font download" on the Internet. To test various fonts and find one you like, select a sample paragraph, copy it, and paste it into a blank document several times, one after another. Then go to a font selection menu (Top toolbar or Format>Font or Character) and apply likely looking ones to the different paragraphs. Print out your completed sample. The monitor doesn't reliably show how a font will look on the printed page.

Besides the font itself, you can change font size. Most books use 10 pt. or 11 pt. type. If you use a font with large lowercase letters, such as Bookman Old Style™, you can comfortably drop a point. A dainty font such as Garamond™ calls for a larger size for easy reading. Here again, print samples and ask for opinions from a few people before making your decision.

Line spacing

Adding a small amount of extra space between lines makes print easier to read by providing a wider "path" for eyes to follow as they sweep back to begin a new line. The white space between lines of print is called leading. For most practical purposes, it is the same as line spacing.

Microsoft Word	OpenOffice	WordPerfect
Format>Paragraph. Set Line spacing to "at least" and increase point setting until you are happy with the result.	Format>Paragraph. Set Line spacing to leading. Adjust setting as desired.	Format>Typesetting> Word/Letter Spacing. Click Adjust Leading and adjust amount as desired.

In Word and OpenOffice you can access the paragraph format menu with a right click. Experiment to see whether your adjustments apply only to the paragraph where your cursor is positioned, or from there through the document. You may need to select the area you want to adjust.

When you set leading by increments of an inch, a little bit goes a long way, as shown in Figure 18. Start at .01 and work your way up. The old typewriter standard was 12 point line spacing, which fit 6 lines of print into the space of a vertical inch. (A point is 1/72" or .014".) This measurement included both the height of the letters and the space (leading) between. Default leading varies considerably for computer fonts. The font used for this book is Century 731 BT™, 11 pt. The line height must be set higher than 13 pt. for any adjustment to occur. This book, created in Microsoft Word, uses line spacing of "at least" 16 pt. This is art, not science. Select whatever looks best to your eye and pleases a test reader or two.

Paragraph style

There is no single correct way to format paragraphs. The most common format for stories is to single-space between paragraphs, indenting the first line of each. When using a typewriter, five spaces, or half an inch with pica type, is the standard indentation. You can stick with that setting on a computer, or set it narrower. Books typically use around .2" for a standard tab setting.

Most people double-space between paragraphs when they type letters. Some also indent the paragraphs after double spacing. Double-spacing between paragraphs works in letters, but in stories it interrupts the flow of the eye and makes the story feel choppy. Save the double, or even triple spaces to indicate a break in time, action, or thought. You may also skip the indentation for the first paragraph following a title, subtitle,

Line Spacing Sample:
Times New Roman, 10 pt. type

14 pt.	14.75 pt.	15.5pt.
In Microsoft Word, adjust line spacing on the paragraph menu. Selecting the "at least" option allows for extra line height to be added for larger type sizes, such as titles and headers. For uniformity, *edit the normal style* rather than individual sections. In OpenOffice and WordPerfect, you can adjust either line height, or leading size itself, independently of the line spacing. Use the typesetting menu under format to adjust leading. Adjustments as fine as .015 or .02 make a visible difference.	In Microsoft Word, adjust line spacing on the paragraph menu. Selecting the "at least" option allows for extra line height to be added for larger type sizes, such as titles and headers. For uniformity, *edit the normal style* rather than individual sections. In OpenOffice and WordPerfect, you can adjust either line height, or leading size itself, independently of the line spacing. Use the typesetting menu under format to adjust leading. Adjustments as fine as .015 or .02 make	In Microsoft Word, adjust line spacing on the paragraph menu. Selecting the "at least" option allows for extra line height to be added for larger type sizes, such as titles and headers. For uniformity, *edit the normal style* rather than individual sections. In OpenOffice and WordPerfect, you can adjust either line height, or leading size itself, independently of the line spacing. Use the typesetting menu under format to adjust leading. Adjustments as

Figure 18: Line Spacing Sample

or break, as I have done in this book. If you want to get fancy, you can use an oversized initial letter for the opening paragraph, raising it high or dropping it into two or three rows below. Both of these options are accomplished by means of the Drop Cap function, found on the Format or Paragraph menu. Whether you decide to double-space or single-space with indentation, use drop caps, or any other variation on paragraph formatting, be consistent from one story to the next within a collection.

Title style

Books have several types of titles: the title on the cover of the book and the inside cover, chapter titles, and subtitles or headers. Word processing lets you select styles for each element, to set it apart from the text that follows, and to help readers know at a glance how the book is organized.

Many people stick with the same font for the title as they use in the body of the text. If you do this, make the titles bold, and increase their size by at least two points with each level up the scale. You may prefer a sans serif font such as Arial™ for contrast, and cover titles are also a good place to use a more decorative font, chosen to reflect the tone of your book. See page 259 to learn how to use Styles to make it easy to experiment with title font and formatting changes without spending hours going through and redoing each one individually.

Poster Bodoni
Academy Engraved Letters
BERTRAM
Fun Stuff
GALLERY CAPS

Find appealing books on your bookshelf and copy layout features such as margin settings, type styles, page headers, and page numbering treatment. Chapter titles are generally set in much larger type, and may include some sort of graphic adornment. They may be centered, or justified to either right or left. They may be numbered, or not. Find something you like and copy shamelessly.

Page numbers

Sooner or later someone will want to find one specific story in your book. Use a Table of Contents and page numbers to help them do this easily. This will add pages at the beginning, and the stories will not start on page one. If this concerns you, instructions follow for resetting the page numbers.

Microsoft Word	OpenOffice	WordPerfect
Go to Insert>Page Numbers. Format and set value. Or, create a header or footer, View>Header and Footer, and insert # field.	Insert>Footer> Default. Insert>Field>Page Number. Format the page number as you wish.	Format>Page> Numbering. Select position, format, and anything else that appeals to you. Set page number on Set Value.

Page numbers can be placed in headers or footers, and you can format them as you wish, with a larger or smaller font, or a different font, centered or on a corner. Some people like to add symbols surrounding the page number, for example, ℘ **54** ℘. (Those particular symbols are from the Webding font.) You can insert special characters by going to Insert>Symbol or Special Character. Choose the font and character in the menu that pops up. An en-dash works nicely too.

Page headers

Not all books use headers. More commonly, the title of the book is placed in the header on the left-hand (even-numbered) pages, and the title of the chapter or section is in the right-hand header on odd-numbered pages. Some are elaborate, with graphics in the header, but most are simple. If you want to use them, check your bookshelf to find a layout you like.

Keep the font size for headers relatively small. Using all caps in the same size as the body text or italics will set it off. You may use a horizontal line running from margin to margin to set the header apart from the text. Whether or not you use a line, allow enough space below the header to make the division from body text clear.

Microsoft Word	OpenOffice	WordPerfect
View>Header and Footer. Use the toolbar or menu that opens to define the header. Use the Next function on the toolbar to define a header for the alternate pages and format as above.	Insert>Header. Format text after entering. Control from Header tab on Page formatting menu.	Insert> Header. Select from options on menu.

Changing headers from one chapter to the next varies enough between programs and versions that you should check your help documentation to make sure you get the correct instructions for your use. On older programs, you may discover that you need to lay each chapter out as a separate file and use a Master Document to pull them all together. This is not as tough as it sounds. Read the help files carefully and take it one step at a time.

First-page format

If you look at commercially published books, you'll see that they don't have headers or page numbers on the first pages of chapters. This is how you make that happen.

Microsoft Word	OpenOffice	WordPerfect
Go to File>Page Setup. Look through the tabs to find the "Different first page" option. Section breaks activate new first page.	Right-click the page style field near the left on the bottom status bar. Select First Page. Repeat for each chapter.	Format>Page> Suppress. Select anything you don't want printed on first page. Repeat for each chapter.

This first-page format will be activated when you insert a section break.

Working with Style

People often pale at the mere mention of the term styles. The concept sounds intimidating even to veteran computer users, yet it's simple to grasp. What styles boil down to is putting an invisible label on the various parts of your document. You are telling the program that this is a chapter title, that's body text, there's a story title, and down here are comments about my story. The process is not complicated:

- Select text, i.e., a title.
- Format the text the way you want it.
- Tell your program this is a new style and give the style a name.
- Click on another title.
- Click on the title style name to apply the style "label."
- Formatting is automatically applied.

Unless you say otherwise, the new style will be defined from all text in that paragraph (anything between line breaks). We aren't going into the otherwise part here. To define a new style, place your cursor in the formatted text area, then:

Microsoft Word	OpenOffice	WordPerfect
Format>Styles and Formatting. Click button to open New Styles menu. Name style. Click OK.	Format>Styles and Formatting. Right menu button options: New, update ... Select New. Name style. Click OK.	Format>Styles. Click Create. Name style. Click OK.

If you decide to change the way your titles are formatted, you change the formatting in one title, then update the style to match, and all the titles are changed in a flash, even if you have hundreds.

Update styles by changing the formatting on one item, say a title. While your cursor is still inside the reformatted area, you update its style to conform to the reformatting. No, no! Don't run off into the woods. It isn't hard. Reformat that title, then:

Microsoft Word	OpenOffice	WordPerfect
Format>Styles and Formatting. The active style will be highlighted. Right-click the definition and select Update to Match Selection.	Format>Styles and Formatting. Right menu button options: New, update ... Select Update.	Update function not available, as of Version 9.

To edit within the style definition, open the menu you used to name the style and use formatting options found on that menu.

To apply a style, place your cursor in a paragraph you want to apply it to, such as a new title. You may find a toolbar field along the top that displays the style currently active. Click on the tiny arrow to the right of this field to open a drop-down list of available styles. If you don't find such a field, open the regular style list as described above. Click on the style of your choice. The paragraph will magically be formatted to match all the others. Using styles will prove to be quite a timesaver if you make major changes like switching fonts, making an element bold, changing paragraph formatting, or similar things.

While you are in the style formatting menu, find the field for "Style for following paragraph." In nearly every case, this will be the style you use for body text. With this setting, after you format a title and press Enter, the next paragraph will be ordinary body text. You won't have to apply a new style to that.

Now that you understand how to format a style, you can change the way all the body text is formatted by changing the normal or default style. Format a paragraph the way you want it, with line spacing adjustment, font, or anything else you select. Use the process above to update the Normal or Default style. You'll need to create a paragraph style for WordPerfect and apply that. Don't worry about changing every document on your computer when you change the Normal style. The change only applies to the document you are working on.

That's it. That is how you work with styles. I think you can see how this can save you time, and it will also make sure you don't miss anything. You'll have the freedom to be as creative as you wish, with just a few clicks. I'd suggest that you resave a copy of your document with a new name to play around with styles. That way you can copy the new formats you like without running the risk of losing the old one you may like better.

Templates

This Geek option saves me time and confusion. I have hundreds of story files lurking in various places on my computer and backup disks. Finding a file again can be tricky, so I made a template that I call Lifestory.dot (.dot signifies the file is a Word template). When I begin a new story, I open the template rather than a blank document. This template has a default title in place, formatted to my specifications. It has the body text font I like, with a little extra leading between the lines. I added a header for all pages after the first that includes the story title and the page number (to make things simple in case I drop a pile of thirty-eight multiple-page stories). I won't have to spend hours wondering which page two goes with which front page.

The final items below are found at the end of the story. I've included my name, the document name, the date I began writing the story, and the date of the most recent edit. The final result looks like this:

— Sharon Lippincott
Too old for ice cream.doc
Created, 6/24/2004
Edited, 7/16/06

I delete the last three lines before sharing stories. Working backward, here's how to add those data lines at the end, then how to create the template and open it. Add the document name and dates by inserting field definitions, place your cursor where you want the information to appear, and then:

Microsoft Word	OpenOffice	WordPerfect
Insert>Field> FileName.	Insert>Fields> Other > File name.	Insert>Other> Filename.
Insert>Date and Time. Check box to update automatically or leave un-checked for a fixed date.	Insert>Fields> Date or Insert> Fields> Other> Date>Date (fixed)	Insert>Date/ Time. Check box to update automatically.

Each program gives you options about formatting the field as you set it up. Using a template keeps things consistent from one document to another. I only use the file name, because I may move the file from one folder to another, and I'll back it up a couple of places. A search will proceed faster with a file name than it would with body text. I have two date fields in my template because I like knowing when I started a story, as well as how recently I worked on it. Obviously the creation date needs to stay the same, so that field must be "fixed." The edit date is set to update automatically each time I save the file. Check carefully when you enter these fields in your template to make sure you set them accurately.

How to create a template

To make a template of your own:

1. Open a document that has a story in it, or write one and format the title. Update the default Header 2 style to match it.
2. Format the body text the way you want, updating the Normal style to match it.
3. Create a second page header if you want one. Follow the earlier instructions to set a different first page, and insert

your header, using filler text like "Story Title." You can place the page number in the header if you like, or have it at the bottom of the page.

4. Add your name to the end and format as you wish.
5. Add any fields you want below your name. Format these to suit yourself. The filename field will remain empty until you've saved the file, and it will remain empty in a template file. The edit date will be the same as the creation date until you open the story later.
6. Replace the story text with the words "Start story here."
7. Highlight the title and replace it with "Title."
8. Click on File>Save As. Select (program name) Template as the file type.

That's it. Your template is finished. Your program may store it in the template directory automatically. If it doesn't, you may need to dig around a little to find it. Look in C:\Program Files\(Program Name) for a Template folder. If that doesn't work, check the "save as" field and notice the extension, i.e., .dot for Word templates. Search your C: drive for ".dot" to locate the files. Move or store your new template there.

If it's too confusing to figure out where to put the finished template, there is another way. Do all the things listed above to get the template ready. Save it as a regular document in a place you'll remember. Then immediately open My Computer and browse to that file. Right-click the file name and select Properties. Click the box that says Read-Only. When you open a Read-Only file, you'll see a warning that you'll have to save it with a new name. Click okay. That's the idea. The only difference between this file and a formal template file is that you don't get that warning with a template.

I love templates—they keep me from saving new files over old ones if I forget to rename them. In ages past I had a business letterhead formatted with great care to print with my letters. Before I learned about templates, I would open a random old letter, delete the contents, and write a new letter. I hate to think about the number of times I forgot to *rename* the file when I saved it—probably dozens more than I realized. Fortunately I never came to any grief because of this. In any event, I'd rather lose an old business letter than a story any day.

How to use your template

Using your template is much easier than creating it. The process of opening a template varies even from one version of a program to another. You may find it on the File>New menu, or you may find it on the New file icon. Search the Help file if all else fails. Once you open your template, your formatting will be done, and the end information in place. Highlight the title and type in your new one. Then highlight the "Start story here" text and begin your story. When you get to the second page, you'll need to type the title into the header.

If you want to change a template, find the option to open it for editing. The location of this option varies. The simplest way is to open a story created with the template, change the formatting as you wish, then replace the contents as described in the steps for creating a template. Save it as a template, as described above, and allow it to save over the existing one. Changing template settings will apply to future documents, but it won't affect existing ones.

Adding Photos to Text Documents

A photo or two can make all the difference in a brochure and add pizzazz to lifestories, family history, or your annual newsletter to friends. You aren't limited to photos. The steps listed below work for adding any type of graphic—maps, scanned documents, clipart, or any image stored on your computer (you must save e-mailed photos to disk before inserting them). Once you learn this easy process, you'll probably use it often.

Microsoft Word	OpenOffice	WordPerfect
Place your cursor on the line where you want to insert the picture.	Same	Same
Click on Insert>Picture>From File. A small file browser will open. Find your picture. Select it and click on Insert.	Insert>Picture>From File	Insert>Graphics>From File
Click to select the picture that appears, and right-click over it to open the tabbed Format Picture menu box.	Right-click to activate fly-out menus.	Right-click for pop-up menu. Image Tools is similar to Word menu box.
You can resize the picture on the Size tab, but for best results, have it as near the size you want as possible before you insert it. Image ratio is retained by default so you can resize by dragging a corner with the mouse.	Same. Shift key retains image ratio while resizing.	Same. Image ratio retained by default.
The Layout tab allows you to decide how text wraps around the photo. For photos less than ⅔ the width of the page, you can put them on one side and let text wrap to the other. Wider pictures look best centered, with no side text. It's confusing to have text wrap on both sides, so you'll want to wrap above and below centered pictures. To make most efficient use of your space, place the picture against one of the side margins.	Select Wrap on right-click menu.	Select Wrap on right-click menu.

Microsoft Word	OpenOffice	WordPerfect
Clicking on the Advanced tab gives you options about picture placement. You can have it move with the text or remain locked in a specific position. Locking may be important for a brochure, but you'll want it to flow for a story or letter. Explore the options, and use help as necessary.	Select Anchor on right-click menu.	Select Position tab on right-click menu.
The Picture tab has some cropping options. I do not recommend using this. You'll get best results by cropping in a photo editing program!	Select Picture on right-click menu, Crop tab on Picture window.	Select Image Tools on right-click menu. Use Zoom tool to crop.
Click on Colors and Line tab to add border to picture.	Select Borders tab on Picture menu.	Select Border/Fill option on right-click menu.

Adding captions is a nice touch for photos and other illustrations in stories. Position your picture, then follow these steps:

Microsoft Word	OpenOffice	WordPerfect
With image selected, Insert> Reference> Caption.	Select Caption on right-click menu. Edit options. Apply border to picture after adding caption. Start fresh and right-click picture.	Select Caption option on right-click menu. Edit options.

In each case, the caption can be edited onscreen later. You may find it easiest to add your pictures after you finish everything else. Pictures are set to move with the text by default, but if the paragraph moves near the bottom of the page, weird things can happen. Should you run into this problem, click on the picture, copy it, then cut it, place your cursor in another paragraph, and reinsert it. You may need to move it up or down with the arrow keys or edit the position to place it to your liking.

A final piece of advice about pictures is to make them large enough to be seen. They don't have to be huge, but three inches on the smaller dimension is a good rule of thumb as a minimum. Especially on full-size pages, very small pictures look out of balance. Better to have fewer, larger pictures than dozens of thumbnail-sized ones.

That's It!

You have learned more than you ever wanted to know about layout and formatting. Have fun with it, and best wishes for every success with your whole project.

Appendix 4:
Bibliography

Books Cited in This Volume

Allen, Stephanie West, JD, *Creating Your Own Funeral Or Memorial Service: A Workbook.* Lulu.com, 2006.

Auster, Paul, *The Invention of Solitude.* New York: Penguin, 1988.

Bryant, Roberta Jean, *Anybody Can Write.* Barnes & Noble, 1999.

Dimbleby, Jonathan, *The Prince of Wales.* Thorndike, Maine: Thorndike Press, 1995.

Frey, James, *A Million Little Pieces.* New York: Nan Talese/Doubleday, 2003.

Fowler, H. Ramsey and **Jane E. Aaron**, *The Little, Brown Handbook, (Fifth Edition).* HarperCollins, 1992. (Several editions available)

Goldberg, Natalie, *Wild Mind: Living the Writer's Life.* New York: Bantam Books, 1990.

Jakiela, Lori, *Miss New York Has Everything.* New York: Warner Books, 2006.

Karr, Mary, *The Liar's Club: A Memoir.* New York: Viking, 1995.

Kelley, Kitty, *The Royals.* New York: Warner, 1997.

Kotre, John N., *White Gloves: How We Create Ourselves Through Memory.* New York: Free Press, 1995.

Kotre, John N., *Make It Count: How to Generate a Legacy That Gives Meaning to Your Life.* New York: Free Press, 1999.

Krasnow, Iris, *I Am My Mother's Daughter: Making Peace With Mom Before It's Too Late.* New York: Basic Books, 2006.

Lamott, Anne, *Bird By Bird: Some Instructions on Writing and Life.* New York: Pantheon Books, 1994.

Mack, Karin, PhD and **Eric Skjei,** *Overcoming Writing Blocks.* Los Angeles, Calif.: J. P. Tarcher, 1979.

McCourt, Frank, *Angela's Ashes: A Memoir.* New York: Scribner, 1996.

Moses, Anna Mary, *Grandma Moses: My Life's History.* New York: Harper, 1952.

Murdock, Maureen, *Unreliable Truth: Turning Memory into Memoir.* Avalon Publishing Group, 2003.

Dillard, Annie, *An American Childhood.* New York: Harper and Row, 1987.

Strunk, William, Jr. and **E. B. White,** *The Elements of Style, Third Edition.* New York: McMillan, 1970. (Several editions available)

Toffler, Alvin, *Future Shock.* New York: Random House, 1970.

Waller, Robert, *The Bridges of Madison County.* New York: Warner Books, 1992.

Williamson, Hal and **Sharon Eakes,** *Liberating Greatness: The Whole Brain Guide to Living an Extraordinary Life.* Tarentum, Pa.: Word Association Publishers, 2006.

Additional Resources

Albert, Susan Wittig, *Writing from Life: Telling Your Soul's Story.* New York: G. P. Putnam's Sons, 1996.

Barrington, Judith, *Writing the Memoir: From Truth to Art.* Portland, Ore.: Eighth Mountain Press, 1994.

Bender, Sheila, *Writing Personal Essays: How to Shape Your Life Experiences for the Page.* Cincinnati: Writer's Digest Books, 1995.

Borg, Mary, *Writing Your Life: An Easy-to-Follow Guide to Writing an Autobiography, Third Edition.* Cottonwood Press, 1998.

Cameron, Julia, *The Sound of Paper.* New York: Jeremy P. Tarcher, 2004.

Conway, Jill Ker, *When Memory Speaks: Reflections on Autobiography.* New York: Alfred A. Knopf, 1998.

Daniel, Lois, *How to Write Your Own Life Story: The Classic Guide for the Nonprofessional Writer.* Chicago: Chicago Review Press, 1997.

Dixon, Janice T., *Family Focused: A Step-By-Step Guide to Writing Your Autobiography and Family History.* Wendover, Nev.: Mount Olympus Pub., 1997.

Elgin, Duane and **Coleen LeDrew,** *Living Legacies: How to Write, Illustrate and Share Your Life Stories.* Berkley, Calif.: Conari Press, 2001.

Gornick, Vivian, *The Situation and the Story: The Art of Personal Narrative.* New York: Farrar, Straus and Girous, 2001.

Hauser, Susan Carol, *You Can Write a Memoir.* Cincinnati: Writer's Digest Books, 2001.

Jacob, Dianne, *Will Write for Food: The Complete Guide to Writing Cookbooks, Restaurant Reviews, Articles, Memoir, Fiction and More.* New York: Marlowe and Company, 2005.

Klauser, Henriette Anne, *With Pen in Hand: The Healing Power of Writing.* Cambridge, Mass.: Perseus Publishing, 2003.

Klauser, Henriette Anne, *Put Your Heart on Paper: Staying Connected in a Loose-Ends World.* New York: Bantam, 1995.

LeDoux, Denis, *The Photo Scribe: A Writing Guide: How to Write the Stories Behind Your Photographs.* Lisbon Falls, Maine: Soleil Press, 1998.

Ledoux, Denis, *Turning Memories into Memoirs: A Handbook for Writing Lifestories, Third Edition.* Lisbon Falls, Maine: Soleil Press, 2005.

McDonnell, Jane Taylor, *Living to Tell the Tale: A Guide to Writing Memoir.* New York: Penguin Books, 1998.

McKeithan, Elsa, *Writing the Stories of Your Life: How to Turn Memories into Memoir.* Trafford Publishing, 2005.

Metzger, Deena, *Writing for Your Life: A Guide and Companion to the Inner Worlds.* San Francisco: HarperSanFrancisco, 1992.

Phifer, Nan, *Memoirs of the Soul: Writing Your Spiritual Autobiography.* Walking Stick Press, 2001.

Piercy, Marge and **Ira Wood,** *So You Want to Write: How to Master the Craft of Writing Fiction and Memoir.* Wellfleet, Mass.: Leapfrog Press, 2005.

Reahm, Thelly, *About Life Story Writing.* Cardiff-by-the-Sea, Calif.: Thelly Reahm, 2000. (P.O. Box 387, Cardiff-by-the-Sea, CA 92007)

Selling, Bernard, *Writing from Within: A Guide to Creativity and Life Story Writing.* Alameda, Calif.: Hunter House, 1997.

Spence, Linda, *Legacy: A Step-by-Step Guide to Writing Personal History.* Athens, Ohio: Swallow Press, 1997.

Stanke, Lou Willett, *Writing Your Life: Putting Your Past on Paper.* New York: Avon, 1996.

Thomas, Frank P., *How to Write the Story of Your Life.* Cincinnati: Writer's Digest Books, 1989.

Wakefield, Dan, *The Story of Your Life: Writing a Spiritual Autobiography.* Boston: Beacon Press, 1990.

Zinsser, William K., *Writing about Your Life: A Journey into the Past.* New York: Marlowe & Co., 2004.

Zinsser, William K., ed., *Inventing the Truth.* Boston: Houghton Mifflin, 1987.

Index

About the Author

Sharon Lippincott is a lifestory writing instructor and coach, and the author of *Meetings: Do's, Don'ts and Donuts.* In recent years, she has focused her attention on creative nonfiction, specializing in lifestories. An active member of several writing groups, both real-time and on the Internet, she has written over 500 stories and essays about her own life experiences and observations. She  holds workshops and lectures on lifestory writing all around the country and lives in Pennsylvania.

Sharon's professional background is in training and development. After graduation from Boston University, she earned a master's degree in psychology from Central Washington University, where she received the Distinguished Thesis award. An enthusiastic supporter of Toastmasters, International, Sharon holds the Distinguished Toastmaster award. She claims the conceptual organization skills she learned in Toastmasters have helped her writing as much as her oral communication.

You can e-mail Sharon at slippincott@yahoo.com, and visit her on the web at her website, http://www.sharonlippincott.com, or her lifestory writing blog, http://heartandcraft.blogspot.com.